The Sacrifice of Socrates

Studies in Violence, Mimesis, and Culture

The Sacrifice of Socrates

Athens, Plato, Girard

Wm. Blake Tyrrell

Michigan State University Press · *East Lansing*

⊛ The paper used in this publication meets the minimum requirements of ANSI/NISO
Z39.48-1992 (R 1997) (Permanence of Paper).

Michigan State University Press
East Lansing, Michigan 48823-5245

Printed and bound in the United States of America.

18 17 16 15 14 13 12   1 2 3 4 5 6 7 8 9 10

LIBRARY OF CONGRESS CATALOGING-IN-PUBLICATION DATA
Tyrrell, William Blake.
The sacrifice of Socrates : Athens, Plato, Girard / Wm. Blake Tyrrell.
pages. cm. — (Studies in violence, mimesis, and culture series)
Includes bibliographic references and index.
ISBN 978-1-61186-054-2 (paperback : alkaline paper) 1. Socrates. 2. Plato—Criticism and
interpretation. 3. Girard, René, 1923– 4. Athens (Greece)—History—Thirty Tyrants, 404–403
B.C. 5. Greece—History—Peloponnesian War, 431–404 B.C. I. Title. II. Series: Studies in
violence, mimesis, and culture.
B316.T97 2012
183'.2—dc23
2011050523

Book by Charlie Sharp, Sharp Des!gns, Lansing, Michigan
Cover design by David Drummond, Salamander Design, www.salamanderdesign.com

Cover art is a detail from School of Athens, from the Stanza della Segnatura, 1510-11 (fresco)
(detail of 472) by Raphael (Raffaello Sanzio of Urbino) (1483-1520) located in Vatican Museums
and Galleries, Vatican City, Italy. Image courtesy of Giraudon, The Bridgeman Art Library.

green   Michigan State University Press is a member of the Green Press Initiative and
press   is committed to developing and encouraging ecologically responsible publishing
INITIATIVE
practices. For more information about the Green Press Initiative and the use of recycled paper in
book publishing, please visit *www.greenpressinitiative.org*.

Visit Michigan State University Press at *www.msupress.org*

For Larry Joe Bennett

April 1, 1949–April 20, 2006

Son, Brother, Soldier, Husband, Father, Pa, Nephew,
Uncle, Cousin, Friend, Colleague

Contents

Preface

In the late 1980s Larry Joe Bennett and I began researching the Socrates of Plato's *Apology of Socrates* as a *pharmakos* figure. Encountering resistance to our nonhistorical approach, we turned to Aristophanes' *Knights*, whose underlying structure we believed was that of the *pharmakos*. After overcoming prejudices against the Cambridge School, whose "heresies" we were charged with reviving, we published our study of *Knights* in *Arethusa* (1990). In the meantime, our interest had shifted to the influence of funeral oratory in Sophocles' *Antigone*. By the time that we had worked out our interpretation in *Recapturing Sophocles' Antigone* (1998) and were out from under the weight of accepted knowledge about the play, we had been away from the Socrates idea for some fifteen years. We were getting back to it when one morning in April of 2006 Joe died. With him perished the direction that the study would have taken. I returned to the hypothesis of René Girard that proved to be useful in reading Sophocles' *Ajax* (*Arethusa* 1985) and *Antigone* (*Contagion* 2009). From there, I moved to the present endeavor, an essay of Plato's project from the perspective and methodology of Girard's mimetic mechanism. It is intended as a contribution to Girardian studies and, in particular, his theories on the origin of culture in mimetic rivalry and victimization. In what follows, I attempt to apply René Girard's theory, his mimetic mechanism, to Plato's therapy for the social ills of his society that forms a major purpose of his dialogues. Often I have been surprised, thrown into wonderment, actually, on how Girard's thesis overflows the banks of literature.

◆   ◆   ◆

All translations, unless otherwise noted, are mine. Abbreviations for classical works are standard and may be found in Henry George Liddell and Robert Scott, *A Greek-English Lexicon*, 9th ed., edited by Henry Stuart Jones (Oxford: Clarendon Press, 1940).

Introduction

"If I am not mistaken, we are being approached by a man who bears on his head Mambrino's helmet about which I swore that vow."

"How can I be wrong, you doubting Thomas?" said Don Quixote. "Tell me, do you not see that knight coming towards us, upon a dapple-grey steed, wearing a helmet of gold?"

—CERVANTES, *Don Quixote de la Mancha*

Squire Sancho may "make out a bloke on a donkey, brown like mine, with something shiny on his head," but his master espies the enchanted helmet of the Moorish king Mambrino and has to have it for his own.[1] With it, Don Quixote can become a knight. Rather, he desires to become a knight like his model, Amadis of Gaul, and since his model desires the helmet, he desires it, for he imitates his model's desires as he imagines them. Girard calls this dynamic "mimetic desire."[2] Without ado, Don Quixote descends upon the fellow, a barber from a nearby village, "at Rocinante's fastest pace, his pike couched low, with the intention of passing him through and through."[3] The barber, narrowly escaping a skewering, abandons his basin, and the knight errant acquires his golden helmet. Don Quixote's model, Amadis, although remote and removed from rivalry himself, arouses in him no less desire for the object, and that desire sends him careening at the barber. When subject and model are in close proximity, mimetic desire confounds their roles and turns them into rivals, "doubles" in Girard's terminology, who are imitators of one another. Their rivalry over the object quickly leads them into conflict over acquiring the object. Girard maintains that Cervantes understood this mechanism, the transition of mimetic desire to acquisitive desire, while Plato, author of the formative theory of mimesis for Western philosophy, did not. In fact, Girard believes that Plato "never uncovers its [mimesis's] empirical reason for being" because he has no stated theory of acquisitive desire: "Plato never relates conflict to acquisitive mimesis, that is, with the object that the two mimetic rivals attempt to wrest from one another because they designate it as desirable to one another."⁴ Greeks thought the causes of war to be self-evident and consequently did not develop theories of war.⁵ Acquisitive desire in the form of envy (*phthonos*) was endemic to Plato's culture, as may be illustrated by a pivotal scene of Aeschylus' *Agamemnon*. Although Plato never expressed his awareness in the form of a theory, he shows clearly his understanding of its dynamics in an episode from his *Gorgias*.

◆   ◆   ◆

In 458 BCE, Aeschylus produced the *Oresteia,* a moment sufficiently important in the history of tragedy at Athens to allow Aristophanes to capitalize upon it for his *Frogs* fifty-three years later. Aeschylus put mimetic desire leading to acquisitive desire and scapegoating at the heart of his monumental scene of Agamemnon's return to the house that his wife, Clytemnestra, now rules (*Ag.* 810–975, esp. 908–945). Agamemnon enters with Cassandra and is surrounded by an entourage of attendants and soldiers. Mounted upon a four-wheeled wagon drawn by horses, he towers over his wife, who stands before the door. She greets him at length and then orders her slaves to spread richly embroidered vestments on the ground before him. She beckons to him to walk upon them to the house "he never expected to see," an appeal whose menace lies beyond his ken. He demurs, protesting weakly and in pieties hollowed by his prolonged stay in the land of foreigners and the lust for glory that drove him there. Clytemnestra asks, "What, do you suppose, Priam would do if he did what you did?" "Walk on the vestments. No doubt." She prods, "The man free of envy is the man without anything to envy." Agamemnon the Greek knows better than to tread the wealth laid out before him.

But he has been too long in the East. His model for behavior has changed. He desires what the foreigner, a non-Greek, would desire. He imitates Priam, once a close and now a remote model, whose influence in the land of Greeks, who know their place before the gods, proves deadly. Agamemnon walks to the house upon the brownish-red robes evocative of Iphigenia's blood and to his death as Clytemnestra's sacrificial victim that establishes her power in her household and Argos. Agamemnon concedes to Priam the desire to walk upon the vestments and then, in envy of the man and his desire, he allows himself to imitate that desire.

Clytemnestra's orders put the watchman on the roof of Agamemnon's house to await the signal fires declaring the fall of Troy (Aesch. *Ag.* 8–10). "A woman's man-counseling heart expectant ordains" (10–11). Clytemnestra has the power that put the watchman on the roof; this Clytemnestra is not the preyed upon and seduced wife of Homer's epic (*Ody.* 3. 263–272). Clytemnestra envies Agamemnon for the power over the household that he wielded before leaving for Troy and that she has seized in the meantime and for his sexual freedom, which she has emulated by taking a lover, Aegisthus. She brought Aegisthus into the house for sexual purposes, as Agamemnon brings Cassandra.[6] Mimetic rivalry has wiped away the significant differences between king and queen, husband and wife, man and woman.

Mimetic rivalry defined the Greek as a man in a contest system where rewards of victory were few and the stakes were fought as a winner-take-all.[7] Men learned from their youth the objects to be desired by watching others and, in particular, their fathers. From others, a man derived his sense of worth. Thus his desire learned from others drives him into conflict with them; at the same time, those with whom he competes are the source of his self-worth and identity.[8] Moreover, it was incumbent upon a youth to surpass his father in deeds and fame.[9] The father's age and respect owed him kept the rivalry as an external mediation and generally ended positively.[10] But the ethics of mimetic rivalry fail to establish a curb upon the son's desires. Nothing fixes absolutely the son's surpassing of his model and obtaining the object. Sophocles explores this flaw in his *Ajax,* produced in the 440s, through Ajax, who has been denied the weapons of the dead Achilles.[11] Ajax held them as the consummate proof of his valor, not before his peers in the army, but in his father Telamon's eyes upon him. He magnifies his father's exploit in Heracles' campaign against Troy: from Heracles Telamon received Hesione, the daughter of the Trojan King Laomedon, as a reward for flattering Heracles. Ajax believes that the son should imitate the father: "O son, be more fortunate than your father, but in all else be like him" (Soph. *Ai.* 550–551). By the time of Achilles' death, Ajax has fulfilled the expectations of a son, having far surpassed his father. But Ajax esteems Telamon's glory beyond proportion and without regard for what he actually accomplished. In the place of a real father to rival, Ajax has fabricated an idealized father that has no meaning outside of his own fantasy. Mimetic desire that cannot be satisfied drives him to irremediable shame before his model, madness, and suicide.

Girard looked for acquisitive desire in Plato's treatment of mimesis, but it is in his discussion of rhetoric that Plato lays most clear his understanding of this form of desire. Socrates describes for Gorgias the course of a discussion gone bad:

> I suppose, Gorgias, that you have experienced many discussions and have seen something like this. Men, after laying down definitions, learning and teaching one another regarding what they are trying to discuss, cannot easily end their colloquy. They differ about something. The one says the other is wrong or unclear in what he says. They get angry. Each supposes the other speaks competitively (*kata phthonon*), striving for victory and not seeking what is proposed in the discussion. Sometimes, they depart, abused (*loidorêntes*) by one another, saying and hearing things about themselves that causes the bystanders to be angry with themselves for providing them an audience (*Grg.* 457cd).

Socrates has engaged the famous rhetorician Gorgias in the elenchus, an exchange of questions and answers. It soon becomes apparent that Gorgias is unfamiliar with the medium. The professional in him, however, desires to make a good show of himself before Socrates and the prospective students listening, and the elenchus turns competitive. Socrates respects the man, although not his rhetoric of belief above knowledge, and has before suggested that they end their discussion (*Grg.* 453b). Gorgias labors on, puzzled but ready to tout his skill at some length, enough that Socrates has gained what he searches for: the key to reducing his interlocutor to contradiction. At this point, Socrates prompts Gorgias about his experience in discussions, outlining for him the transition of mimetic to acquisitive desire. After laying

down the rules and exchanging information, the men cannot end because
they have lost the object of the discussion; each has come to desire what he
concedes the other has, the upper hand in the discussion. This is the *phthonos,* the envy they generate because of the pervasive competitiveness inbred
by their culture: it gives them no sense of self-worth apart from the opinion
of others and drives them to validate their worth by imitating those who are
in mimetic rivalry with themselves. They become alike in their protestations
of one another's statements as vague or wrong and angry when the discussion fails to lead to a winner.[12] Their differing strikes the spark of contention;
neither allows the other to seize the object. Quest for victory in the discussion replaces the quest for knowledge. They are no longer "searching for the
thing proposed in the discussion." Meantime, they have been so abused by
one another as to render them alike. This is the effect of the passive participle,
often disguised by translators,[13] that emphasizes their sameness as targets of
the abuse rather than the abusers acting individually, implied by an active
participle. Further violence does not ensue because their behavior disgusts
the listeners, but in an assembly or other public gathering, the violence of the
pair could easily spread to others.

◆   ◆   ◆

"If a man seemingly capable from his cleverness of becoming every sort and
imitating everything should come to our city and want to display himself
and his poems, we would express our deepest respect for him as a holy man,
marvelous and sweet, but we would say that such a man as he has no place
among us in our city, nor is it right for him to be with us" (*Rep.* 398a). Plato
fears the poems of the man of many ways because what they say of the gods
and heroes speaks for the sacred.[14] Poets deceive the listeners and affect their
behavior so that their listeners act wrongfully and cower before death and
Hades. But he excludes the poet himself because of his multiplicity, his ability to imitate and thus acquire anyone and anything. He makes this clear by
the poet he accepts: "a more austere and unpleasant person" who tells in the
fitting style the prescribed types (398ab). Such a poet supports the constitution of the ideal city based not upon "a twofold or manifold man" but rather
upon types of men, "each of whom does one task" (397de). For the same
reason, then, mimesis and its purveyor fail to convey the single truth: both,
copies far removed from the Ideal, have acquired many false and misleading

images. Their motivating desire imitates the truth, produces manifold and, like the beds of different painters, differing copies of it, and threatens the loss of hierarchy and difference. It is the crisis into which Plato grew up; the civil war in Corcyra occurred in the third year of his life, an event so catastrophic that Thucydides claimed that it undermined language itself (3.82.4): words used before of immorality and wickedness came to be used for approval, and moral good and honesty were described in terms of blame and censure.[15] It is the crisis that brought him to maturity; the civil war of the Thirty fell in his twenty-fourth.

Plato feared mimesis, for he lived in a society rampant with acquisitive desire in the form of envy. In his view, no *polis* was well governed (*Ep.* 326ab). His remedy involved not only the creation of a new form of constitution but also a new form of human being to live under it. In the process, Plato retraces what Girard calls the "mimetic mechanism," which, Girard believes, is ultimately responsible for the hominization, the transition of animal to man, and formation of men into stable groups. This process begins with mimetic desire—that is, a desire for something that the subject learns from another, as when, for instance, a baby, watching her mother's delight in eating chocolate, wants it for herself, not from a sweet tooth but because she has learned that chocolate must be good. Mommy wants it, and now, having learned from her mother, so does she. Mother will eventually stop the supply, and the baby may react by crying. This is the reaction of thwarted acquisitive desire, violence, albeit infantile. The child might reach out to take the chocolate, the mother resists, a struggle ensues.

On a social level, acquisitive desire spurs many pairs of rivals locked into rivalry over an object that, in the crescendo of violence linking them, is forgotten. This cascade, or "reciprocal violence," sweeps away order and with it the group itself. Some societies discovered the mechanism to halt the plague of reciprocal violence. All seize upon a victim, someone different in some way or someone who can be made different, and, falling upon him/her in common, remove him/her permanently. The means does not matter as much as its unanimity and finality. He/she unifies reciprocal violence, and his/her removal reifies it as action taken by the group against the individual. The latter, made responsible for the violence whose true cause, if there is one, no longer pertains, is eliminated, and with that death, whether literal or social, as in banishment, harmony is restored.

At first, the community regards their victim as polluted, contaminated with the contagion of the violence that threatened social order and the existence of the group. But they come to see him/her as the one who redeemed them from destruction of forces beyond their control that they often imagine as a plague or other unspecified evil. Then they come to revere their victim as savior with cult and a form of divinity. They remember, and the next time their society confronts a disaster that undermines hierarchies and structures, they seek out a scapegoat, a *pharmakos* or human drug in its ancient Greek apparition, for society's ills; and from what must have started as a hodgepodge of acts and words, they fashion and formalize the pharmacy that is ritual. It follows, as Girard supposes from his hypothesis, that those groups that did not achieve this innovation perished. Accordingly, members of surviving groups have the mechanism instilled in them as part of their acculturation in workings of the world, however they transform the ritual that puts it into performance.

Plato retraces this mechanism in the dialogues *Euthyphro, Apology of Socrates, Crito, Phaedo*, and, to some extent, *Gorgias,* often considered another defense of Socrates.[16] His Socrates functions as the *pharmakos,* the human drug, for the *pharmakon,* the poison/cure that is Plato's written words. In setting out to devise a new constitution and with it a new society, Plato found the need to re-create a new kind of human being. This human being is motivated by the knowledge of justice and the other virtues that are aspects of justice. In doing so, Plato retraced the hominization, *mutatis mutandis,* of humankind. His call for a new city involved the reprisal of its founding mechanism, the scapegoat. He found his scapegoat in sacrificial offering of Socrates at the hands of the Athenian demos. In asserting this thesis, I make clear that by Plato I mean the author of the dialogues, not the real man, in the awareness that his dialogues reveal little about either the author or the real man.

Plato lived in a victimage society. Girard found his access through triangular become mimetic desire in the works of select European novelists.[17] But the mechanism far predates either of them. Evidence, while abundant, is not obvious, and, while striking, has proven easy to overlook. The mechanism is a continuum in the form of a circle, Girard explains, "and one has to choose a point of entry into this descriptive circle, which isn't self-evident."[18] One hops on and grabs a horse. That jump, the arrival into the horse's spinning world, came for Plato with the persecution and legalized murder of Socrates, a man Plato believed to be "the most just of men alive today" (*Phd.* 118; *Ep.* 424d). He explains in the *Seventh Letter* how he became disenchanted with the prospect of a life in politics as he realized how much harder it was becoming to govern a city (325cd). Suitable friends for support were not available. Laws and customs were being corrupted as rule was no longer carried out in the way of the fathers. He turned to philosophy for a perspective that led to the founding of his ideal city with the *Republic.* This process began with a founding murder, that of Socrates, and that began with κατὰ . . . τινα τύχην (*Ep.* 325b). This phrase, "by some chance," conceals the "victimary sign that signals a villain" that leads to "an expulsion/killing of the victim (which is also represented as a hero because he/she eventually saves the community)."[19] We will unpack this τύχη, this chance event, but for now, I take it as a piece of circumstantial evidence that, with others, corroborates the usefulness of Girard's theory for interpreting Plato's project.

Aristophanes' *Clouds* and Plato's *Apology of Socrates* are of especial importance. The *Clouds* presents a Socrates not unlike Plato's, rather, sufficiently like Plato's for the latter to bring the Aristophanic Socrates into his defense at the price of what seems precarious chronology. Aristophanes' Socrates abets the sacrificial crisis in Strepsiades' house and, by his death, restores order. He plays the role of Girard's Satan.

Plato's *Apology of Socrates* provides much information about the historical Socrates and, accordingly, has been received by readers of all sorts as Plato's version of Socrates' actual speech. To read it as a historical text secures a ready and convenient explanation: Socrates said such and such so we must accept it as given. For reasons set forth here, however, I contend that Plato's *Apology of Socrates* is just that, Plato's. All methods of dating its composition, whether internal stylistic or stylometric tests or external historical evidence, at best place it among the so-called early dialogues.[20] I follow Mario Montuori who considers the *Apology of Socrates* to be Plato's first published dialogue, written at Megara after Socrates' death, where Plato and other Socratics had fled for refuge out of fear "for the savagery of the tyrants."[21] These "tyrants" cannot be the deposed Thirty but their democratic successors.[22] Montuori considers Plato's *Apology of Socrates* "as a document of evidence of Plato's reaction to the judicial accusation against Socrates and his defense of the Master's memory and of the Socratic community itself," for "the condemnation of Socrates was also a condemnation of his followers."[23] Plato was a son among the sons of the wealthy who attended upon Socrates; he was liable to prosecution for being corrupted by him. He created a Socrates aimed primarily at defending himself and made a monumental mythic figure. It is generally agreed that Plato wrote the *Apology of Socrates* soon after Socrates' execution. By placing it very soon afterward, I gain a marvelous context for its composition. Plato and the others, huddling in Euclides' house, engaged in mimetic rivalry not only for each to seize Socrates for his own but also to defend themselves against the charges of being contaminated by his teaching and allowing his unnecessary death to besmirch the new regime.

At the end of this beginning, I reprise Girard's question in concluding his monumental *Things Hidden since the Foundation of the World*: Does it work?[24]

CHAPTER 1

Mimesis, Conflict, and Crisis

In the contest system, men's satisfaction with their own position decreases to the extent that others' positions are improved. The good things that happen to others are therefore hurtful to them. This is precisely the nature of envy, which is a feeling of dissatisfaction that arises from the success of others.

—ALVIN W. GOULDNER, *Enter Plato*

In the Greek contest system, all men share, relative to their social position, the roles of subject and model, for all desire to possess all the goods of society for themselves, and anyone can be an object of envy. One aristocrat differs little from another, and they all desire the same things, the implements of honor and excellence. When one among them puts his personal worth together with an accomplishment, victory in the Olympic chariot races or prominent leadership in the assembly, for example, he stands as a model that attracts the envy of others. The others, subjects in Girard's terminology, desire what he has gained and react as if suffering a diminution of their personal esteem and success. "The bitter competitiveness of the contest system," Alvin W. Gouldner continues, "induces men to relish openly the defeat of their foes—thereby making subsequent reconciliation all but impossible."[1] On the other hand, envy from the side of the victorious savors the satisfaction of having gained all in the contest at others' expense. The contest system, inspired by acquisitive desire, motivates victor to continue winning and motivates the defeated to humiliate and impoverish him and take what he has from him— both motives for violence. Agamemnon arouses envy for having destroyed Troy. Yet he is in mimetic rivalry with Priam. He wants what Priam as king and as subject would have in his lust for glory—the prerogative of striding upon clothes from the house, richly made and purchased for silver, and fit only for the foot of a god. Plato as an aristocrat could not have been unaware from his earliest youth of the conflictual aspects of imitative desire.

Plato became a philosopher while writing *Sôkratikoi logoi,* Socratic conversations or discussions, in competition with other followers and admirers of Socrates. Some Socratics showed their desire for the man by following him around the city. Some adopted his lifestyle. Aristophanes points out that the latter "were sick with Socrates," as if Socrates were a disease, or "desired to become Socrates." His word *esôkratôn* denotes both meanings.[2] These Socratics actually copied him, wearing the same kind of clothes and mimicking his gait and manner of speech. Some like Apollodorus spent time with him daily, wanting "to know what he said or did" (Pl. *Sym.* 172c). Others less ostentatious wrote accounts of Socrates beginning around the time of his death. (Even before then, if Diogenes Laertius may be trusted,[3] Simon the cobbler wrote down what he could remember of the conversations Socrates had in his shop with his customers.) Aristotle called their writings *Sôkratikoi logoi* and classified them as mimetic (*Poet.* 1447b11–3). Evidently, he held that they re-presented Socrates' words and deeds, although not necessarily for philosophical purposes. Xenophon's Socrates, less philosophical than Plato's, is a man of self-control and perhaps a more faithful copy of the original. *Sôkratikoi logoi* in the form of narratives or dialogues circulated privately among what was a highly competitive circle of devotees. Little is known, of course, about their activities, but the titles that remain suggest a keen rivalry over representing Socrates.

Aeschines, a constant companion of Socrates, won praise for his depiction of his idol with works entitled *Callias, Axiochus, Aspasia,* and *Alcibiades.* These are names found in the Platonic corpus. Aeschines also appears to have written about Socratic *eros* before Plato so that Plato could have had Aeschines before him in composing the *Symposium.* He undoubtedly knew the work and, while adopting the idea of a female expert, changed the actor for the role from the hetaera Aspasia to the priestess Diotima.[4] Aspasia wrote the funeral oration in his *Menexenos*. Another prominent early Socratic was Antisthenes, an Athenian like Aeschines, who composed an *Aspasia*, *Menexenos*, and *Alcibiades*. Their writings exist in fragments. Plato and Xenophon were minor Socratics at this time.[5] Indicative of their rivalry, however, is the absence of mention of Xenophon by Plato and Xenophon's sole reference to Plato as Glaucon's brother, as well as Xenophon's shared titles, *Apology of Socrates* and *Symposium*—titles, Diskin Clay observes, "clearly meaning to rival the homonymous dialogues of Plato."[6] The silence is compelling, especially beside the willingness of both to name others of Socrates' companions and acquaintances.

Socrates was alive in 414 BCE when Aristophanes produced *Birds*, with its observation on men who wanted to become Socrates. They could have encountered their subject on the streets of Athens. Socratic writers wrote about Socrates from firsthand knowledge of the man but not with the intention of reproducing him faithfully. Rather, in concert with contemporary notions of biography, they could not have imagined the prospect of recording Socrates as an individual.[7] Biography formalized uniqueness into typicality, a process that the comic poets had begun before his death.[8]

Afterward, the rivalry of the Socratics took the form of what Girard calls "external mediation," in that Socrates was removed from them by his death. They could not enter into conflict with him, and so as model he could function positively for the individual. But external mediation easily slips, even in the case of a dead model, into "internal mediation."[9] From imitating Socrates, which they definitely did, they could easily take that small step to the desire to imitate him more closely and in better fashion than the others and, finally, to acquire him in one's version for one's own. (This is, after all, what happened with the Platonic Socrates.)

In this way, the *idea* of Socrates mediates among Socratics internally—that is, within their circle—for it would be accessible to all, and all were disposed to acquire it exclusively of the others. Girard explains that the model in a situation of "internal mediation" is close at hand to the subject:

> Due to the physical and psychological proximity of subject and model, the internal mediation tends to become more and more symmetrical: the

subject will tend to imitate his model as much as his model imitates him. Eventually, the subject will become the model of his model, just as the imitator will become the imitator of his imitator.[10]

In this case, the model is the written Socrates of the subjects. They imitate the Socrates of their desire, the one of their experience and imagination, in an effort to acquire him exclusively. By so doing, in time they defined an arena of topics within whose competition they were made alike. This accounts for the appearance of the same titles; each writer is trying to capture the definitive Socrates as his own.

◆   ◆   ◆

Plato once wanted to be a poet whose tragedies would carry off the prize for entertaining and instructing Athenians in the values of the demos. Tragedy at Athens conformed to the same institutional model as its assemblies and courts and functioned no less as an instrument of democratic ideology. The young Plato evidently desired what poets enjoyed from time immemorial: authority as teacher and voice of wisdom. Then he encountered another voice, a voice capable of instructing the people in another way, and he went into another direction with his writing. But the desire to have what the poet has appears to have abided. He later engages himself in another mimetic rivalry, which he deemed an "ancient quarrel between philosophy and poetry" (*Rep.* 607b). It is a "quarrel" that has left no trace in Greek literature and culture before Plato. It is most likely a Platonic invention, in Andrea Wilson Nightingale's words, a "part of a bold rhetorical strategy designed to define philosophy and invest it with a near-timeless status."[11] Poets traditionally were educators of the people concerning gods and men. Through their songs, heard, memorized, and repeated from earliest youth, the Greek was acculturated as Greek, and Greeks were bound together in communities. Poets, foremost among them Homer, inculcated moral virtues and values, illustrated modes of behavior, and provided information of all sorts and kinds. They had no quarrel with philosophy, for philosophy in Plato's sense did not exist before Plato. It is, as Nightingale says, "Plato's private quarrel . . . which is retrojected back onto the ancients in *Republic* 10 and thereby made to escape the contingency and specificity of Plato's own historical moment."[12] In this process, Plato's philosophy is undoubtedly the newcomer. Poetry and rhetoric wielded power over audiences long before Plato had arrived to conceive of philosophy and continued to do so as long as Athenian culture remained essentially oral. The desire for that power had to have been shown to Plato by those other genres/media. That is, as newly arrived on the block, Plato could only have learned the desire from its established residents. Thus, Plato is the subject who feels the desire to imitate the models, the poets, in exerting authority over audiences as voice of wisdom. The story in Diogenes Laertius, although not likely historical, expresses this dynamic by having Plato desire first to be a poet and only then turn to philosophy and Socrates as the better way to attain that desire, for, as the story implies, the wisdom was better. Although he no longer wanted to be a tragic poet, he craved the poet's influence for his philosophy.

◆   ◆   ◆

To the end of usurping the authority of the poets with that of his philosopher, Plato deconstructs the beliefs of the morality they popularize in their songs. One avenue of attack is the elenchus, the process of question, cross-examination, and refutation practiced by Socrates.[13] The elenchus begins with a request for information—that is, knowledge. "Do we believe that there is any such thing as death?" (*Phd.* 64c). "When someone loves someone, which of the two is the friend, the one loving the beloved or the beloved of the lover, or does it make no difference?" (*Ly.* 212a). Socrates rarely asserts that he has any worthwhile knowledge and looks to others for instruction.[14] "I do not say with knowledge what I say but I am searching in common with you" (*Grg.* 506a). "How could anyone answer who does not know and keeps saying that he does not know. . . . It is more reasonable for you to speak, for you say that you know and can tell us" (*Rep.* 337e). "We are all now equally in perplexity," he avers in forestalling the invitation to tell the nature of courage (*La.* 200e). His request comes in the form of a question that establishes Socrates in the role of the subject which, in turn, casts the answerer in the role of the model. Socrates looks to Euthyphro, for example, for knowledge of piety. "Tell me what you say the pious is and what the impious?" (*Euthphr.* 5d). By becoming the student of Euthyphro, expert on piety, he explains, he will know what he knows and so copy him in being an expert in piety. Thus Socrates could say to Meletus, "If you acknowledge that Euthyphro is wise in these matters and believes in them correctly, consider that I too do and do not prosecute me" (*Euthphr.* 5ab). There is, of course, nothing serious in this on Socrates' part. Yet, if Euthyphro were an expert, and Socrates were to acquire the object of his desire, the result would be that Socrates would be like Euthyphro. Similarly, Socrates looks upon Callicles as the model who holds the same opinions as he, for their agreement would yield likeness as well as "the truth itself" (*Grg.* 487a). In different ways, Socrates imitates his model to acquire knowledge.

The initial question provokes others whose answers are self-evident, so much so that to withhold assent would be perverse and provocative. Socrates insists that the answerer reply sincerely from his beliefs. "See to it, Crito, in agreeing with these matters, you do not agree against your opinion" (*Cri.* 49c). "This thing that you are thinking, since you know how to speak Greek, would you say what it appears to you to be?" (*Chrm.* 159a).[15] Socrates explains to Gorgias at length his idea of an elenchus:

> I consider myself among those men who are glad to be refuted if I am saying
> something not true, and would gladly refute another if he says something
> not true and for whom it is not less pleasant to be refuted than to refute.
> Yet I consider the former the greater good in releasing oneself from a very
> great evil than to release another. (*Grg.* 458a)

Forthrightness in stating one's opinion is another aspect of the elenchus that Socrates lists for Callicles:

> I think that the one who is going to examine correctly concerning the
> soul, whither it lives correctly or not, should have three qualities that you,
> Callicles, have, knowledge, good will, and forthrightness of speech. (*Grg.*
> 487a)

In this way alone, the elenchus remains legitimate search for truth rather than a game like that of a lawsuit with arguments and witnesses (*Grg.* 471e–472b). That is, the elenchus is a contest with the person's beliefs and self-esteem as the stakes and, unless truthfully and openly conducted, will not reach to the quick of the responder.

However far removed subsequent questions seem to be from the starting query, they eventually land the answerer in a contradiction and the collapse of his first answer or definition. Commentators have remarked upon Socrates' skill in framing questions and have drawn conclusions about his knowledge, but this is to displace the author. Plato gets to play both sides of the chess board unrestrained by a time clock. The contest is renewed, often aided and always prompted by Socrates, with a new definition that ends in contradiction and failure. Socrates may declare his willingness to begin anew, but with *aporia* (perplexity) the elenchus ends with the answerer's abandonment of his position. *Aporia,* on the one hand, marks the answerer's total defeat in the zero-sum of the contest. Socrates emerges with all of the prize— namely, whatever, if anything, has been learned and the stakes, which are the answerer's profession of his ignorance and with it his sense of worth.[16] On the other hand, *aporia* evinces the cessation of the answerer's role as model. He has been shown to lack the desired object, the knowledge of what piety is, for example. Socrates is willing to continue, but, as if the river between them has disappeared, their rivalry ends.[17]

The shrewdness of Socrates' questions strikes his interlocutor that he knows both where the inquiry is going and what lies at its destination. Socrates always desires knowledge but also always denies that he has any of his own. "You behave towards me as if I admit to knowing these matters about which I ask you, and if I wanted to, I would agree with you. This is not the case, but I am seeking along with you what is set before us because I myself do not know" (*Chrm.* 165b). Socrates would shift the blame, for that is what it appears to be, for the refutation from himself to the argument. "I mainly examine the argument [*logos*]," Socrates tells Protagoras, adding, however, "it turns out perhaps that I the questioner and you the answerer are being examined" (*Prt.* 333c). But familiarity with his methods, among his friends, precludes such innocence. "You clearly have not encountered Socrates since he has grown older," Nicias warns Laches (187e). "The denial that he is conducting an elenchus," Richard Robinson states, "is insincere, and constitutes what is known as the Socratic slyness or irony."[18] Robinson goes on to explain Socrates' purposefulness as hardly happenstance.[19] The biographical approach looks for answers in Socrates as a person and dismisses the author who, in arranging the questions toward his objective, employs irony to palliate their purposefulness and to diffuse the hostility that a "fixed" contest would arouse. The elenchus is a contest in the form of a mimetic rivalry between Socrates the subject who desires the object and the answerer as model who has it. Their rivalry over the object potentially arouses anger between them. Plato tries to head off conflict by integrating Socrates as a fellow seeker but at an ironic distance. This is to say, irony positions Socrates outside the rivalry inspired by his question.[20] The answerer becomes irritated by his failure to display his knowledge, but as long as the irony of Socrates' ignorance holds, remains unaware of the contest and unprovoked by his inability to display his prowess. Whether Socrates actually knows is not the issue. Should his victims think that he is pretending not to know, then violence breaks out.[21] Whereas Euthyphro is left wondering why his words circumambulate (*Euthphr.* 11b), and Meno likens his state to numbness induced by the sting of an electric eel (*Men.* 80ab), Thrasymachus and Callicles penetrate Socrates' pretense of ignorance and strategy of asking questions and not offering information. He lives in a child's world without villains (*Grg.* 521–522). He should come out and answer questions (*Rep.* 336bc). These are victims who become, Robinson says, "angry with Socrates and ill-disposed towards him."[22] Each believes that he knows the answer, asserts his claim to the object by fighting Socrates for it, and refuses to allow him the freedom from the fray (*Rep.* 337a). It is no accident that the elenchus falters with these answerers, who in seeing through Socrates' "accustomed irony" (*Rep.* 337a) become violent and lash out at him.

More than the question, however, is at stake in the elenchus. Socrates examines how well and good the answerer has lived his life. Nicias elaborates for Laches on his observation:

> You do not seem to know whoever comes very close to Socrates and converses with him must, even if he begins by conversing about something else, not stop being moved around by him in speech until he falls into giving an account of himself, how he lives now and how he lived in the past. (*La.* 187e–188a)

Socrates' victim is supposed to profit from the elenchus. He should leave knowing that he does not know what he thought he knew. For, once shown the flaws of his way of living, Socrates contends, the answerer will cease to be ignorant and change for the better.[23] Many years of the elenchus, however, did not result in a community of enlightened citizens in pursuit of the best sort of life. Plato has Socrates admit in his *Apology* that many of them resent and hate him (23a). Both effects, enlightenment and hatred, derive from Socrates' activity. One is not the side effect of the other. Rather, they are conjoined, like cure and poison, in the *pharmakon* of the word written by Plato and administered to his readers by his *pharmakos*, his human drug.

We return to Socrates as *pharmakos*.[24] In the context of mimetic rivalry, it suffices for now to see that the perplexity over the philosophical question at hand pales before the loss of center and self that the victim suffers at Socrates' dispensation. The Euthyphro who complaisantly but self-assuredly states, "What help would I be in me or in what way would Euthyphro differ from the many men if I did not know accurately all such matters" (*Euthphr.* 4d), is not the Euthyphro who declares on the run, "Another time, Socrates, I'm in a hurry and it's time to go" (15e). The latter Euthyphro has learned that praying and sacrificing preserve the family (*Euthphr.* 14b). His conversation with Socrates has made him a better person in this regard, but Socrates did not inquire beforehand whether Euthyphro wanted to be that, surely diminished, person. Each elenchus causes a sacrificial crisis that envelops the individual in the loss of differences that imperils his identity and place in his city and the cosmos. The proliferation of such crises leads to realignment of the community against the one and the induction of the sacrificial mechanism, a ready expedient for a victimizing society and the fate of the Platonic Socrates.

The task for what remains of this chapter is to trace the operation of acquisitive desire in selected dialogues. I have chosen to examine Plato's desire to seize the authority of the poet for his philosophy in *Ion,* the quarrel that arises in *Laches* over rivalry induced by the elenchus into what is courage, and the clash of Socrates and Callicles as enemy brothers in *Gorgias.*

◆　◆　◆

Plato's quarrel with poetry brought his philosophy into conflict with Homer's epic. It is a mimetic conflict in which Plato seeks to strip the poets of their weight as a source of knowledge and authority. Homer permeated Greek culture, while Plato's native city had especial ties to his poems. Ever since the mid-sixth century, rhapsodes had been performing at the Great Panathenaea every four years and probably were to be found in the city at other times as well. Hipparchus, younger son of the tyrant Pisistratus, "brought the epics of Homer to the land [of Attica] and compelled the rhapsodes at the Panathenaea to go through them in order and in succession" ([Pl.]

Hipp. 228b). Evidently the tyrants found in epic a congenial voice that promulgated respect for hierarchy and authority, and rhapsodes became part of the Athenian landscape. The author of the spurious *Hipparchus,* whose languages denote that he lived in the fourth century, adds "just as they do even now."[25]

Rhapsodes, "stitchers of songs," received their name from their ability to string together lines of spoken as opposed to sung poetry.[26] Some of them may have included something of their own in their performances, but the rhapsode was known for declaiming from memory the standard verses of Homer's *Iliad* and *Odyssey.* Some in an Athenian audience, hearing them all their lives, would have caught instantly improvisation or mistakes. But the rhapsode did more than recite Homer. He enacted the parts, speaking a language remote from the Attic of every day, and held his audiences spellbound. Standing before thousands aloft upon a bema and dressed in embroidered finery and crowned with gold, he inspired his audience to laugh or cry with him. He worked them like an actor, throwing himself into the role while maintaining a presence of mind to evaluate his impact. "I have to pay close attention to them, since if I get them weeping, I myself will laugh as I get the silver, but if they laugh, then I'll weep myself for losing silver" (*Ion* 535e). It was a moment that was repeated enough times over the centuries to have become, as it were, a "text" familiar to Athenians, so that everyone knew how it went. Plato comes to it with his *Ion,* not to dismember Ion the rhapsode, but to use Ion as a model to take over the plot line and essence of the tale itself. The mimetic rival retells the story in words of his source, putting them to his use, in order to take the mantle of knowledge from rhapsode and the Muse from the poet. What remains, then, is the *logos* of the philosopher who, in Plato's pages, has acquired the desideratum, truth as he, not the poet, would have it.

The *Ion* begins with Socrates falling in with Ion somewhere in Athens. Ion has just come from Epidaurus, where he took first prize in the contests for rhapsodes and is in town for the Panathenaea. Socrates confesses his envy of men like Ion (*Ion* 530b–c):

> I have often envied you rhapsodes, Ion, for your craft [*technê*]. The fact that
> it fits your craft to be always dressed up and appear as beautiful as possible
> and that it is necessary to spend time [*diatribein*] with many good poets

and, in particular, with Homer, best and most divine of poets and *to learn thoroughly his thought* not merely his words. All this is enviable. *A rhapsode could never* become good unless he understood what was being said by the poet. For *the rhapsode must be* an interpreter of the poet's thought for the listeners. *It is not possible* to do this well while not knowing what the poet is saying. All of this is worthy of envy.

Socrates confesses his envy of the rhapsode—that is, his desire to have the rhapsode's craft and knowledge of Homer and other poets. This combination of personal attributes and knowledge reproduces Girard's definition of envy, the coveting of "the superior *being* that neither the someone nor something alone, but the conjunction of the two, seems to possess."[27] However, Plato has so ironized Socrates' admission—nothing should have less appeal to Socrates, whose idea of dressing up is a bath and shoes (Pl. *Sym.* 17a), than to stand before a crowd and act out a memorized script—that no one takes the admission of the desire to imitate Ion seriously. Even if little doubt exists that Socrates will acquire the object, knowledge of Homer as he defines it, from either Ion or the genre of rhapsody itself, the desire is genuine. It is real for the philosopher who imitates the rhapsode's control over the minds of the audience by reaching out for it with his *logoi* (words, arguments).

Plato defines Ion's supposed craft, not in terms that relate to Ion and what he is doing, but in terms of his own philosophy. *Diatribein*, Penelope Murray points out, is "a phrase more often used of a life spent in philosophy."[28] To have a *technê* is to have mastery over the subject-content, principles, and reasons of a skill. Ion will prove to have a craft but not a skill, not a *technê,* because he does not possess a body of knowledge based on reason and rational principles that can be applied to creating a service or a product. The cobbler creates visible sandals, and the lyre player, invisible music, because each has the necessary knowledge (*epistimê*) of the techniques (*technai*).[29] (This distinction between *technê* as skill based on knowledge and a craft or knack, often called a *technê* but never accepted as such, runs throughout the dialogues and is fundamental to Socrates' thinking.) Ion cannot interpret all poetry because he lacks the knowledge and skills of interpretation. Ion, however, never conceives of what he does in these Socratic and philosophical terms. Rhapsodes have been successful in what they do for generations, and Ion is particularly talented in the art.

By defining Ion's art, his craft, in terms set by the philosophy, Plato reaches out and takes that art away from Ion. Whatever Ion says of his art will fall short of that art as defined by Plato for his philosophy. We are in the presence of mimetic and acquisitive desire. Plato expresses his desire in terms that imply it will be thwarted: "to learn thoroughly his thought," "a rhapsode could never," "the rhapsode must be," and "it is not possible." For the reader gleans from the first that Ion is not going to have this knowledge. In terms of philosophy, the lack of that knowledge allows philosophy to acquire the interpreting of poetry from him. Thus acquisitive desire achieves by the end of the dialogue what it sets out to obtain: the power to interpret Homer and the poets.

Successful at this craft, Ion accepts that Socrates would envy him. A prize-winning rhapsode, to judge from the contests of the Panathenaea, he carried off a small fortune from Epidaurus.[30] But rhapsodes like Ion are dismissed by ancients and moderns alike as dimwitted. "Do you know a bunch of men sillier than rhapsodes?" Xenophon's Antisthenes asks of Niceratus whose father had him memorize all of Homer (*Sym.* 3.6; also *Mem.* 4.2.10). Pointedly, Socrates twits Ion for being "forgetful": "It would not be a good thing for a rhapsode to be forgetful," to which Ion responds in huff: "And just what have I forgotten?" (*Ion* 539e–540a). When reminded of a point in the argument, Ion's curt "I remember" shows the low priority he places on remembering that stuff. This view of Ion is reprised by modern scholars who react by deeming the *Ion* as spurious or, after abandoning that approach, as a product of Plato's earlier, immature period, when he first began to write dialogues. This attitude arises with the devaluation of memory and the encyclopedic functions of the bard. Ion is surely overmatched in this discussion with Socrates; in fact, he has little idea of what is happening. When Socrates tries to impute that Ion is possessed, however, he demurs: "I would be amazed if you could speak so well as to convince me against my will that I praise Homer while possessed and maddened" (53d). Ion is no fool but the representative of a kind of knowledge that Plato wants to destroy in order to replace it as a voice of authority with philosophy and its definition of inspiration. Ion the man is not dim of wit: he is outside Socrates' grasp because he is confident in his worth and the worth of his craft.

Socrates puts off to another time Ion's offer to perform with the question "Are you skilled only concerning Homer or also concerning Hesiod and Archilochus?" (*Ion* 531a). Thus Socrates engages Ion in the elenchus, the dialogue of question, answer, and refutation that aims to stir the interlocutor to perplexity (*aporia*) while arousing an appetite for philosophy and to demonstrate for audiences of listeners and readers that those who pretend to have wisdom are not really wise. The elenchus breaks down the confidence of the interlocutor, usually a figure of authority, to a state of helpless ignorance. Euthyphro, self-professed expert on piety, is revealed as both pedantic and conventional in his beliefs. Few understand, fewer agree with Socrates, and no one actually follows Socrates in the pursuit of philosophy; rather, most become agitated and argumentative. Euthyphro runs away: "Some other time, Socrates." Diogenes Laertius speaks of Socrates getting into fistfights and hair-pulling (2.21). The second purpose, the educative function of the elenchus, tends to become lost in the effects of its negative intention, that of demonstrating ignorance, and the adversarial approach by which Socrates goes about it. He tries to head off conflict by being very friendly, but the attitude in the Greek contest system bespeaks intellectual and personal dominance. Socrates belittles his understanding of the subject, but after a while his pretense appears disingenuous and may be received as deliberately ironical. Irony in the elenchus functions to forestall conflict by concealing Socrates' acquisitive desire as long as possible beneath his guise of ignorance and eagerness to be taught. Although Socrates often professes that he, too, has no idea where the argument will end, Plato does. The dialogues, we must remember, may be realistic, but they are not real. They are the products of Plato's imagination, and he imagines the end from the beginning and directs Socrates to that end. The question Socrates poses to Ion predicates the ending that Ion has no craft and therefore lacks the skills, rational principles, and techniques to criticize all poetry as one whole (532c). The elenchus is Plato's way of working his way to the goal of destroying the expert's authority. Conflict arises when Socrates' desire to obtain information from his rival clashes with the rival's inability to satisfy his questions and thus assert his authority. Not every elenchus is of this type—what Girard calls "internal mediation"—because Socrates does not press those who are not his peers, youthful interlocutors and the less thoughtful or worthy, like Euthyphro and Ion. Still, conflict is hinted at by Euthyphro's exasperation at the argument moving in a circle (*Euthphr.* 11c) and Ion's refusal to accept Socrates' contention that he composes while entranced (*Ion* 536d) but does not erupt because

Socrates' ironic stance and the deficiencies of his interlocutors keep them at
a distance.

In *Ion,* the first round of the elenchus quickly brings Ion to this point. In
fact, Ion remains perplexed as to why he can interpret only Homer. Socrates
has to tell him that he could speak about all poets if he spoke in accord with a
craft. Then, evidently suspecting Ion's failure to comprehend, Socrates asks if
he needs clarification. Ion agrees, but then adds, "for I enjoy listening to you,
the wise" (532d). The comment has no preparation. With it, Plato intrudes to
give Socrates a second form of discourse. "Would that you spoke truthfully,
Ion, I would like it, but you rhapsodes and actors are wise" (532d). Socrates'
discourse is to speak the truth. "I am saying nothing other than the truth as
is likely for an ordinary person to say (532d)." *Sophos* (wise) has always been
said of poets but is now contrasted to *alethês,* "true," said of the philosopher's
reason. "Let us resume with reason" (532e).

Socrates continues with the elenchus, hammering Ion with the same
question. Have you ever heard of anyone who can elaborate about the works
of one artist and not those of another of the same sort? Ion cannot answer
Socrates, but he knows that it is true of him. Reduced to perplexity, he cues
Socrates: "You figure it out" (533c). Socrates proceeds to do so in what is
often denoted as the great speech in the middle of the dialogue. But it is less
a speech than a performance after the manner of the rhapsode that destroys
the rhapsode's manner. Socrates stitches together words that he puts in a new
order and in prose that "touch Ion's soul" as he misses what they do to his
craft and that of the poets (534de).

Although some rhapsodes performed their own poetry, the audience for
their art expected the faithful repetition of a song that few in the audience
had not heard before. The actor also acted out the lines, as Ion makes clear
(535de), and added his own "thoughts" (530d). It is not clear from the *Ion*
what these thoughts consisted of, but by comparing Ion to Metrodoros of
Lapsacus and other of his ilk, Plato implies that they were allegorical interpretations of meanings hidden in Homer's characters as well as questions of
grammar.[31] Thus by revealing the hidden force in Ion's inspiration, Plato is
probably imitating the performance of a rhapsode (533d):

> This speaking well about Homer that you have is not a craft (as I already
> told you) but a divine power which moves you just as the stone that

Euripides called a magnet, but most people call the stone of Heraclea. This
stone attracts not only the rings themselves, ones made of iron, but it puts
power into the rings so that they are able to do the same thing that the
stone does, to attract other rings, so that sometimes a very long chain of
iron pieces and rings is suspended from one another. For all of them, the
power is dependent upon that stone. So also the Muse makes men inspired
herself and through these others being enthused, a chain is strung out.

The poet composes not from knowledge of what he is saying but from inspiration from the Muse, like the attraction of a magnet to iron rings. The Muse
first possesses the poet, then the rhapsode, and finally the audience. Murray
suggests that Plato was the first to apply the image of the magnet to poetry.
"The idea that poets are inspired is, of course, age-old, but the notion of
ἐνθυσιασμός which P[lato] here introduces is strikingly new."[32] Plato apparently took the word and the idea of *enthusiasmus* from Democritus, the earliest source of the word: "Whatever the poet writes with *enthusiasmus* and the
holy spirit is very fine" (fr. 18). Whereas Democritus allows the poet to create
under the influence while in possession of his technique, Plato contrasts the
two states: "All the poets of epic—the good ones—do not say all these beautiful poems from craft but by being inspired and possessed, and in the same
way the lyric poets" (533e). Poets are reduced to lumps of iron, as it were,
controlled by a force that lies beyond human understanding.

Plato, however, imitates by invention. The poet as a Bacchant enthused
with Dionysus (533e–534d) is his idea. Archilochus connected Dionysus and
wine with poetry, but the poet's "wineless Bacchic ecstacy . . . seems to have
begun here."[33] Indeed, as Murray says, Plato evokes the poet's state of mind
with a sentence that "as a whole enacts its own meaning, as the clauses are
piled up one on top of the other and the reader is carried away by the stream
of words":

All the poets of epic—the good ones—not from craft but by being
enthused and possessed, say all these beautiful poems, and the lyric poets,
the good ones, in the same way as the Corybantes dance while not in possession of their senses, so too the lyric poets do this, not being in their
minds, but when they enter into harmony and rhythm, they act like Bac-
chants, possessed, as the Bacchae draw honey and milk from rivers, being

possessed and not in their senses, and the soul of the lyric poets accomplish this, which they themselves say.

Plato took the phrase "the Bacchae draw honey and milk" from Aeschines, a fellow Socratic writer, who used it of Socrates (fr.11c Dittmar):

> Through the passion that I felt in passion for Alcibiades, I experience nothing different from the Bacchae, for the Bacchae, whenever they are filled with the god, draw honey and milk from wells that others cannot draw even milk from.

Plato reproduces the same verb for "draw" and the same order for its objects. Murray sees this as "a more original comparison" that highlights "the irrationality of the poetic process."[34] Nonetheless, Plato steals the language of a fellow writer of *Sokratikoi logoi*—a theft that might have gone unnoticed but indicates that Plato read the works of other Socratics. Plato finally imitates the poets' self-referential language of poetic inspiration (534b–d):

> Of course, the poets tell us that from springs flowing with honey out of some gardens and glens of Muses, they cull their poems and bring them to us like bees, and so they too are on wings. They are telling the truth, for a poet is a light-weight thing, winged, and sacred. He is not able to create poems until he is inspired and out of his senses. Until he has this possession, every man is incapable of making a poem or a prophesy. In as much as poets do nothing by craft, while saying many beautiful things about the deeds of men, just as you do about Homer, by divine allotment, each one is able to make beautifully that to which the Muses impelled him, whether one makes dithyrambs, another hymns of praise for victors, another dances set to music, another epics, and another iambics. Each one is run-of-the-mill regarding the other types, for they do not say these things by craft but by a divine power, since, if they knew by craft how to speak beautifully about one of them, they would know how to do so concerning all of the others. For this reason, the god, removing their mind from them, uses them as servants, both soothsayers and divine seers in order that we, the listeners, know that these in whom a mind does not reside are not the ones who are saying these things through them.

Speech as a flowing river and its associations with honey are as old as Homer. They are found in Pindar, Bacchylides, and Callimachus. Aristophanes refers to the poet as a winged bird, Pindar and Bacchylides as an eagle, and all poets speak of being inspired. The lightness of the poet and his words have been asserted many times, as has been drawn the connection between poetry and prophecy. The performance of traditional language deeply moves Ion, and he agrees that "all good poets seem to me to act as mouthpieces of the gods for us" (535). But if he listened more carefully, he would hear that the poet cannot create until he is inspired—a state that even he denies (533–534a)—and out of his senses, and then only that type of poetry sanctioned by his Muse. Plato grants poets a link to the god, but he strips them of any claim to truth. Rosemary Harriott explains "what he has taken away":

> He has disposed of the belief that the poet transmitted knowledge, that he was in control of his material, that he was concerned to communicate with an audience. The matter-of-fact acceptance of poetry conspicuous previously has vanished, without a single destructive word being spoken.[35]

Philosopher becomes rhapsode to destroy the authority of the poetic tradition itself. He takes over the language of poetic inspiration and revises it into his prose with an argument that is itself flawed like the poet's wisdom. For everyone knows that poets do not compose in a frenzy, and many write more than one kind of poem. Further, though Ion is touched by Socrates' poetic statement, he leaves no doubt that he is not inspired when performing. "I think that I would not seem so to you if you heard me speaking about Homer" (536d). Thus the connection suggested by the image of the magnet is broken and with it the poet's linkage with the Muse as source of truth.

◆ ◆ ◆

The conversation of the *Laches* begins and ends peacefully, but the interim traces a crescendo of mimetic rivalry. Lysimachus and Melesias have taken the generals Nicias and Laches to watch an exhibition of fighting in hoplite armor. Since the hoplite fought in a formation, individual fighting was specialist training. Afterward, Lysimachus and Melesias explain their motive in requesting their presence at the performance. They want the advice of the military men on whether they should have their sons pursue such an education. The generals seem to be friends and comfortable with themselves as generals of the Athenians. Surely they would make admirable advisers in military affairs. As we discover, Laches appears as an ordinary Athenian who has learned things about fighting, courage, and war from his military service, while Nicias, more refined and sophisticated, has been studying with the sophist Damon.

The rivalry begins with Lysimachus' request, which becomes the first object over which Laches and Nicias contend: "Your role now is to advise us whether our sons should learn this lesson or not" (*La.* 180a). Laches suggests that Nicias and he may not be the best advisers since, like Lysimachus' and Melesias' famous fathers, they neglected their family in their duty to the city. He points to Socrates, until now a silent presence for the reader, as someone who has experience in the education of the youth. Laches adds that Socrates accompanied him on the return from the Athenian defeat at Delium. "If the others had wanted to act like this one, our city would have stood up and not have fallen so" (181b). The scene serves to establish Socrates' authority of sorts regarding the subject at hand (180bc) and bravery, thus putting his word beyond reproach. The military experience that Lysimachus and Melesias sought in Laches and Nicias, we should note, henceforth resides in Socrates. The latter, with a strategy from the dynamics of the elenchus, puts off speaking until he has heard what his elders say and, in the process, has gained material for questioning and refutation.

As it turns out, however, the generals differ absolutely, with Nicias praising fighting in hoplite armor as a means of self-defense and a first step to advancement in military science, and Laches seeing nothing of value in such a display. Lysimachus asks Socrates to decide the issue by casting his vote. Socrates refuses to submit a question of knowledge to the will of the majority (*La.* 184d) and encourages Lysimachus and Melesias to consider the matter very important since it concerns the welfare of their children. He brings the conversation around to an inquiry on how the souls of their sons may be as good as possible (186a), heading them toward the elenchus by averring that he has not been able to teach himself on this matter and has had no teacher, although he has been interested in education from his own youth, because he lacks the money to pay a sophist. On the other hand, the generals could have learned about these things from sophists, for they have greater means and have lived longer. For now, Socrates flatters their knowledge, thus drawing them into a discussion of education, for, he contends, "they never would have spoken out fearlessly concerning the practices good and bad for the young, if they weren't sure that they knew sufficiently" (186d).

Lysimachus suggests that Nicias and Laches submit themselves to Socrates' questions, since, as he said at the beginning, they believe that the generals have given care to the education of their sons. Nicias replies that Lysimachus does not know what he is bargaining for. Once someone starts conversing with Socrates, he will not escape until he has given an account of his life. Nicias has suffered this experience and will gladly do so again, "it being neither strange nor fearful to be tested by Socrates. . . . But see how Laches is disposed about a thing of this kind" (*La.* 188b). Nicias' father made his fortune in mining silver, and Nicias himself was not above using his fortune to gain influence.[36] He surely has had the "best education," continues to attend to the sophists, and has spoken with Socrates. Nicias touts his superiority, brandishing his "weapons," as it were, on the field before the battle. He lets go the challenge, for this sounds like "I triple double dare you." Laches, irked and put on the defensive because he has never heard Socrates speak, replies that he is "of one mind, no, rather, two regarding conversations" (188c). He can only listen to a good man of proven worth and not his opposite. He has experienced such a man in Socrates and is ready to face his inquisitor, although he expects that Socrates will learn from what he knows (189b).

The lines are drawn over the education of the souls of the sons of Lysimachus and Melesias. How long this remains the object, and the object remains between them, remains to be seen. Not very long, as it turns out, for within less than two of Stephanus' pages, Socrates has changed the subject/object with a suddenness for which Plato apologies: "Perhaps you don't understand what I'm saying" (*La.* 189e). Now the object lying between Nicias and Laches is the question what is *aretê* (virtue, goodness). Socrates gets Laches to agree that he knows what it is, but assessing the inquiry into the whole of *aretê* to be too large, he narrows it to the part that concerns instruction in weapons—namely, *andreia* (courage, fortitude). The issue now is one that they should know. Athenians chose many of their administrators by lot, but generals they elected for their expertise. It could not have been good for Socrates, if such a conversation had actually happened, to reduce two of their stellar leaders to schoolboys. As it is, Laches jumps right in to begin this, as many *elenchoi* have begun, on an example of the virtue instead of a definition (198e).

We needn't follow Laches through Socrates' questions. They bring him to the contradiction between his definition of courage as thoughtful endurance and his admission that those who endure foolishly are more courageous than the wisely courageous (193d), and to *aporia*, the interlocutor's destination. Our concern lies with his reaction. He endeavors to keep going,

> although I am unaccustomed to conversation of this sort, buta rivalry (*philonikia*) over what has been said has seized me, and I am truly annoyed at not being able to say what I think. I seem to discern what courage is, but I do not know where it has escaped me just now, so that I couldn't seize it with my words and say what it is. (*La.* 194ab)

His is the reaction of the interlocutor, but we need to pay attention to his disclaimer. He says he will continue, "although I am unaccustomed to conversation of this sort" and its cause, a rivalry or contention. "You are contentious [*philonikos*]," Callicles accuses Socrates, who replies, "No, I do not ask out of contention [*philonikia*] but I truly desire to know" (Pl. *Gorg.* 515b). Callicles is openly rivaling Socrates, but Laches turns his failure upon himself. His disclaimer points to the cause of his failure, that of not being as good at argumentation as he imagines his model Nicias to be and so failing to gain the prize that his model in his estimation desires. As Nicias will soon tell him (200b), Laches looks to others, not himself, and even now desires the victory that he imagines Nicias will obtain.

Laches, though eager to continue, is out of his element, and Socrates turns to Nicias. "Come, Nicias, aid your friends. They are floundering in a storm of words and at a loss (*aporousin*)" (*La.* 194c). Nicias asserts his experience by quoting Socrates and then defines courage as a kind of knowledge. Nicias is trying to imitate Socrates in defining courage—that is, he is in mimetic rivalry—not with Laches but with Socrates. Laches does not understand his responses and, at Socrates' prompting, questions Nicias. Nicias' replies strike him as "nonsense" (195a). For Laches, rivalry over the object has given way to rivalry with Nicias. He is scolded by Socrates for reviling Nicias rather than teaching him, the ostensible purpose of the elenchus (195a). But the object has "disappeared in the heat of rivalry," and doubling, as we shall see, begins to occur. Girard describes the way that

the two rivals become more and more concerned with defeating the opponent for the sake of it, rather than obtaining the object, which eventually
becomes irrelevant, as it only exists as an excuse for the escalation of the
dispute. Thus, the rivals become more and more undifferentiated, identical: doubles.[37]

Throughout Nicias' exchange with Socrates, Laches claims not to understand. He proposes that "Nicias does not want to fess up like a noble man
that he is saying nothing and twists here and there, trying to conceal his
aporia" (196b). He accuses Nicias of decking himself with words as if he
were in court trial (196b, 197c). Then he learns from Socrates that Nicias
repeats what he learned from Damon. "Such stuff befits more the sophist,"
Laches pronounces, "than the man who the city deems worthy of leading
it" (197d). Their quarrel takes the form of the plain man against the sophisticated, but what matters here is how quickly it sprang up between settled
men of distinction.

   Within the dynamic of Nicias in mimetic rivalry with Socrates, and
Laches in conflict with Nicias, the rivals have been moving toward symmetry. "One is always moving towards more symmetry, and thus always towards
more conflict, for symmetry cannot but produce *doubles*."[38] Theirs is not a
free-for-all but, as it were, a managed conflict. Socrates has been guiding the
conversation with Nicias to Nicias' *aporia*. His bravery in the retreat from
Delium has placed him outside the struggle. The effect is that the generals
come into conflict with one another without their realizing Socrates' role
in their frustration and failure. They are ordinary Athenians in never having
thought through their values, but with the desire of each to obtain the object
desired by their model in their fancy, they quickly fall into a dispute that
renders them the same. Both prove to be ignorant of the quality upon which
their profession depends:

SOCRATES: We have not discovered, Nicias, what courage is.
NICIAS: We appear not to have. (*La.* 199e)

Symmetry is complete. Laches and Nicias are doubles in ignorance
of what is courage. Laches attempted to imitate Nicias by entering into

arguments with Socrates. He wanted what Nicias could do—namely, discover what courage is. He says that he thought Nicias could do this with the wisdom gained from Damon (*La.* 200a). Nicias replies with a speech that summarizes the first stages of mimetic rivalry:

> It is alright for you to think that it's no big thing that you yourself appeared just now knowing nothing about courage, and you look at this, whether I will appear another such ignoramus. And it will make no difference to you that you and I know nothing about things, knowledge of which it befits a man to have to some degree. You seem to me to do the truly human thing: not looking to yourself but to others. (200ab)

At the outset, Laches looked to Nicias as someone who knew about courage. He took Nicias as his model and, although unacquainted with argumentation, desired to obtain the object that he imagined—correctly, as it turns out—Nicias desired. Laches is a mimetic rival of Nicias. Once Nicias is identical to him in ignorance, Nicias no longer serves as a model. Laches did not want the object from his own desire but in imitation of Nicias. As Nicias tells him, he looks to others. It is the human thing. Hence, when Nicias no longer serves as someone to look to, Laches gives up his *philonikia,* and the rivalry ends abruptly. The river has disappeared.

It is worth noting that Socrates removes himself immediately as a model:

> If in the conversations just now I appeared to know something, and you did not, it would be perhaps just to call me to this task [of improving the youth], but now we all equally are in *aporia.* (200e)

The quarrel may end, but the crisis, one of disquiet over the generals' ignorance and anxiety it may arouse, goes unresolved except for the promise to meet tomorrow to consult. The discussion in *Laches* begins with an appeal for advice over a lesson in fighting and becomes, thanks to Socrates' questions, "a lesson for the sake of the souls of the young men" (185e). Both generals surely would have been satisfied, perhaps after some refinements by the sophist-educated Nicias, with Laches' definition of courage: the man who stands in formation, faces the enemy, and does not give way to flight (190e). It is the mantra of hoplite fighting heard from its earliest recorded exponent,

Tyrtaeus of seventh-century Sparta (fr. 10). But Socrates turns the discussion to the *therapeia psychês,* the therapy of the soul. Allowed by his bravery and ignorance (186c, 200e), he remains outside the inquiry and its treatment. His questions, his elenchus, are like the *pharmakon* (drug) for treating the eyes:

> Whenever someone inquires about a *pharmakon* for the eyes, whether one should be applied or not, do you think the counsel is about the *pharmakon* or about the eyes? (185c)

"Counsel is directed toward the thing about which one inquires and not about that thing concerning which he inquires for the sake of something else" (185d). Like that of the *pharmakon,* Socrates' interaction escapes inquiry because its purpose is *therapeia*—in this instance, *therapeia psychês.* Socrates' elenchus is, then, a *pharmakon,* a drug that cures the souls of Laches and Nicias of their ignorance. It is also a poison that debilitates the souls of men in command of other men by undermining their sense of self. In discussing Shakespeare's *Troilus and Cressida,* Girard observes how "in a disciplined and efficient outfit, each soldier looks up to the rank immediately above his own in the hope of a promotion. Each soldier takes his commanding officer as a model and a guide." But when the upper ranks fail, the imitation of their failure runs down through the chain of command, the "degree" in his discussion, to facilitate "the contagion of disorder when disorder appears."[39] Disorder appeared in 413 BCE when Nicias deferred to the seers over an eclipse of the moon and postponed the retreat from Sicily. Thus he allowed the fleet of the Athenians to be contained and destroyed in the harbor of Syracuse (*Thuc.* 7.50.4). The general's *aporia* over the nature of courage is set in a time before the Sicilian expedition and was written many years after its defeat. Plato's view that "the seer not lead the general, but the general the seer" (199a), probably refers to the crisis of degree that Nicias suffered in the harbor of Sicily between the superstitious man that he was and the educated man who "should have recognized eclipses as a natural phenomenon."[40] The fictional crisis implies the historical crisis; both result from ignorance of something that someone in command should know. Fiction and history are mixed up like this in Plato's therapy, a masala to be soon savored again.

As Girard contends, Plato has no expressed theory of acquisitive desire and, knowing the dangers of imitative behavior, he "eventually refuses mimesis."[41] Plato, however, did not need a theory, as its avatar in his society, envy, was ubiquitous. As Plato's Nicias observes, looking to others for what one wants is only human.

◆ ◆ ◆

By the time he came to writing *Republic,* Plato could speak without rancor of how politicians who pander to the people in poorly governed cities are honored by them as true public servants (*Rep.* 426cd). In the earlier *Gorgias,*[42] however, he was far more energized, charging the giants of the Athenian past, Themistocles, Cimon, Miltiades, Pericles, with pleasing the people and making them worse rather than better (503cd) and creating the crisis in Athenian society. Gorgias and Polus are historical figures, and, although nothing is known of Callicles of Archarnae outside the *Gorgias,* he is believed to have been a real person.[43] In his way, each is an exponent of the crisis. Gorgias contributes its efficient cause, rhetoric; Polus, unthinking acceptance of the power of politicians who wield it; Callicles, the aspiration to use it as a politician to deceive and milk the people. Plato involves them in an elenchus with Socrates that moves toward greater hostility until it breaks down with Callicles. Polite but probing against Gorgias, he abandons his studied ignorance against Polus to define rhetoric as a form of pandering that deceives the souls of men. He exhausts himself in an effort to dissuade Callicles from adopting a lifestyle of the politician in a democracy. Plato contrasts their conversation with the conflict of the enemy brothers, Zethus and Amphion, in Euripides' *Antiope.*[44] Enemy brothers, however, are a symptom of the crisis, not its cause. For this, we must examine Gorgias and the rhetoric for which he serves as a model, a method of speaking that ambitious men pay to imitate.

Socrates and Chaerephon, held up in the agora, arrive too late to hear Gorgias' exhibition, Callicles' "elegant feast" (*Grg.* 447a). No matter, for Socrates has not come for speeches but to "feast" upon Gorgias with his question. It is the same question as that of the *Apology of Socrates,* now directed at Gorgias: "Who is he?," quickly emended to "What is his *technê,* and what do we call him?" "Rhetoric" and "rhetor, or rhetorician," are the answers, establishing Gorgias as the model of a kind of speaking that, as he readily, even gleefully, concedes, confounds the differences between knowledge and belief.

Gorgias' character reflects his *technê* (as it turns out, his is no *technê* but a knack, a mystical power comparable to creating tasty fish relish), which explains why Plato spends so much time on his portraiture. A foreigner from Leontini in Sicily and a famous rhetor, Gorgias is a guest at the house of Callicles, young, wealthy, and ambitious.[45] The opening scene implies that Gorgias is meeting Socrates for the first time.[46] Socrates may have heard of him. Gorgias came to Athens with a delegation from his city in 427 BCE and caused a sensation in the Athenian assembly with his style of speaking. He garnered many students and left town, Hippias says, with loads of the locals' money.[47] At any rate, Socrates treads lightly with the distinguished gentleman (*Grg.* 453c, 454c) while pressuring him to perform in unfamiliar ways. Gorgias is no less on display today as a speaker and advertisement for his wares than on that day in 427. Such is the life of the itinerant professor that he must be aware of himself at all times. Several from his audience have remained behind (458c) to listen to the conversation and, as Socrates mischievously notes, there may be among them potential students too embarrassed to ask questions themselves (455c). How Gorgias comports himself matters because he does not teach through theory but by having the students imitate him by memorizing his practice exemplars and speeches.[48]

Success has made Gorgias complaisant, as his comment to Chaerephon reveals: "No one has asked me a new question in many years" (*Grg.* 448a). Gorgias consents, in part, to answering Socrates' questions because he has no knowledge of the phenomenon, but, more so, because he is satisfied with himself. He freely admits that he enjoys the "great ease of not knowing other skills but this one and being in no way inferior to the practitioners" of those skills—that is, the experts (459c). He grants that his rhetoric consists of words that are intended to persuade, have no basis in knowledge, and yet create belief in audiences ignorant of the subject. His greatest influence, he admits, lies with those empowered with governance, judges in courts, councilors in the council, and assemblymen in the assemblies. Shaped by success and a skill shared by few, he has become his own institution, rendering him pompous (451d, 455d) and vain (449a, 463d). E. R. Dodds sees the Platonic Gorgias as "a well-meaning but somewhat muddleheaded old gentleman" self-satisfied with the comforts his life's exertions have bestowed upon him.[49] But Gorgias is also a model for an oratory that Dodds admits "put a deadly instrument into the unscrupulous hands for the corruption of simple people who are morally only children."[50]

To this man comes Socrates, gift of the god, for, although Plato mentions neither Apollo's oracle nor Socrates' interpretation, the Socrates of Plato's *Apology of Socrates* must have been familiar to Plato's audiences. Socrates has a question that, surprisingly, he has Chaerephon ask: "Who is he?"[51] Chaerephon hesitates, uncertain of Socrates' meaning, but, when prompted, readily understands Socrates to mean "what is his *technê,* and what do we call him?" But before he asks Gorgias, Polus, a young Sicilian rhetor, interrupts. Chaerephon, he says, should ask him. Gorgias has talked a lot already. "Do you think, Polus, you could answer more beautifully than Gorgias?" Polus' response, "What is the difference, if I answer sufficiently for you?" (*Grg.* 448b) reveals his stance on speaking: it is the means to gratify and persuade the listener. Chaerephon accepts his condition, and Polus responds:

> Chaerephon, many skills exist among men, discovered from their experiences through their experiences, for experience makes our mortal existence (*aiôn*) proceed according to skill while inexperience through chance. Some share each of these skills in some ways, others, others in other ways. The best share the best, and among them is Gorgias here, and he shares the most beautiful of skills. (448c)

Repetitions, balanced phrasing, and poetic allusions (*aiôn*) reprise Gorgian style.[52] Polus shows his ability to imitate his master and propensity to flatter him. Socrates rejects a description of Gorgias' *technê* as a definition of its nature. This brief skirmish, initiated by the boorishness of a man true to his name, "Colt," brings out the essential difference between them: Polus' rhetoric, cause of the crisis as speech that seeks persuasion and indulgence, and Plato's remedy, Socrates' speech that seeks the truth.

Chaerephon's acceptance of Polus' claim that the persuasive answer serves rather than the one derived from dialectic and the rational search for truth, it is worth noting, isolates Socrates from even as frail an ally as Chaerephon the "Bat" (Ar. *Av.* 1296).

Socrates eases Gorgias along through their definition of rhetoric, for he does not understand dialectic, but he knows that rhetoric consists of words. Although uncertain what words, he perceives their function. They convey to the rhetor freedom and the power to rule over others (*Grg.* 452d). Rhetoric, he says, is

persuading by words jurymen in the court and councilors in the council-
chamber and assemblymen in assembly and in every other gathering which
concerns city business. And indeed, through this power, you will have the
physician as your slave and the trainer as your slave and the financier will
be seen making money, not for himself, but for another, you who wield the
power to speak and to persuade the multitudes. (452c)

The response of the Platonic Gorgias, besides reflecting the convictions
of the historical rhetor,[53] implies that the words themselves, their content,
truth or falsity, matter less than the influence they wield upon others. Their
function is to persuade and to convey upon the rhetor the power to reduce
others to becoming his slaves. Gorgias' statement is strong, provocative, one
recalling again the historical Gorgias,[54] in a slaveholding society—namely,
that one free man can render another his slave. For Gorgias, rhetoric is less a
means to convey information than a weapon to subjugate. They are "power"
words that resemble the truth but are not the truth.

Socrates confirms that Gorgias means to say that rhetoric produces
persuasion and has no other power. This entails, as we see, that rhetoric does
not teach or convey wisdom. Its words, then, are unlike any of those used
in the skills (*technai*), for a *technê* is based on principles of truth that can
be stated. Yet the rhetor is not alone in persuading, Socrates goes on; the
arithmetician persuades with his statements about numbers. Gorgias refines
rhetorical persuasion to that which is produced in the courts regarding
issues of justice and injustice (*Grg.* 454b). While the arithmetician produces
knowledge through his *technê,* the rhetor does not teach knowledge to the
courts but produces belief without knowledge (454e–455a), since he lacks
the expertise and knowledge of numbers or of any skill. At this point in the
discussion, Socrates reminds Gorgias of potential students in the audience.
His observation awakens the showman. Gorgias rises to the challenge and
boasts: all that the architect built, the docks and walls and edifices of the
port, came about through the rhetoric of Themistocles and Pericles and
not from the craftsman. This is to say that the power of speech wielded by
Pericles outshines that of the experts. In response, Socrates butters him up
by remarking that the "power of rhetoric is almost demonic (*daimonia*) in
its magnitude" (456a). Without thought for the sarcasm,[55] Gorgias slips

into what seems to be his "pitch" to students. He recalls how the rhetor, although he lacks the expert's knowledge (456c), prevails in every instance over the expert because of his power to persuade. With thoughts of students looming in the background, however, his apprehension over their activities pops into his head: his responsibility for how they use what he teaches. The thought betrays Gorgias' awareness that his rhetoric may be used unjustly. But "responsibility" may be too strong a word for the self-absorbed model of rhetoric. "Blame" fits better (remembering how sensitive Polus was to rhetoric being blamed [448e]) as he becomes exercised over the fact that "those who have taught are not wicked nor is their skill culpable [*aitia*: also 'blameworthy,' 'responsible'], but the wicked are those who do not use rhetoric correctly" (456e). Gorgias concludes that the rhetor should use his skills justly; he who does not use what he has been taught justly may be "justly hated, banished, and slain but not the one who taught him" (457c).

It would not be speaking outside the evidence to say that the Platonic Socrates lives for a moment like this when his interlocutor waxes eloquent. The usual respondent interacts with the world through traditional wisdom, the legacy of the "village." He is bound to be the victim of inconsistency and contradiction, since both are inherent to received wisdom. This explains why Plato steps aside after Gorgias' speech for Socrates to rehearse for him the frequent descent of a discussion into acquisitive desire ending in violence (*Grg.* 457cd). Socrates is preparing him for the embarrassment of being caught in a contradiction. Gorgias would rather end the session whose tiresomeness he attributes to the throng of listeners, but caught by their enthusiasm and his own self-image as the answer man, he labors on. He soon falls into Socrates' trap, his failure to explain how a rhetor given to justice and just deeds can perpetrate the unjust deeds Gorgias attributes to him (460d–461a). Before the denouement, however, Socrates submits Gorgias to an elenchus that ends with his admission of another element of the definition of the rhetoric: the rhetor's ignorance of the subject at hand (458e–459c).

The rhetor wields his persuasive power before the multitude because the multitude consists of those ignorant of the skills in question. Gorgias adds that the rhetor is at a greater advantage in persuading the ignorant if he himself is ignorant of the subject. Socrates clarifies: the rhetor has more power to influence the patient than the physician because of his ignorance of medicine (*Grg.* 459b). Gorgias agrees: "Does it not prove a great advantage, Socrates, that, although not knowing the other skills but this one, he is no less inferior to the craftsmen?" (459c).

Gorgias' personality is of a piece with his rhetoric: self-absorbed. The professional man needs to be liked and so becomes exercised over how he is perceived through his students' behavior. He knows the difference between truth and belief and says nothing about lying, for rhetors do not lie as such. He believes that knowledge is always true (*Grg.* 454d), but he demonstrates no interest in knowledge. He reinforces Socrates' statement that the rhetor acts best in total ignorance of the subject at hand and without concern for truth. It is perhaps the most striking aspect of his rhetoric, its lack of regard for truth, reality based on fact and knowledge. Yet truth is synonymous with wisdom, and rhetoric works best in ignorance. He cares far more to represent himself as having knowledge before those who lack the knowledge and the means to identify his ignorance. To escape exposure, he confines himself to the masses of the ignorant—namely, the men who hold sway over the decisions of public policy, jurors, council members, and assemblymen. Because of their ignorance, these men who pass judgment only with the yea or nay of a pebble or hand are at the mercy of men like Gorgias and the politicians who learned from men like Gorgias. Although Gorgias may express the belief that the rhetor should use his skills justly (457b), he harbors no illusion that his students concur. He glories in the "freedom" (452d), implying with his next words public power, but the rhetor is primarily a man of words. The liar's lies are conditioned by the truth and play off the truth, but the rhetor's "mode of creativity" is more expansive and independent, with more spacious opportunities for improvisation, color, and imaginative play. This is less a matter of craft than of art. Hence the familiar notion of the "bullshit artist."[56]

Plato's view of rhetoric, especially its neglect of truth, reproduces the salient features of Harry G. Frankfurt's inquiry into the phenomenon of bullshit.[57] Plato, it may be said, traces the crisis in his society to the politicians' incessant bullshitting of the people with the utter disregard for the differences between knowledge and ignorance, truth and falsehood, reality and illusion, for which we need look no further than the Sicilian expedition. The crisis cascaded throughout society, reducing values and substance to bogus words and empty beliefs.

People resort to bullshit, Frankfurt speculates, when they have to speak about some topic that exceeds their knowledge of the facts. "This discrepancy is common in public life, where people are frequently impelled—whether by their own propensities or by the demands of others—to speak extensively about matters of which they are to some degree ignorant."[58] Gorgias, model for rhetoric, readily admits his lack of knowledge and glories in the freedom it confers. Yet the rhetor, no fool in Socrates' estimation, is "shrewd at sizing others up, gutsy, and silky smooth at schmoozing people in gatherings."[59] He has no skill, for skills (*technai*) are based for Plato on knowledge. His is "an acquired knack," born of his personality, of procuring gratification for himself and pleasure for his auditors (*Grg.* 462a–c).

Polus, who has taken over the conversation from Gorgias, thinks that to be *kalon*, "a good thing." Bored with defining, he wants to skip ahead to commending the qualities of rhetoric in the kind of performance he inflicted upon Chaerephon. Socrates reins in the Colt by applying the same definition to the preparation of *opsa* (*opsopoiia*). An *opson* was anything added to bread—for example, meat, vegetables, sauce, or relish. The Greek diet divided between bread made of wheat or other grain and wine fermented from the grape.[60] *Opsa* confounded the categories since it belonged fully to neither. James Davidson explains in *Courtesans and Fishcakes* why *opsa*, a part of a Greek meal with a real and defined "space," upset philosophers:

> The philosophers' efforts to neglect, elide or reduce *opson* to the status of a vacuum are evidence of a profound nervousness about the whole category. The dangerous supplement threatens to divert eating away from sustenance and into pleasure, and even to usurp the place of bread as the bedrock of existence.[61]

Opsopoiia deceives the body by replacing (supplementing) nourishing food with pleasurable "junk food" (465bc).[62] It does not consider what is best for the body but gleans what delights the consumer. In a similar fashion, rhetoric harbors no regard for what is best for the soul. Both are aspects of *kolakeia*, which "aims at the pleasant without concern for what is best" (465a). Usually translated as "flattery," *kolakeia* is better rendered as "pandering," "toadyism," or "brownnosing," because of the propensity of the *kolax* to suck up out of desire for personal enrichment.[63] Like rhetoric, *opsopoiia* is an acquired knack that consists of sizing up the consumer and titillating his palate without thought for his nourishment or health. It is, Socrates contends, the destructive complement to medicine (465c). Whereas medicine is a *technê* directed at restoring the health of the body, *opsopoiia* is but its *eidôlon* (463d), its fleshless double that deceives the body into feeling good. Similarly, rhetoric is the sham of justice that maintains the health of the soul. Far from *kalon,* it is *aischron,* base, in that it is not concerned with the benefit of the body (463d). The effort at definition ends at this point as Socrates leaves it at an analogy between *opsopoiia* and rhetoric (465d), and Polus insists that the man who wields such power in the state, whether rhetor or politician, is a person of great power in the cities.

Polus has demonstrated his admiration for Gorgias and esteem for rhetoric, "most beautiful of skills" (448c), as well as his ignorance of dialectic. He is shocked at Socrates' estimation that "the good (*agathoi*) rhetors" are "toadies in the cities" (466b). Polus is a victim of both the bullshit of his own profession and the tribal origins of his society's view of *aretê.*[64] The code of the Homeric warrior may have originated during the tenth or ninth centuries, but it continued through the classical period to dictate what meant the "good life" through its popularity in epic song and acceptance by the elite, who modified its emphasis on military prowess to fit their arenas of competition. The warrior led a household in rivalry with others, whose survival depended upon his skills in killing the enemy. For him, *aretê* by necessity meant the ability to kill the enemy. In his zero-sum world, success was paramount and required at any cost; defeat brought humiliation and extinction. The successful hero was envied for his wealth and reputation, which nonetheless depended upon the approval of the people. The *dêmou phatis,* "talk of the people," carried far more weight than communal safety or order. Hence Achilles let many of his fellows die because of Agamemnon's trespass upon his honor, and Crito urges Socrates to shuck the laws and their justice and flee.[65] Justice and moral right have no bearing on the need to succeed, for only through victory in the struggle, whether in war or elsewhere, can there be survival and the good life.

By deeming the rhetors *agathoi,* Polus aligns himself with the *anêr agathos,* "brave/good man," the *summum bonum* of the warrior system of values that draws the individual's loyalty from the community to his family and friends. Polus accordingly praises the rhetor's manipulation of others for his own gratification. He attributes great power to rhetors because he sees that when they speak, men lose their lives, property, and citizenship (*Grg.* 466bc).

He discounts the atrocities that Archelaus committed to seize the throne of Macedon in favor of the good life and envy of all men (470d–471d). It would seem, therefore, somewhat surprising that Socrates would consider such a man his friend, but twice in their discussion he admits to being his friend (470c, 473a).

Let us not be misled by realism. The movement of the *Gorgias* is from the polite but distanced relationship with Gorgias, to friendship limited by Polus' being a foreigner and dull of wit, to a nearness with Callicles, friend, citizen, intelligent, that Plato uses to establish a continuum to join Socrates and Callicles as enemy brothers. At trial, Socrates criticized Athenians in effect for being men like Polus, men who care for money, reputation, and honor, the very things that validate the good life in the eyes of the warriors' *aretê.* Socrates said that whenever he encountered someone who claimed to care for what he held as important—wisdom, truth, and the condition of his soul—he would not let the fellow go but would question, cross-examine, and refute him, adding that he would do this for anyone, young, old, foreigner or townsman, "but more so for townsmen for they are closer to me in kin" (Pl. *Apol.* 29e–30a). In this way, Socrates performed the service imposed by the god as his gift to Athenians.

Now Plato defends Socrates by having him confront, with the hope of improving the Sicilian, Polus, who is a friend mired in the superficialities of his profession and his society's view of the good life. He sets out in the ensuing conversation to guide him, through the question-and-answer of dialectic, to an understanding of what rhetoric truly is, and to show him that the rhetor, confined by his need to toady, never gets to do what he wishes. Since rhetoric is a knack, not a *technê,* he lacks true knowledge based upon reason and logic and can easily fall into behavior that is harmful and against his best interests. A man like Archelaus cannot be happy because he has acted unjustly. Socrates toils with the stupid and crude Polus to bring him to this insight. He cannot escape the rigor of Socrates' arguments and proofs, and in the end Socrates gains his approval for the conclusion that rhetoric has no value except to punish oneself or dissuade and so harm one's enemy by keeping him from punishing himself. But Polus deems Socrates' proofs "absurd" (480e), and Socrates' service to the god and Polus ends, as does his service to Athenians, in failure.

❖ ❖ ❖

The theme of enemy siblings focuses the sacrificial crisis on a pair of implacable opponents. Each embodies a position, natural or sociological, that cannot be reconciled with one another. Its violence is consonant with that generated by the birth of twins. "It is only natural that twins should awaken fear, for they are harbingers of indiscriminate violence, the greatest menace to primitive societies."[66] Argeia, wife of the Spartan king Aristodemus, assaults the laws of royal succession by exploiting the identical appearance of her sons so that both can become kings instead of the elder (*Hdt.* 6.52). Twins, identical twins in particular, manifest sameness naturally by being two individuals who occupy a space, their mother's womb, that belongs to each but which neither can possess exclusively. There are two in places normally held by one—namely, the womb, mastery of the house, and throne of the kingdom. The doubling of occupants causes violence—or rather the doubling that sweeps away the norms of reproduction and primogeniture creates a sameness that manifests itself as (and in) violence. Aglaia's sons, Akrisios and Proitos, "began quarrelling with one another while still in the womb, and the violence inherent in their twinness continues unabated, for when they matured, they fought wars over the kingship."[67]

Myths of twins point to a time when Greeks feared the sameness of identical twins. Their mythmakers diffused the violence by normalizing the twins through imposing differences. Pelias is no sooner born than he receives from the blow of a horse's hoof the livid mark that distinguishes him in appearance from his brother, Neleus. Twins are said to live apart: Pelias in Thessaly and Neleus in Pylos. Akrisios and Proitos divide Argos but remain apart in Argos and Tiryns. These strategies of mythmaking are combined in the monumental twins, Castor and Polydeukes. They are distinguished in the womb: Castor is the son of the mortal Tyndareus and Polydeukes of the god Zeus. They practice different arts, war, and boxing peacefully. In the end, they are separated by the extremes of life and death, immortality and mortality. After Castor was killed, Polydeukes would not accept immortality. Zeus granted that they live alternately, one among the gods for a day and the other among the mortals.[68] Their sameness is thus diffused by not being in the same state or place at the same time.

The sameness of twins in itself, Girard points out, expresses the loss of difference but need not symbolize the violent loss of differences, as twins are no more violent than other men.[69] Brothers, on the other hand, in particular enemy brothers, while losing the element of identity, compensate for that loss with their gain in realism.[70] The proximity of brothers in familial relationships, rights, and obligations are intensified in the case of Oedipus' brothers/sons, Polyneices and Eteocles. Incest produces a circularity, reverting to a sibling of the parent rather than moving forward to a descendent. Incest puts them on a par with Oedipus as his brother and with one another as heir to the throne of Thebes and mastery of its royal household. It renders them incapable of overcoming the other's claim and immerses them in conflict whenever they meet. But their sameness and equilibrium generates the sacrificial crisis. Girard points to the encounter of Polyneices and Tydeus in Euripides' *Supplices*.[71] They meet before the gate of Adrastus, king of Argos, and fall immediately into a ferocious fight that reconstitutes Polyneices' relationship with his brother. Together, they project loss of identity that leads at first contact, like germs to pestilence, to a sacrificial crisis. Aeschylus opens *Seven Against Thebes* with the siege of Thebes in progress. As long as the walls separate the brothers, Eteocles remains in control of himself. Once a messenger penetrates the wall with news of Polyneices, it is as if he brings Polyneices himself. The curse, the miasma of reciprocal violence, consumes him: "Alas for me! now truly the curses of my father are coming to accomplishment. . . . Trusting in Justice, I will go and face him in person. Who else could do so with better right?" Eteocles calls for his armor and weapons, and an arming scene follows that renders Eteocles identical in appearance to the absent Polyneices. Eteocles becomes what the young women of the chorus fear:

> Do not, most beloved of men, child of Oedipus, become
> like him in temperament who is spoken of so badly. (677–678)

That is, like an enemy brother.

Girard does not include in his assessment of the Oedipus myth feminine relationships, yet the same redundancy that characterizes the males marks the females.[72] Jocasta conjoins in one person multiple and redundant social roles: she is the mother and wife of the same person, for which she hangs herself, leaving for Oedipus "many pains that a mother's furies fulfilled" (Homer *Odyssey* 11.279–280). Her daughters, their father's sisters, manifest kinship redundancy in two persons. That the reciprocity of the violence between Ismene and Antigone has gone unnoticed is understandable in view of the familiarity of the conflict between their brothers. Males in Greek society pursue difference by striving to excel as *aristoi* in competition for prestige, wealth, and power.[73] Whenever Eteocles and Polyneices come together, each asserts a right to Oedipus' household and throne that is equally matched, and violence ensues from the equilibrium. On the other hand, Greek women were not supposed to compete with one another for distinction.[74] They wove wool for clothes, maintained the household, cared for the children, the sick, and the dead, activities that required cooperation away from public view. Proximity with other women was the norm and desideratum. Moreover, lawgivers like Solon based their funeral legislation on the premise that every woman wanted to participate in mourning.[75] For the sake of public tranquility, legislators tried to limit the number of women participants by imposing restrictions according to degrees of kinship—for instance, to children of fifth cousins. In this context, women are interchangeable, and the places they hold—birth, coming of age in wedding ceremonies, and death—are open to more than one woman. Closeness and sameness among women are the norm.

To express reciprocal violence in a feminine relationship, the mythmaker Sophocles adopted a narrative strategy characteristic of Greek mythmaking. To tell the myth, he reversed something concrete, something Greeks knew, to create something other and opposite, thus employing a common narrative strategy found, for example, in the myths of the Amazons and the *barbaroi* of the Persian Wars. These myths reverse the reality of the Greek/male/free/hoplite to create myths of mirror images, the Amazon, foreign/female/warrior, and the Persian, foreign/unmanly/slave/archer.[76] Sophocles reversed the dominant form of activity among women, that of cooperation over ritual obligations and duties to the household. Each time Ismene and Antigone come together, he unites them as a pair and then has them differ verbally. They separate, separation causes more verbal violence, and they spring farther apart. The incest that effaces differences vital for selfhood and social identity manifests itself in the sisters' inability to cooperate with one another to tend to their dead kinsman and embroils them in futile verbal combats to establish differences where none exist. Their efforts to erect differences in justifying their individual claims to proper action lead, in turn, to the dismantling of other differences that brings about the dissolution of the household with the death of Creon's son, Haemon. Sophocles' dynamic supports Girard's observation: "When they [differences] no longer serve as a dam against violence, they serve to swell the flood."[77] Antigone and Ismene become enemy sisters.

❖   ❖   ❖

The crisis in Plato's community predates his birth, intensified with the war and its aftermath, and it became ever fixed in his mind with the execution of Socrates. It consists, no less than a natural upheaval brought on by plague or drought, of the loss of order caused by its democratic form of government and failed system of leadership. In *Gorgias,* Plato traces failure to the propensity of leaders to bullshit the people and offers Socrates as the only true politician, in that he tells them what is best for them to hear. His reference to Socrates as the lover of Alcibiades (*Grg.* 481d) may be intended to recall the role of Alcibiades as corrupted student in Socratic writings and hence defend Socrates through his efforts to dissuade Callicles from a public life of pandering to the people. With greater moment, however, Plato presents Socrates as the true politician through the theme of enemy brothers locked in a conflict over the best way of life under the democracy (500c, 512e). His initial acrimony with Callicles intensifies as they move into what resembles a siege. Callicles barricades himself behind the views stated in his first speech, and Socrates comes against him, a Polyneices against an Eteocles, with an elenchus that has one major flaw: to be successful it requires the cooperation of Callicles, who has been listening with growing impatience and disgust to Socrates' questioning of Gorgias and Polus. When Polus agrees with Socrates that he who commits injustice is more wretched than he who suffers it, Callicles asks: "Tell me, Socrates, are we to put you down as being serious or joking around?," for if you are serious about what you're saying, "the life of men would be turned topsy turvy" (*Grg.* 481c). Callicles has been annoyed at Polus' complacency and Socrates' philosophy. Socrates has also been aroused, for he begins by addressing him with his name: "O Callicles, if there weren't some common experience among men, we could not reveal what we think to one another" (481c, paraphrased). The initial rather than embedded vocative calls out pointedly. Here it anticipates the abruptness and forthrightness and, perhaps, surprise of Socrates' next words: "You and I have had the same experience of loving (*erônte*) two things. I love Alcibiades, son of Clinias, and philosophy, and you two things, the demos of the Athenians and Demos, son of Pyrilampas" (481d). Socrates goes on to accuse Callicles of not being able to speak independently of his lovers, "so that if someone, on every occasion when you were saying what you say because of them, would wonder at the absurdity, you could say (if you wanted to tell the truth) that until the objects of your affections stop talking, you won't stop talking yourself" (481e). George Kimball Plochmann and Franklin E. Robinson remark: "It is hard to think of a similar assault mounted by Socrates before any serious discussion has begun, in the other dialogues."[78] As a politician, Callicles in Socrates' view is an *erastês* (lover) wooing the affections of his *ta paidika,* "beloved," and, as Socrates ironically remarks to Euthyphro, "It is necessary that the lover follow the beloved wherever he leads" (*Euthphr.* 14c). His next sentence reveals his mood: "Believe that you must hear different things from me, and do not wonder that I am the one saying these things: it is philosophy, my *ta paidika*" (*Grg.* 482a). Plato anticipates the clash of enemy brothers. His Socrates comes to the discussion aroused by the impudence of Callicles' question from a man who trims his words to curry the favor of the demos. He is uncharacteristically blunt and challenges Callicles to refute his philosophy, which looms more monumentally than usual.

Plato alludes to Socrates and Callicles as lovers, but he spends more effort in developing them as a pair of combatants by framing their exchange as a clash of enemy twins. Callicles, who reprises Socrates' initial vocative with one of his own (482c), responds: "I feel fairly friendly towards you, Socrates, but I run the risk of feeling toward you as Zethus of Euripides' tragedy did toward Amphion whom I mentioned just now" (*Grg.* 485e). Callicles readily accepts the role of Zethus, as does Socrates his of Amphion (*Grg.* 506b). The brothers in *Antiope* dispute about the active versus the contemplative life.[79] Zethus contends that the study of music "takes a man distinguished by nature and makes him worse" (186 Nauk). It is an idle pursuit, useless and given to wine. It renders a man capable of subtleties but not of hard work in the fields and in war (fr. 188 Nauk). His nature deserts him, leaving him worthless to help his household, friends, and city. Amphion accepts the obligation to help friends and his city,[80] but he replies that "one wise plan outweighs many hands, and stupidity with the crowd is the worse evil" (fr. 200 Nauk). The man withdrawn from public life, Amphion retorts, is better able to help the city, for he does not act overly bold. Zethus prevails over his brother, but Amphion is vindicated by Hermes, who foretells that his music will raise the walls of Thebes. Thus in Euripides' mythmaking, each brother gains a victory, but Amphion's music trumps Zethus' politics. Since Antiope's twin sons do not descend into violence, we may accept Callicles' profession of regard for Socrates despite his behavior (*Grg.* 486a).

Callicles enters upon a long speech. Socrates has objected to speeches in his hearing (449bc), but Callicles, it becomes clear, equally objects to Socrates' conversation by question and answer. He attacks his method as the exuberance of a stripling and the rabblerousing of a mob orator (482c). He accuses Socrates of delighting in tying up Gorgias and Polus in contradictions and forcing them into silence. "You truly, Socrates, import vulgar banalities into your discussions by always claiming that you seek the truth, things that are beautiful not by nature but by convention" (482e). With this charge, Callicles moves to his main and formidable weapon, the opposition of nature (*physis*) and convention (*nomos*). Whichever side his opponent adopts, he contends, Socrates questions him from the other, and contradiction between a true polarity is bound to result. That it is more just to be wronged than to do wrong, the last topic agreed upon by Polus, flies in the face of everything natural, as may be seen in the world of the animals and in relations between cities. The stronger and superior, animal, city, or man, by virtue of being stronger and superior, seizes by nature and deserves to have by nature the greater share of power, possessions, and all else over the weaker and inferior. Callicles argues and defends this position, his "natural justice," against all of Socrates' devices. For Callicles, philosophy bedevils the wits of adults with subtleties that crowd out the things he needs to know to live long and prosper. It hobbles him in public, exposing him defenselessly against lawsuits. Callicles appeals for support to Zethus' admonitions to his brother, Amphion. Out of good will for Socrates, he says, he warns him against advanced study of philosophy:

> Now if someone should arrest you and summarily haul you off to prison, alleging that you acted wrongfully when you had not, you realize that you would lack the necessary means and would flounder about and stand there with your mouth open because you have nothing to say. When you went to court and encountered a disreputable and unscrupulous prosecutor, you would die, should he want to call for a penalty of death. (486ab)

"How is it wise," Callicles closes by quoting Zethus, "that a pursuit (*technê*) take a man distinguished by nature and make him worse?" (486b). He concludes by stating his version of the good life: "wealth, reputation, and many other goods" (486c).

Again, Plato surprises his reader. As Antigone comes to Ismene, confident in her aid in burying their brother, Socrates expresses delight in finding in Callicles, because of "his education, good will, and freedom of speech" (487a), his touchstone to truth. As the stone reveals gold, their agreement guarantees "truth itself" (486e). But confidence and delight are thwarted by the rivalry between enemy brothers. Over the lengthy course of their exchange, Socrates and Callicles agree on nothing substantive. Callicles says that philosophy does not suit a mature man and, accordingly, he refuses to engage Socrates in the inquiry into his notion of natural justice. He reaffirms his belief, however, with his original verve and bluntness (491e–492a). Socrates wants to persuade him in the virtues of the life lived in an orderly and moderate manner (493c) but to no avail. Callicles, always irritated by the quibbling and vulgarity of Socrates' approach, answers with growing reluctance, and then perfunctorily, and finally not at all. In the end, he admits:

> I do not know in what way you seem to speak correctly, Socrates, and I have the experience that many have: I am not at all convinced. (513c)

Socrates endeavors to persevere, saying that the demos has captured his heart. But by his refusing to answer, Callicles reduces Socrates to delivering speeches and, in effect, kills the man of the elenchus. Ironically, Plato defeats the intention to defend Socrates against the charges of corrupting the youth with this elenchus. Socrates fails to convince a youth who is well disposed to him and cares for his safety.

To return to Euripides' enemy twins: Zethus prevails over his brother. The active life, among mortals at least, promotes greater prosperity and safety for a man and his household and affords him the greater resources to benefit his friends and city. The need for friends alludes to the dangers of the democracy, the world of Euripides' audience, but his Zethus and Amphion live in the world of tragedy, where, in the final scene, a god may appear to balance the dysfunction of human frailties and ignorance. Hermes vindicates the power of music; Amphion builds the walls of Thebes with his lyre. Plato's enemy brothers, however, are immersed in the democracy whose demos acts by whim and whose leaders favor it with flattery and extract from it rewards and honors. Callicles desires to be such a person, believing by his doctrine of natural justice that the superior and stronger may and should take what he wants from the weaker. Callicles sees Socrates' devotion to philosophy as his downfall, for, when brought before a jury, he will not know how to defend his life. Socrates, in turn, sees Callicles' dedication to the people as exposing him to their whimsy. To survive, Callicles will need to imitate the demos, a tyrant whose evil ways will corrupt him. Like Amphion, Socrates accepts the premise of the citizen's duty to serve his city. No advocate of the retired life, Socrates sees himself as the sole man capable of improving the citizens and so the only true politician (521d). Other politicians, including the great men of the past, like Themistocles and Pericles, corrupted them by flattery and giving them what they want (518e–519c). In essence, both Callicles and Socrates become politicians who crystallize the crisis with their conflict over leading the people. Each brother fights for his version of the best life and leadership; each cautions the other against the consequences of maintaining his present course. Yet, whether to imitate with Callicles the tyrant that is the people or to oppose that tyrant with Socrates, the end is the same. Serving the citizens of the Athenian democracy is a dangerous undertaking. The chaos of their city renders them symmetrical, balanced in their differences, and united by their deaths.

Imagined through the motif of enemy brothers, Socrates dies the death dictated by the crisis in Athenian society. He is its victim no less, no more, than Callicles for trying to lead the demos. He dies, as he says, like the doctor on trial before a jury of children.

CHAPTER 2

Plato's Victimary Culture

The worshipper experiences the god most powerfully not just in pious conduct or in prayer, song, and dance, but in the deadly blow of the axe, the gush of blood and the burning of thigh-pieces.

—WALTER BURKERT, *Homo Necans*

Religious activities were embedded in every aspect of a Greek's life. Children across Hellas had watched and participated in sacrificial processions as long as they could remember. Processions that led a victim to the god's altar happened every day. Few thought particularly about them. They were the way of things. Processions consisted of two or three people and an animal victim, a goat, sheep, or cow, or the whole population of the community and a herd of victims. Their purpose was always the same: to escort the animal calmly to the altar. Sacrificers kill the victim. In this, they are *homines necantes,* men killing, but not *homines necantes,* men murdering, the distinction fundamental to their ideology of sacrifice.[1] The demeanor of the animal, therefore, caused much anxiety, for, were it to balk or resist, the pretense of its cooperation and willing participation would be undone. Once at the altar, the sacrificers sprinkled the altar, themselves, and the animal with water, a sign of unanimity but also the first act in a crescendo of violence toward it. They waited until it shook its head, indicating its consent, and would not proceed until it had done so. The animal wants to rid itself of the water, but *homines necantes* deceive themselves into believing that the victim consents to what is to come, a pretense Karl Meuli calls "a comedy of innocence."[2] Aggression mounts: they pelt the animal with barley grains and clip hairs from its head and throw them into the fire on the altar. Then the *mageiros* (butcher) or *sphageus* (slaughterer), the man among the sacrificers most skilled with the knife, plunges it into the victim's throat. Women scream out, shrilling, wailing, "ololu, ololu, ololu." Their shrieks punctuate the violence and salute the spontaneous release of mingled joy and terror at the god's advent. This instant when the life is taken is never depicted in art or discussed. Homer, for example, in narrating Nestor's sacrifice to Athena, says:

> *The men lifted the cow from the broad-wayed earth*
> *and held it. Peisistratos, leader of men, gored her throat veins.*
> *After the black blood flowed out and the spirit left her bones*
> *instantly they carved her.* (*Ody.* 3.453–456)

These rituals of *thusia,* ubiquitous in Greek culture, comprise a sacrificial mode through which mortals communicate with their gods and, more so, among themselves through the viscera of a slaughtered domesticated animal.[3] Greeks commonly considered it a kind of commerce. Euthyphro, one of Plato's average Athenians, believes that "sacrificing is giving gifts to the gods, and praying is asking the gods for something" (*Euthphr.* 14c). Mortals send the gods the savor of the viscera roasted in the fire on the altar that ascends to the gods in the smoke (*thuein,* "to make smoke"). The rituals of *thusia* consist of two sets of activities separated by a moment charged with *numen,* met with eerie keening, and otherwise shrouded in silence. Those of the first act prepare the victim and ensure its placidity and the participants' freedom from the pollution of murder. Those of the third act, performed over the carcass, extract the internal organs, beginning with the heart, in an order that imitates the movement of political power in the *polis* from its center in the agora to individual citizens in its territory.[4] The viscera are roasted without salt, a memorialization of the transition from the raw of bestiality to the stew of boiled meat and vegetables that culminates the celebration.[5] But it is the marginal zone of the second act that holds the *mysterium* of *thusia*. At this moment differences and hierarchies that erect the human condition are obliterated by the advent of what mortals deem god. With the sudden thrust of the goring knife and the release of blood, the animal "passes without transition from the state of a live quadruped to that of a mass of meat to be shaped."[6] "From the procession, *pompê,*" Jean-Louis Durand continues, "the moment that takes one to the sacrifice, *thusia,* the moment the blood gushes, belongs to the gods. Men seek no omen in it, no sign."[7] The scholar cooperates with the sacrificers in concealing the moment when reciprocal violence congeals upon a single victim, the moment members of the community thrust their murderous violence upon the sacred that transforms it into the creative violence of carving the meat. The rites of *thusia,* conducted at altars stained with the blood of countless victims amid a miasma of stench and swarming flies, are a bloody business. Girard theorizes that these rites release violence, constructing a society around the victim. They reproduce the founding murder through the flesh of a domestic animal without the pollution of wrongful bloodletting. They enable the sacrificers to believe that they do not murder the victim and allow them to disavow the fatal moment as the gods' concern. In this, they provide "the collective violence revolving around a false interpretation, governed as it is by the unanimous illusion of the persecutors."[8] The sacrificers deceive themselves over the victim's willingness and unite to take its life by rites that scrupulously distinguished sacrifice from murder and whose chicanery they refuse to recognize. Their very scrupulousness implies, however, that the rites imitate a founding murder. More so, the rites offer proof of original savagery by retracing the acculturation that occurred in the time of first beginnings when the world and the human condition were being fashioned.

Sacrificial Ideology Exposed in the Bouphonia

Girard makes the point that the celebrants of sacrifice must not understand what they are doing by substituting an animal for themselves. They cannot knowingly put the onus of their violence upon the gods, much less upon something as nebulous as the sacred. On the other hand, what they are doing must not be so hidden that it disappears from view:

Once we have focused attention on the sacrificial victim, the object
originally singled out for violence fades from view. Sacrificial substitution
implies a degree of misunderstanding. Its vitality as an institution depends
upon its ability to conceal the displacement upon which the rite is based.
It must never lose sight entirely, however, of the original object, or cease to
be aware of the act of transference from that object to the surrogate victim;
without that awareness no substitution can take place and the sacrifice
loses all efficacy.[9]

In the festival of the Bouphonia, or Ox Murder, celebrated on the fourteenth
of Skirophorion (May/June), priests in the precinct of Zeus on the Acropolis carried out this sacrificial charade on behalf of all Athenians. The use of
the double ax and a bronze table, implements prominent in the Mycenaean
period, suggest an origin before 1200 BCE. By the time Aristophanes produced his *Clouds* in 423 BCE, Athenians paid little heed to the proceedings,
dismissing them as "full of cobwebs."[10] Yet, they continued to celebrate them
at least into the second century of the common era. Clearly, they remained
vital to the existence of the community because they were "a deliberate act of
collective substitution performed at the expense of the victim and absorbing
all the internal tensions, feuds, and rivalries pent up within the community."[11]
Athenians depended upon sacrifice to maintain social stability. The rites of
the Bouphonia appear to test the notion of substitution and the tenets of
their sacrificial ideology that sacrifice, though a killing, is not murder. In fact,
the rites serve less to test these fundaments of sacrifice than to question in
order to reaffirm them.[12]

The most extensive source for the ceremony is Porphyry's *On Abstaining
from Living Things*:

At the public sacrifice in Athens, after the meal in honeyed oil and incense
had been set out on the table in plain sight, ready to be sacrificed to the
gods, one of the oxen coming in from the fields is said to have eaten some
of the meal and to have trampled on the rest. A certain Diomos or Sopatros, not a native but someone farming in Attica, became enraged at what
happened. He seized an axe that was being sharpened nearby and struck
the ox. The ox died. When the man recovered from his anger and realized
what he had done, he buried the ox and went of his own accord into exile

in Crete as one who had committed impiety. Then the rain stopped falling, and the grain no longer grew. Delegates were sent by the city to Delphi to inquire of Apollo. The priestess of Apollo responded:

> the exile in Crete will redeem these [drought and barrenness], and vengeance having been taken on the murderer and the dead having been resurrected in the same sacrifice in which [the dead] died, those who taste the dead and do not hold back will be better off.

A search was undertaken, and the man responsible for the deed was located. Sopatros reckoned that he would be released from the unpleasantness of being polluted if they all did these measures in common. He told those who came to him that the ox had to be slain by the city. Since they were at their wits' end over who would be the slayer, he offered them this possibility: if they enrolled him as a citizen, they would share the murder with him. Agreement was reached on these terms. When they came back to the city, they arranged the affair in the way in which it remains today.

They chose girls to bring the water. They fetched the water used for sharpening the axe and the knife. After the sharpening, one man delivered the axe, another struck the ox, and a third thrust the point of the knife into the throat. They skinned it, and everyone tasted the ox. Afterwards, they sewed up the hide of the ox and stuffed it with hay and set it to the plow as if ready for work. Assembling a trial for murder, they summoned everyone who had participated in the deed to offer a defense. The water-fetchers charged that the sharpeners were more to blame than they. The sharpeners said the same about the axe-deliverer, and this one of the throat-cutter, and this one of the knife which, lacking a voice, was condemned for murder. . . . They threw the knife into the sea. (2.29–30)

The rituals of the Bouphonia, which create sacrifice out of a primal murder (*phonos*), depend upon the heightened metonymy of the bestial and the human. Verlyn Klinkenborg, in speaking of plow oxen, observes: "In one way or another I've been among animals all my life, and over time I've learned that there is almost no closer bond on Earth than the one that exists between a human and an animal that works along with him."[13] Athenians, in fact, held slaying a plow ox to be a crime.[14] Sopatros slays no ordinary animal. Its contact with men has rendered the plow ox "too human" and thus unsuitable for sacrifice, for human beings are not to be eaten—the commensal meal being an essential aspect of *thusia*. If the sacrifice of a victim so close to men is not murder, then the sacrifice of other domesticated animals cannot be murder. At the same time, the rites do not conceal that the underlying primal murder was of a human being, for Sopatros treats the slain ox as if it were human: he buries it and goes into exile as a murderer.

After the sacrifice and tasting the meat, the community conducts a trial. The ritual trial denies a murder took place by the strategy of directing blame for the murder at member after member. The unity created by its violence against an animal is shattered as each participant accuses the other of the crime of murder. Sacrifice has disappeared into murder, and with it the distinctions between the ox as a sacrificial victim and a murder victim, as well as those between sacrificer and murderer. All participants are equally guilty, yet each would distinguish himself by erecting the difference as innocent/guilty where no such difference is possible. There results an outburst of violence that effects a vicious circle of reprisals.[15] Reciprocity ends—that is, violence ceases to go back and forth among identical parties and is focused again on a common victim with the establishment of a difference, that between voiced and voiceless. The knife is different from the other participants: it cannot speak. No more guilty than any other, it has no voice to pass on the blame and to stave off becoming the victim by substituting someone else. All focus on this difference to identify the knife as the culprit. All condemn it and cast it into the purifying sea.

The myth accompanying Porphyry's description of the Bouphonia places the murder of the ox at a time before blood sacrifice, when gods received bloodless offerings, cakes, and grains. It belongs to the tradition that pictures sacrifice as terminating men's innocence of bloodshed and distancing them from the gods. The myth explains sacrifice by strategies that divert responsibility for its origin away from the community. The murder of the ox and ensuing sacrifice are inflicted upon the Athenians by outsiders and third parties. Sopatros is a foreigner, an alien working for hire as a farmer in Attica. He does not slay the ox deliberately but while deranged by anger. The ox is to blame for its death, for it desecrates holy things. The ax seems to be a fault for being handy.

Sopatros buries the ox as if it were human and, believing himself to be polluted with murder, flees into exile in Crete. Barrenness and drought oppress the land. As phenomena of the physical world, barrenness and drought threatened the community with extinction; as religious signs, they reveal hidden contamination that must be rooted out to restore harmony with the gods. But as elements in a myth, they signify pollution as a loss of differences and can do so because they kill indiscriminately, breaking down the order of things normal to human life.[16] They destroy the young before the old, the strong before the feeble, children before parents, doctors before patients. In Sophocles' *Oedipus the Tyrant,* a comparable disaster, a plague, afflicts the city of Thebes. Oedipus, ruler over Thebes, consults the oracle for aid in identifying the cause. Apollo's oracle directs the Thebans to "drive out the miasma nourished in the land and not to support it beyond remedy" (*OT* 97–98). The god tells them in ambiguous language how to restore community, and Oedipus launches a search for the man who slew Laïus (139). In the myth at hand, the Athenians receive an oracle from Apollo that sets forth a cure. It directs the community to atone for the loss of the ox's life with that of a man. "Vengeance having been taken on the murderer" can have no other meaning than killing Sopatros. The community searches for the one responsible for the ox's murder and the ensuing barrenness and drought. After they find the culprit, they are stymied, for the oracle's instruction to "taste the dead and not hold back" compounds murder with cannibalism. Sopatros, however, atones for his deed and rids himself of pollution by deceiving the god with his reading of the god's oracle. "The dead having been resurrected in the same sacrifice in which [the dead] died" could also refer to the ox. The subject of the verb translated as "died" is not specified: it could be either the ox or Sopatros, since both would be dead at this point. Sopatros substitutes an animal for himself; it dies and is eaten, and the life of the human is spared by animal blood. The myth denies a murder took place by spreading responsibility for killing the ox among all members of the community, but it does not suppress the other victim, Sopatros.

Human Victim

However the celebrants of *thusia* rationalized the willingness of the animal to be sacrificed, they had to have realized that rather than nodding its head in consent, it was shaking itself dry. True consent could come only from a human victim who consciously offers him- or herself.[17] Girard's hypothesis postulates such a time when the community victimized one of its own in celebration and remembrance of the primordial murder.[18] Mythmakers worked on this problem through stories about young women whose often fatal service to their husbands and his family in child birth was readily assimilated to death by self-sacrifice.[19] Their deaths, not always by sacrifice, are accepted as an offering to the citizens. For example, Antoninus Liberalis, a mythographer of the second century CE, recounts how all of Boeotia was gripped by a plague, and many were dying (*Metamorphosis* 25). Ambassadors were sent to the oracle of Apollo at Gortyn in Crete. The oracle declared for them to propitiate two deities of the earth. "Apollo said that they would stop the wrath if two maidens willingly became offerings to the twain." The oracle does not specify the women by name or offer any details. No women come forward. The daughters of Orion are weaving at the loom when they learn of the oracle. Identifying themselves as the women of the oracle, they seize their shuttles and thrust them into their necks. Similarly, on the verge of a war with Orchomenos, Thebans receive an oracle promising them victory if the most distinguished of the citizens in reputation from his descent agrees to die by his own hand (Pausanias 9.17.1). Antipoinos answers the description but refuses the role. His daughters, heirs to his noble lineage, recognize themselves in the oracle and kill themselves. They are honored by the citizens. Athenians honor Leon with a shrine in Athens because he gave away his daughters, Praxithea, Theope, and Eubole, as if brides in marriage, so that their sacrifice, as declared by Apollo's oracle at Delphi, would save the city (Aelian, *Miscellaneous Stories* 12.28). In accord with an oracle, Erechtheus, king of the Athenians, agrees to offer one of his daughters to secure victory in the war with the Eleusinians.[20] His other daughters, swearing an oath, join their sister in being sacrificed. Another version concerning this war has the daughter of King Cecrops hurling herself from the city walls.[21] During the war against King Minos, Athens is beset by famine and plague. The Athenians consult an oracle that directs them to sacrifice the daughters of Hyakinthos,

Anthea, Aiglea, Lytaia, and Orthaia, on the tomb of the Cyclops Geraistas (Apollod. 3.15.8). Heracles' daughter Macaria voluntarily surrenders her life for those of her brothers when the Athenians sheltering them come under siege by her father's mortal enemy, Eurystheus (Eur. *Heracl.* 407–629).

These myths exhibit an underlying pattern. A crisis befalls the city, whose citizens consult an oracle. The god responds with a remedy stated in vague and general terms. A search is undertaken. A young woman interprets the oracle as designating her, and she willingly offers herself. As with any pattern, it should not be expected that all of its elements will be represented in every version.[22] By "pattern" is meant a general formulation of phenomena whose message may be decoded regardless of the details. Leon gives away his daughters as if in marriage; not every victim is sacrificed; the daughters of Hyakinthos are mentioned by name, but their sacrifice fails to avert the crisis. Scholars have squandered much effort and obfuscated insights looking for fixed patterns. Deceit, for example, is an element of sacrifice from its inception with Prometheus' trick of wrapping bones in fat for Zeus (Hes. *Th.* 538–541). Deceit appears in Aegisthus' sacrifice as Orestes' disguise, in the sacrifice of Iphigenia as a sham marriage, and in Menoeceus' beguilement of his father, Creon (Eur. *Phoen.* 991–992). What matters is that deceit be conveyed, not its specific form, since deceit belongs to the message. Conversely, a pattern builds expectations in those formed by myths embodying it. Listeners of such "daughter/sacrifice" myths develop a familiarity with the type, and so the whole pattern can be invoked for them from a single reference, as "walking on water" conjures Jesus Christ.

The common element is substitution of a virgin young woman for an animal that has been assimilated to the human condition. At stake for sacrificial ideology is the attenuated difference between sacrifice and murder. As in the Bouphonia, whose myths approximate the pattern underlying these myths, the community consults an oracle in response to a crisis whose origin comes from outside sources. (The Minos myth varies the pattern, the cause being the Athenians' slaying of Minos' son.) The oracle identifies the remedy in terms that can refer to any number of women. One woman, or more as the case may be, accepts as her own the identity suggested by the oracle, thus reducing the generic to the specific. Her acceptance consequently has the plausibility denied that of an animal victim. The oracle as interpreted by the community acting under the auspices of the god and his divine knowledge declares her responsible for the crisis. There is no deceit on her part—she accepts—and her willingness to be immolated alone separates her death by sacrifice from murder. For its part, the community discovers the cause of the crisis, which bears the *sacrificetur* of the god and acts without suspicion of unrighteousness or the innocence of its victim.[23]

Iphigenia as Victim

The best known myth of this type is Agamemnon's sacrifice of his daughter Iphigenia. The story is ancient, known to Homer (*Il.* 9.145). The myth appeared in the *Cypria,* a cycle of epics treating events leading up to the Trojan War, and in the *Ehoiai,* a catalog of women's genealogies. Dating to the seventh and sixth centuries and extant in fragments and summaries, these epics established the outline of the story. Proclus in *Chrestomathia* summarizes the events of the sacrifice as related in the *Cypria*:

> After the fleet had gathered at Aulis for the second time, Agamemnon went hunting and shot a deer. He said that he had surpassed Artemis. The goddess was enraged and sent winds, preventing them from sailing. Calchas declared the goddess' wrath and ordered the sacrifice of Iphigenia to Artemis. They summoned Iphigenia on the pretext of marriage with Achilles and tried to sacrifice her. But Artemis snatched her away and carried her to the Taurians and made her immortal. She put a deer on the altar in place of the girl.[24]

The earliest versions emphasize Agamemnon's culpability and the substitution of a human victim for an animal. Murder is forestalled by a second substitution that replaces Iphigenia with an animal, proper victim of sacrifice, and the gift of immortal life.

In *Agamemnon,* the opening play of the *Oresteia* trilogy, Aeschylus omits the stag, but his chorus of Argive elders shows vividly the father's brutal substitution of his daughter for a goat:

> *After Agamemnon put on the strap of necessity,*
> *breathing an impious turn of mind,*

impure, unholy, from that moment
he changed to thoughts of utter daring.
Madness, prelude to shameful schemes,
first cause of pain, emboldens mortals.
He dared to become the sacrificer
of his daughter, succor
for wars to avenge a woman,
preliminary rite for the ships.

Prayers and cries of "Father"
and her maiden's life
the war-loving priests set at naught.
After a prayer, the father told the priests
to lift her on high over the altar,
face downward like a goat,
falling upon his robes with a suppliant's heart,
and to check her voice,
a source of curses for the house,
with a guard upon her beautiful mouth.

With the violence of bridles, speech-dumbing strength,
she poured her saffron-colored robes to the ground
and struck each of her sacrificers
with a piteous shaft from her eyes,
appearing as if in a painting, wishing
to address them, since many times
in her father's sumptuous banquet halls,
she had sung. A heifer not yet put to the bull, with pure voice,
she paid honor lovingly to her loving father's
joyful paean at the close of the feasting. (218–247)

Whereas sacrificers festoon the victim of *thusia* with woolen fillets to have it approach the human condition, Iphigenia is dehumanized as a heifer and slaughtered like a goat. Agamemnon, moreover, tries to bestialize her by muting the voice that called him father and sung the paean for him and thereby fulfilled her part in his household.[25] Alexander Gurd imagines an

Agamemnon who "would . . . hope that something will transform or translate
Iphigenia, so that the impossible act would itself be transformed into something possible, as Isaac was replaced at the last moment beneath the blade of
Abraham."[26] The myth contains such a rescue through Artemis' substitution
of a deer. Gurd points out that Agamemnon seeks on his own to convert
Iphigenia into a beast and erase the atrocity of his act and desires.[27] Despite
the rituals, the gag stigmatizes her death as the murder of an unwilling victim. The ritual, although corrupted, averts the crisis momentarily but does
not end the round of vengeance, because Iphigenia's mother, Clytemnestra,
refuses to disregard her daughter's humanness and exacts vengeance that
recalls the wrongness of the primordial murder. "With no respect for her
life," Clytemnestra exclaims, "as the death of a beast, [this man] sacrificed his
own daughter, most beloved birth pang for me, for a charm against the storm
winds of Thrace" (*Ag.* 1417–1418).

Euripides had in mind Aeschylus' "strap of necessity" when he composed Agamemnon's realization that he cannot escape sacrificing his
daughter: "Into what yokes of necessity have I fallen?" (*IA* 443). Agamemnon's plan to sacrifice Iphigenia in secret has been exposed, and his ruse of
marriage with Achilles disclosed to both Achilles and Iphigenia's mother.
Clytemnestra refuses consent to the rite and has enlisted Achilles as her
champion. Iphigenia begs for her life: "To look upon the light is sweet"
(1218). The army which represents the community in the play has been held
at Aulis by both Artemis' wrath and its leaders' refusal to supply the victim
necessary to appease the goddess and allow sailing. Without winds to drive
their ships, the men become restless and their unity begins to fragment.
The army threatens from its very size. Paris' abduction of Menelaos' wife
has aroused the men to thinking about their own wives left alone, and their
anger, mingled with lust and worry, urges sailing "to put a stop to the sei-
zure of Greek wives at home without children" (808). Achilles' Myrmidons
express the general grumbling among the troops as Agamemnon vacillates
over Iphigenia. They urge their leader:

> *Achilles, why do we remain here? How much time*
> *must be measured until the expedition gets underway?*
> *Do something if you're going to do anything, or lead the army back home.*
> *Don't wait on the delays of the sons of Atreus.* (815–818)

The army, deprived of the sacrifice identified by the goddess as their release from suffering, threatens to seize Iphigenia and immolate her without her consent. Violence verges on breaking from its sacrificial vectors, and the army nearly vanishes into the mob that Agamemnon has long feared (450, 517, 526, 735).

The Greeks at Aulis are enmeshed, Helene P. Foley observes, in "a Girardian 'sacrificial crisis'":

> The leaders of the army have been locked in a competitive struggle for power, or "mimetic rivalry" . . . . Social hierarchy is collapsing; the leaders reject or are inadequate to leadership. Cultural distinctions such as those between the sexes (as when Agamemnon threatens to usurp Clytemnestra's role in the marriage ceremony) begin to be blurred. Mob violence is imminent; the army is gripped by *eros* for war and revenge.[28]

The army is coming to take Iphigenia, and Achilles and Clytemnestra are steeling themselves to receive them. Iphigenia steps forward: "Mother, you must listen" (*IA* 1369). Only the uninitiated in the theater could be ignorant of what's afoot. The action has reached the point in the pattern where the young woman offers herself for the community and, vicariously, for the citizens gathered in the congregation:

> *It is right to thank this stranger [Achilles] for his ardor on our behalf,*
> *but you must see this, that he not be harmed by the army.*
> *We would fare no better, and he would meet with misfortune.*
> *Listen, mother, to what has come to me while I was thinking.*
> *It has been decided for me to die. I wish to do this very thing*
> *with glory, removing what does not befit my birth.*
> *Look again with me, mother, at how well I speak.*
> *All of mighty Greece is looking at me now,*
> *and upon me rest the crossing of ships and the destruction of Phrygians*
> *and the power to keep the foreigners from doing anything to future brides.*
> (1371–1380)

Iphigenia follows with her reasons. Her death will defend Greece and bring eternal glory. To love life excessively is not right. Clytemnestra bore her for all Greeks, not for her alone. How can one life keep "thousands of men, armed with shields and thousands equipped with oars, whose fatherland has been wronged, from fighting the enemy and defending Greece?" There is no justice in this. It is not right that Achilles die fighting the Greeks for the life of one woman. If Artemis claims her body, how can she refuse? (1383–1396):

> No, it is impossible. I give my body to Greece.
> Sacrifice. Sack Troy. Such will be my memorial
> forever. This is my children, my marriage, my reputation.
> It is right that Greek rule foreigners, not that foreigners rule Greeks,
> mother. They are slaves. We are free men. (1397–1401)

"Consent" as an element in the pattern of female human sacrifice consists of two forces working in harmony to achieve the goal of a proper victim. The one is external and public, the demand by the community for its victim. This appears as the threat to drag Iphigenia by the hair to the altar (*IA* 1166–1167); and as the Athenian king's resolve to hand the children of Heracles over to Eurystheus unless one of their own agrees to die (*Heracl.* 492–496); and as the Greeks' decree that Polyxena be sacrificed to honor Achilles (*Hecabe* 220–221); and as Ares' wrath to destroy Thebes (*Phoen.* 973–975). The other force appears internal, the pressure felt by the individual to offer herself. Both forces derive from the mythmaker Euripides, acting on behalf of his community of Athenians. The motives the individual gives for her consent do not well up from her will (a tragic character lacks a will) but is a product of what she is made to say and do in Euripides' mythmaking. Macaria, Polyxena, and Menoeceus refuse to live as cowards—respectively, as an outcast, a slave, a nobody. Euripides gives them no choice, or rather a choice for life that is worse than that for death. Nancy Sorbin Rabinowitz correctly points out the following:

> In a final twist, though, the real glory is reserved for men. For while Eurip-
> ides encourages the audience to think Iphigenia's death is her idea (by
> presenting her as making a choice) and therefore to admire her nobility,
> her death is merely a precondition for the glorification of the army and
> Agamemnon, who gain "the most renowned crown (*kleinotaton stephanon,*

1529) and "imperishable reputation" (*kleos aeimnêston,* 1531). Theirs is the honor that she desired so.[29]

But with one exception. There is no "twist" or unexpected development in the plot. The prosperity of the community was the goal from the outset. An Athenian audience could brook no other outcome in its sacrificial texts.[30] Iphigenia abandons her mother: "I allow no tear to drop" (*IA* 1465). She refuses to allow her mother to corrupt the sacrifice with the tears of dissonance. As the moment of death is concealed in the ritual, so it is in the story:

> *A priest, taking the knife, offered a prayer*
> *and looked at the throat where he would strike.*
> *No small pain entered my breast,*
> *as I stood with bowed head. Suddenly, a wonder to behold.*
> *Everyone could have clearly heard the sound of the strike,*
> *but no one saw where on earth the maiden had vanished.* (1578–1583)

Iphigenia is swept up into heaven, and in her place is substituted a doe: an animal dies for a human. That the community slaughters an innocent for its profit is concealed by a story whose camouflage for her daughter's murder Clytemnestra refuses to accept (1616–1618). Her insight into the murder that is the victimary mechanism awaits its unveiling, as Girard has shown, through the voices of the gospels.

The *Pharmakoi,* Victims of the Athenians

Athenians celebrated the festival of the Thargelia across two days in early summer at the end of their calendar year.[31] On the sixth of Thargelion, they purified themselves and the city by driving out *pharmakoi,* human drugs whose expulsion cleansed the community of its pollution. According to the mythmakers, the Athenians fell sick with plague after they had unlawfully killed Androgeos of Crete or stoned Pharmakos to death for stealing a bowl sacred to Apollo.[32] The rites of the first day of the Thargelia, the mythmaker contends, imitate this original murder.[33] On the seventh of Thargelion, Athenians offered Apollo the *thargêlos,* a stew of first fruits, vegetables, and grains, in his sanctuary on the Ilissos River and sang his praise. H. W. Parke points out that the festival follows the procedure in which the Greeks at Troy rid themselves of the plague sent by an Apollo angry at their leader's disrespect for his priest (Hom. *Il.* 1.312–317): "The two remedies used are for the men to clean themselves and throw the off-scourging into the sea, and then to offer hecatombs of bulls and he-goats to the god."[34] The stew denotes and simulates the fertility and prosperity that the Athenians sought from the god through his protection of their crops ripening in the fields. It is a reflex of the *pharmakos.* Fertility is marked by *thargêlos* and its absence by the *pharmakos,* while pollution, the absence of fertility, is marked by the presence of the *pharmakos* and the absence of the *thargêlos.* Different in appearance, *thargêlos* and *pharmakos* embody the contradictories that constitute divinity. As god of plague, Apollo has dominion over the restoration of fertility.

For some time before the festival, Athenians fed poor and deformed men at the common hearth in the Prytaneum in the center of the city.[35] The men were marginalized by their culture of honor, wealth, and beauty: "worthless men plotted against by nature"; "very low-born and useless"; "very unpleasant, maimed, and plotted against by nature, lame."[36] Athenians sacrificed men like these "for the purpose of being purified from the miasma and from their own evil, and to discover a treatment (*therapeia*) for the evil pressing upon them."[37] These figures display the stereotypes of the victim identified by Girard in *The Scapegoat.*[38] Society, thrown into crisis from a crime that eliminates differences (murder, temple theft), chooses figures susceptible to victimization because they bear marks of the stereotypes of persecution. It is not known how they were selected; they may have offered themselves for the food. At any rate, Athenians in the way of sacrificers deceived themselves, accepting the men arbitrarily as willing offerings.

On the first day, the Athenians dressed two of these men in strings of figs—one wearing black fruit to represent the men, and the other wearing a necklace of white figs to represent the women. The *pharmakoi* bear the city's pollution out of the community. The men are led around the city by a procession and finally escorted outside its walls. They were perhaps beaten on the genitals by branches of sterile plants.[39] Once the *pharmakos* fulfilled his service by removing with himself the city's dark and filthy shadow, he was cast away, left to go back into the obscurity of its alleys and byways with the abruptness with which Herman Melville's Queequeg empties his idol, erstwhile focus of his most solemn devotions, of sacredness: "At last extinguishing the fire, he took the idol up very unceremoniously, and bagged it again in his grego pocket as carelessly as if he were a sportsman bagging a dead woodcock."[40] This is because there is nothing inherently sacred about the victim or the idol.[41] Whether Athenians in fact sacrificed *pharmakoi* in earliest times, as a late commentator contends,[42] is not supported by evidence from the time their rites were practiced. But Greeks tended to be silent even about the goring of the sacrificial animal.[43]

Figs are *hiera* (Latin: *sacra*) fruits, in that they denote both fertility and sterility simultaneously. They combine in one visual sign the twofold nature of the *pharmakoi* that can only be manifested in the real world diachronically. The *pharmakos* removes pollution by simulating the community's pollution through his appearance and lowly circumstances. As such, he is a *katharma*, "something thrown away in cleansing," a *perikartharma*, "refuse," and *peripsema*, "something wiped off."[44] No god is named, and none is needed on this day, as the *pharmakos'* magic is that of the second act of *thusia*. By being different, he becomes the focus of the community's reciprocal violence; by his death or banishment, he restores the city to health. The scourge then turns into hero by the "double transference of the sacred,"[45] which we see next in the sausage seller of Aristophanes' *Knights*. In between the first and third acts, however, he in effect disappears into the sacred with the violence that no mortal wishes to own up to.

Victimage through the *Pharmakoi* Process

The rituals of the Thargelia embody the Athenians' belief that they can rescue themselves from disaster by the banishment of one or more of their members. Athenians confirmed their conviction in this truth of their Weltanschauung through a step-by-step process.[46] These steps occur or are alluded to in some fashion not only in rituals but also in myths, comedy, political institutions,[47] and the dominant mythmaking medium of the later fifth century: tragedy. No ritual need be seen as the source.[48] Artisans drew independently from their acculturation as Athenians and adapted what they took to their medium and purposes. These steps, called "stereotypes" by Girard and "themes" by Todd M. Compton,[49] occurred repeatedly, thus becoming both conventional and associated with one another. As a result, the presence of all is not needed to evoke the belief and signal the victimization. In the same way, mention of "a cross to bear" stimulates comparison to Jesus in a Judeo-Christian society. These steps make up a group of interrelated parts, some familiar from Girard's victimage mechanism that constitutes a process toward obtaining a product. Etically, this group is a critical tool for analysis, but since it derives from evidence obtained from the utterances in myths and dramas in Athenian culture, it must have resided in the culture in a form analogous to Ferdinand de Saussure's interaction of *langue* and *parole*.[50] The entire language (*langue)* is real, residing in the minds of its speakers, but it is manifested only through specific utterances. As no single speech act (*parole)* is the source of language or contains all that can be said, no single manifestation of the *pharmakos* belief is the source of everything that can be said about the belief. Undoubtedly, some expressions are older than others. Tragedy and ostracism did not always exist. Throughout their history, Athenians voiced their belief, educating and confirming themselves as Athenians in the belief through its available forms—presumably, rituals and myths. By the time new expressions were invented, they could recognize the belief through clues, however elliptical or metaphorical, in its new guises in tragedy or comedy. Again the analogy with language. The Greek could say anything he wanted in Greek once he thought of it. When Sophocles told the Oedipus myth through intimations of the *pharmakos,* his audience, confirmed in the belief and educated in earlier expressions, could recognize the clues and respond in ways acceptable to Sophocles and his patron, the demos. In turn, Plato knew the clues and his audience, signaling it to recall what was needed to grasp his meanings.

The procedure begins with the first step: the community is threatened by crisis. Athenians, envious of the victories won by Minos' son, Androgeos, slay him "illegally" and plague besets them.[51] Plague suddenly grips all of Boeotia.[52] Sophocles' Thebes is diseased by plague and barrenness from causes unknown (Soph. *OT* 14–30). The Athenians are beset with war brought by the Dorians.[53] Zeus Idaeus, enraged at the Celaenians, threatens to engulf their city, Celaena, with a watery abyss that "draws down into its depths houses along with the people."[54] In each instance, the crisis consists of the loss of differences. Androgeos is killed by a lawless mob. The abyss accepts all. War and plague kill indiscriminately.

As the second step, the community petitions a god who responds with a remedy usually proffered through an oracle. The Delphic oracle that Aelian relates in *Miscellaneous Stories* identifies the daughters of Leon as the saviors for the Athenians from a crisis that he leaves unexplained.[55] Apollo's oracle probably prescribed the driving out of *pharmakoi* to cleanse Athenians of the pollution of their murder of Androgeos, son of the king of Crete, Minos.[56] The remedy for the Dorians against their defeat in war with the Athenians comes in the form of a prohibition: let the Dorians not kill the Athenian king, Codrus.[57] More often, however, oracles speak vaguely—"The Pythia told the Athenians who were in the grip of plague, to purify their city"[58]—or in terms of the type of victim. "The lord whose oracle is the one in Delphi," observes Heraclitus sagely, "neither speaks nor conceals but gives a sign" (fr. 93 DK). Stobaeus records in *Florigelium* the oracle received by Midas, king of Celaena: the earth will close up if he throws the most valuable thing in human existence into the abyss."[59] Apollo of Gortyne declared to the people of Boeotia that they would propitiate the anger of Persephone and Hades and remove the plague on their land "if two maidens willingly became offerings" to the gods."[60] When Thebes was on the verge of war with the Orchomeneans, an oracle declared that victory would be theirs "if someone who was the most distinguished of the citizens in the renown of his descent agreed to die by . . . hand."[61] Creon returns from Delphi with an oracle in which the god, he says, "clearly commands us to take vengeance on the murderers whoever by male banishment" (Soph. *OT* 106–107).[62] Creon exaggerates its clarity. Sophocles' participle, *andrêlatountas,* translated as "male banishment," consists of *andr-* ("man" or "men") and *lat-* ("driving out"). The participial form renders uncertain the number of men to be banished, whether one or many, by aborting a singular or plural inflexion on *andr-* (*andra,* singular; *andras,* plural). Moreover, the manuscripts have the plural *tinas,* but the tenth-century Byzantine lexicon, *Suda,* offers the alternative, the singular *tina,* a *lectio difficilior* that lends further uncertainty.[63]

In the third step, a search is mounted for the remedy prescribed by the oracle. The people of Celaena throw their valuables, gold, silver, and jewelry, into the chasm in vain. The daughters of the Boeotians refuse to offer themselves. The search occupies the greater part of a tragedy or comedy. The oracles given to Creon leave the search to settle the number as well as the identity of the murderers. At first Oedipus appears to understand that the god spoke of "murderers," for he asks, "where in the land are they?" (Soph. *OT* 108). Moreover, he learns from Creon that the sole witness to the murder said repeatedly that "brigands falling in with him killed him not with the strength of one but with a throng of hands" (122–123). The plurality of murders is repeated later by Theban elders in recalling what was said at the time: "he was killed by some travelers" (292). Despite the ambivalence, Oedipus sets out almost immediately to find the "man" responsible for Laïus' death, "How did the brigand come to such a degree of boldness unless he was acting with money from within?" (123), and replies to the chorus, "I heard that, too, but no one saw the doer" (293). He returns to the plural number in telling Tireseias of the single means of release from the sickness: "that we learn well those who killed Laïus and kill them" (308–309). Jocasta relates the same story, that "foreign brigands murdered him," with one new detail: "at the meeting of the three wagon-roads." Oedipus knows that he is different in one way: he killed men at a crossroads (801–813). Straightway, he leaps to the conclusion that he may have inadvertently cursed himself as Laïus' murderer, and that his only hope is that the herdsman will stay with his story of many—for, as he says, "How can the one be equal to the many?" (845). The search continues, now no longer for Laïus' murderers, however, but for the identity of Oedipus.

The fourth step entails the nature of the person or persons sought: they are liminal figures located on the fringe of the community. Physical deformity renders questionable the ritual of *pharmakos'* status as human, while his poverty besmirches his status as a citizen. Rituals represent the *pharmakos* as low and worthless; myths glorify him. The virgin daughters of Leon, Orion, and Antiopoinos, yet to be acculturated by marriage, are expendable. The handsome Cratinus and royal son Anchurus give their lives for their cities.[64] Their worthlessness, disguised by their high station, comes out in the ease with which they are thrown away.

The victims' acceptance of the identity prescribed for them by the oracle forms the fifth step. Once the victims of myth determine the cure, they seize upon themselves as the party marked by the god and offer themselves. Anchurus determines that nothing is more valuable than a human life and hurls himself into the chasm. Codrus dons the humble clothes of a woodcutter and provokes the Dorians into slaying him. The daughters kill themselves on hearing of the oracle. During his search for the murderer of

Laïus, Oedipus recalls how he slew a man at the crossroads in Phocis who, he is later told, resembled Laïus (Soph. *OT* 122). The herdsman, sole witness of the murder of Laïus, reported back to Thebes that "many robbers" killed him. A despairing Oedipus reasons: "If he still says the same number, I did not kill him, for one could not be the same as many (643–645). But to affirm without hesitation the evidence of such an eyewitness, "a worthy man for a slave" (763), not only flies in the face of Greek distrust of slaves; it also injects certainty into the selection process that belongs to his victimization after his self-selection. At line 1016, "Polybus was no kin to you," the search shifts from who murdered Laïus to who is Oedipus. Oedipus learns that he is the son of Laïus and his own wife, Jocasta, and grasps as well the reverse of this revelation—that the man at the crossroads was his father. He willingly accepts the identity prescribed by the oracle not as the god stated it but as he has interpreted it throughout his own search: one man. The search ends with Oedipus because he is different: he comes from outside and has killed at the crossroads in Phocis, and because from the outset he feels the sufferings of others as his own. Acknowledging that he is the son of Laïus and Jocasta, he dismisses evidence that he may not have slain his father. By allowing himself to be victimized, the one becomes the many, and doubts no longer persist.[65] The backstory, describing the discovery of Oedipus as scourge after he has admitted his responsibility, revises the front story of his possible innocence of the death of Laïus. In identifying himself as the scourge of Thebes, Oedipus finds himself as its legitimate king and is revealed as stranger and citizen, hunter and hunted, husband and son, father and brother, defilement and savior, identities that Jean-Pierre Vernant has shown operate along an axis occupied at the summit by the divine king and at the base by the incestuous parricide.[66] This is the backstory, the revision of Oedipus' actions heaped upon them by his admission of guilt, that Sandor Goodhart has shown is responsible for the issue of the one and the many to be settled.[67] The myth's unequivocal determination of Oedipus as parricide and incest reproduces the Thebans' need for a victim to rid them of the plague, and Oedipus has from the beginning willingly allowed others to foist upon him responsibility for the plague. Thebans of the chorus, once behind Oedipus as their savior, unite against him as the miasma of Oedipus and Jocasta raise doubts about the veracity of oracles (863–910). As they lament with Oedipus, they make the point of connecting him as Laïus' son to the pollution on the city:

Now who is more wretched to hear of?
Who is more wretched living in savage ruin,
in sufferings, with a change in life?
O renowned Oedipus,
for whom the same great harbor
served the son and the father as bridegroom,
how ever, however were your father's furrows
able to bear you, wretch, for so long?

Time seeing all things found you out.
It brings to justice the marriage no-marriage
that for a long time begot children begotten by children.
O child of Laïus,
if only, if only
I had never seen you. (Soph. *OT* 1204–1218)

Thebans need Oedipus as victim to justify their faith in oracles that, however imperfect, serve as beacons to the truth, while Sophocles mediates through his medium what he suggests with his chorus: men, deprived of oracular wisdom, have to secure for themselves whatever is to be known, a specter that he averts for them by manufacturing an answer, the victimization of Oedipus: In the hindsight reading—namely, the myth—Oedipus "is presented as a monstrous exception to the general run of mankind; he resembles nobody, and nobody resembles him."[68] But Sophocles lets his audience, through the interplay of the search and its glomming onto Oedipus, see that what transpires in the myth "seems nothing more than the camouflaged victory of one version of the story over the other."[69] In essence, Tireseias and Creon sell their story to the Thebans, who, desperate for a victim, take Oedipus, who offers himself.

Sausage Seller as *Pharmakos*

Aristophanes' *Knights* (424 BCE) depicts the household of the Athenian peasant Demos in crisis because of his perverted love for politicians. In turn, because his household stands for the "household" of the demos, the play alludes to the poor state of affairs in Athens under its current leadership. Demos has ceded his authority to a slave called Paphlagon after his homeland, Paphlagonia. The members of Demos' household seek a cure to the crisis by retracing the steps of the victimage process. In this scenario, they are dispatched by an oracle to find someone so low, so loathsome that he is not only more corrupt than Paphlagon, but also so far gone that he reverses the process of decay to become the means of renewal and fertility in both household and city.[70]

An actor playing a slave enters from the stage building. He wears a portrait mask that identifies him as the general Demosthenes. He is in pain, he says, from a beating inflicted by a fellow slave. Another actor enters. His mask shows that he plays the general Nicias. The slaves proceed to lament their situation and to ponder escape:

> DEM.: Find a way to dance out of here.
> NIC.: Okay. Say "de" and "sert," joining them into one word.
> DEM.: Desert. There, I said it.
> NIC.: Now say "let" and "tuce."
> DEM.: Lettuce.
> NIC.: Very good. Now, like doing yourself a favor, say "de" and "sert" and "let" and "tuce" slowly, then real fast.
> DEM.: Desertlettucedesertlettucedesert—LET US DESERT! (*Eq.* 20–26)

The slaves abandon this plan: "The hides of slaves who wack off gets wacked off" (29). They turn to the gods whose existence Demosthenes questions, but Nicias knows that gods exist, for he is "god-awful miserable." Then they turn to tell the audience the situation that has them so miserable: the crisis in the house (40–79).

Their master is Demos, "a bumpkin, a rotten-tempered, bean-eating peasant, a dyspeptic old man, a bit deaf" (*Eq.* 40–43). The house, then, represents both the dwelling of this old man and the city of the Athenian demos. Demos bought a slave from Paphlagonia who sized him up from the beginning. Paphlagon fawns on the master, flatters and toadies up to him, and deceives him. He holds him enthralled and refuses to let the other slaves come near him. Demosthenes complains how,

Yesterday or the day before,
I kneaded a Spartan cake in Pylos.
He ran round me villainously and stole it
and served it up himself—what I baked. (54–57)[71]

"Gulp it down. Devour it up. Have three obols," Demosthenes quotes Paphlagon, manipulating Demos to shirk his duty as judge. The food image anticipates the specter of the politician as nurse who treats Demos like an infant, chewing his tidbits for him and swallowing thrice as much for herself (717–718). "Paphlagon would fork over a little bit of what he took and lay up the rest for himself" (1222–1223). Aristophanes further depicts Paphlagon's relationship with Demos as a perverted pederastic affair, which K. J. Dover summarizes as follows: "acceptance of payment, readiness—even appetite— for homosexual submission, adoption of a bent or lowered position, reception of another man's penis in the anus or mouth."[72] The *erastês* (lover) who satisfies his desires by payment and treats his *erômenos* (beloved) as an object for his own pleasure commits wanton and arrogant violence against him and stands liable to social censure and public persecution for hubris. Paphlagon has turned Demos into his *erômenos,* whom he dishonors by paying him for his vote (255) and treating him like a common prostitute. For his part, Demos willingly accepts payment and pleasures from his *erastês* and willingly forfeits all civil prerogatives. "O Demos," the Knights of the chorus tell him, "you like being flattered and deceived, with your orifices gaping open for the speaker" (116–119). Demos has sunk into prostitution, where he joins other sexual marginals, female and foreign male prostitutes. According to his own laws, Demos, a citizen who openly prostitutes himself, cannot participate in governing his own city without being liable to public suit carrying an extreme penalty.

Within Demos' household the master has abrogated power; the slave Paphlagon has usurped Demos' authority for his own gains (*Eq.* 67). Distinctions between slave and slave, master and slave, and citizen and prostitute have been lost. Aristophanes shows a demos that has let itself become the plaything of the speakers, politicians, like Cleon. Conditions in the house of Athens bear no superficial resemblance to the "plague and patricide/incest" afflicting Thebes or an army stalled by a goddess' anger, but each community is imperiled by a crisis that confounds the differences and hierarchies of its structure.[73] Demos' descent into sexual perversion carries "the collective character of the disaster, in universally contagious nature," that Girard identifies with plague in Sophocles' *Oedipus the King,* while parricide and incest that Girard identifies with "violence and nondifference" are limited to one person. In the tragedy, this is Oedipus, the lofty king and savior of the city from the Sphinx. In the comedy, he proves to be someone who is more violent and more marked by nondifference—that is, more corrupt in every moral sense—than Paphlagon.

In *Knights,* Aristophanes attacks the dominant politician of the day, Cleon, son of a rich tanner, for not recognizing his proper place as the son of a tradesman, for rejecting traditional avenues to power and prestige, and for ridiculing the established mores of the city.[74] Since Cleon claimed to be of humble birth and a lover of the demos, Aristophanes eagerly went go along and put him on stage as a barbarian from Paphlagonia and bugger of a senile, bean-eating Demos. But Aristophanes suspends the normal world of political solutions to political problems. Mired in a crisis, Demosthenes conceives the comedy's brilliant idea by drinking wine. He decides to consult the god for a remedy, but no one approaches the deity at his shrine. The second step begins when Nicias slips inside and purloins oracles from a drunken Paphlagon, snoring and farting on a bed of hides (*Eq.* 104, 115). Comedy flouts the scruples of piety and reverence, but the audience is no less alerted to expect a god-sent tonic. Thus, from its beginning, the effort to heal Demos moves away from the political sphere to the religious.

Oracles identify cures in generic terms: "the most precious thing in human life (Stob. *Flor.* 3.7.66)," "vengeance upon the man's murderers—whoever he may be (Soph. *OT* 107)," or "the one who will oust Paphlagon is a sausage-seller" (*Eq.* 143). Their openness necessitates a process of selection. The search and the third step get under way when the slaves espy a seller of sausages coming into the agora "as if in accordance with god" (147) and call out to him as their savior. Anyone selling sausages would fit the identity given by the oracle. It indicates "sausage-sellers" (200), the plural denoting members of the trade, not specifically the one coming into view. The slaves must get *this* seller to accept as his own the identity prescribed by the oracle. In what follows, the knights praise Sausage Seller, not because they accept him—he is a *ponêros,* after all, a man of physical toil (*ponos*), inferior and loathsome, and they are the quality. Rather, their motives[75] for encouraging

him are personal, namely, to rescue themselves and free their Athens from
the crisis:

> *If you [Paphlagon] win by shouting, you get "Hail to the Victor."*
> *But if he [Sausage Seller] surpasses you in shamelessness, the prize cake is ours.*
> (276–277)

In the contests between them, Paphlagon and Sausage Seller profit themselves, but the knights, not the victorious Sausage Seller, reap the rewards of
his victory, for they obtain a savior.

In the ensuing action of the play to line 1263, the community searches for
a victim through a process of selection in which Sausage Seller must prove
himself more loathsome than Paphlagon. He demurs ("I don't consider
myself worthy of great power" [182]), showing that his designation is not
automatic. The oracle even acknowledges that he may prefer to continue
selling his wares (201). His hesitation parallels that of Antiopoinos and the
maidens of Boeotia.[76]

Sausage Seller scores two decisive blows over Paphlagon in the ensuing
food fights. In the dynamics of pederasty, he tops Paphlagon's theft of the
Pylos cake by serving Demos a dish of roast hare snatched from Paphlagon.
The *erastês* commonly presented his *eromenos* with a hare, so that, by accepting it, Demos receives Sausage Seller as his new lover. The second blow
comes through the mechanism of the *pharmakos*. Repeated defeats have
left Paphlagon desperate. He decides to test whether this particular seller of
sausages is the one identified by Apollo's oracle to worst him (*Eq.* 1232–1252).
As often observed, this scene perhaps parodies the recognition scene from
Oedipus Tyrannus in that both probe the oracle as the community arrives at
unanimity over the identification of its *pharmakos*.[77] Paphlagon's questioning of Sausage Seller reveals how much more abominable he is than himself.
On the fringes of society since boyhood, Sausage Seller spent his youth
in the singeing pits and brothels. Trained in stealing and perjury, he now
peddles his own flesh as well as the meat of his sausages at the gates, the city's
edge, apart from the merchants located at its center, the agora. "O me, the
revelation of the god has been fulfilled" (1248). Paphlagon admits defeat,
and Sausage Seller cries out victory to "Hellenic Zeus." Demosthenes, representative of Demos' community, responds: "Hail, glorious victor (*kallinike*)"

(1253–1254). The exchange implies that Sausage Seller has won a victory at Olympia.[78] The games there sought out the best among the very good. The contests in *Knights,* held to decide upon the worst, have discovered among the abominable the best scoundrel. Sausage Seller need only claim the rewards promised by Demosthenes (150–181) and the knights (838–840) and lord over Demos. His parting words enact the acceptance of the fifth step, by proclaiming the scoundrel's intention to confuse and abuse the Athenians far worse than Paphlagon:

> *I'll serve you well, Demos, so that you'll*
> *confess you never saw a better man than me*
> *for the city of gullible, buggered Athenians.* (1261–1263)

In the interim before Sausage Seller's return from Demos' house, Aristophanes inserts a choral interlude. The chorus summarizes in metaphorical language the sickness that has come over the demos from its preference for bad leaders. Its leaders engage in sex for pleasure in perverted ways that preclude fertility. Ships imagined as virgin girls refuse to offer themselves to such men because of their depravity.[79] A choral ode at the end of an episode is conventional. This song, however, acts like the second act of *thusia* to shift the violence from men to the sacred by keeping the focus on the sickness and away from the manner of obtaining a cure. The community has united upon a victim by cajoling and egging on a seller of sausages who was minding his own business. It is their violence that ultimately causes Sausage Seller's victory, which brings about their salvation. They have acted under the guise of fulfilling the oracle, so their actions appear condoned, blessed by the god who has offered them the victim as the means of restoring peace and harmony.[80] The ode hides all this.

When Sausage Seller returns, the scoundrel has disappeared. Everything about the final scene distinguishes it from what precedes. Sausage Seller does not exploit his victory or attempt to dominate Demos. He calls immediately for words of good omen, the customary prelude to a ritual (*Eq.* 1316–1318). Gone are the politician's obscenities: *prôktos,* with its anal homosexual connotations, is replaced by *hypolispha pugidia,* "well-worn little rumps" of hard rowing, dutiful sailors (1368). By surpassing him in lowliness, Sausage Seller should have claimed leadership in order to drive the community more deeply into crisis. What ensues has nothing to do with Sausage Seller. Throughout the selection process, he acts the amoral, ruthless, and perverted *erastês* and politician, different from Paphlagon in degree, not substance. The reversal from the lowest of the low to one whom "you would think a god" (1338) derives not from Sausage Seller but from the process, the mimetic mechanism, itself. Paphlagon and Sausage Seller have engaged in reciprocal violence until the community centers upon Sausage Seller as the "winner." The slaves and knights have run the scapegoat mechanism to obtain the lowest and most marginal of men to be the savior. They have driven the crisis to the bad so far that violence becomes generative and triggers the good. "There is no paradox in a disease that cures a disease. It is a question of augmenting the forces of destructive mimesis in order to channel them toward the sacrificial resolution.... The model that functions in order to perpetuate the status quo is also the model of change, which in any case functions to bring about the return of the same. The crisis must simply be replayed in order to bring about the resolution with its desired effects."[81] There is nothing in Sausage Seller to explain it; the transition does not adhere to the necessity or probability of an Aristotelian plot, and neither does the finale of the *Knights*. It is, rather, an example of what Girard calls "double transference":

> The double transference of the primitive sacred explains the logical flaw that characterizes numerous myths. In the beginning of the latter the hero passes for a dangerous criminal and nothing more. After the violence intended to prevent him or her from inflicting further harm on the community, this same scapegoat appears in the conclusion as the divine savior, though this change of identity is never justified or even pointed out.[82]

The audience accepts the transition that the lowest of the low converts to the highest of the high because in this way they have their savior, and the fourth step continues to unfold.

Sausage Seller enters with Demos, who addresses him by his given name, Agoracritus, He of Disputes in the Agora.[83] Agoracritus wears the rags of the seller of sausages, but Demos has been transformed in appearance. "I've boiled Demos for you and made him noble out of ignoble" (*Eq.* 1321). Demos wears the cicada of the old-time Athenian and smells of libations and myrrh. The knights hail Demos as "the sole ruler of Hellas and this land" (1330).

Demos back in power gives flattering politicians short shrift (1362–1363) and drives the beardless pathics from the agora (1373). The perverted liaison that he succumbed to with Paphlagon is replaced by the proper and socially approved affair with "a betesticled boy" (1385). His authority regained, he has his manhood: he acts the *erastês* to the boy's *eromenos* and lusts after the women playing the role of Peaces.[84] Demos healthy reverses Demos sick.

During the selection process, Socrates and Paphlagon jostle in front of Demos' house and knock his *eiresiônê* (harvest wreath) from its perch above the door (*Eq.* 729). The fillets and figs of the *eiresiônê,* signs of fertility for those within, transpose the fine clothes and strings of figs worn on the sixth of Thargelion by the *pharmakoi* as signs of miasma being removed from within. Together, they embody the totality of the *pharmakos.* In everyday life, people put *eiresiônai* above their doors, where they might be dislodged, and an *eiresiônê* above a stage door remains a prop—until it falls into the action. Then it visualizes for the audience what Sausage Seller emphasizes by saying: "You've broken my harvest wreath to pieces" (729). When seven hundred lines later Demos invites Agoracritus to accompany him to the Prytaneum (1406), Aristophanes expects his audience to remember the *eiresiônê* and the loss of fertility that its crashing to the ground put before their eyes for his visual scene with a frog-green cloak (*batrachis*).

Demos invites Agoracritus to the Prytaneum: "Take this *batrachis,*" he says, "and follow me." The scene is again visual. The audience sees the *batrachis,* but Aristophanes calls attention to it. The *batrachis* is a cloak, green in color after its namesake, *batrachos* (frog), but the translation offered by the standard lexicon, "frog-green garment," does no justice to it or to Aristophanes' stage direction.[85] The scholiast in *Knights* 1406 describes the *batrachis* as "a kind of flowery clothing, having a color like the name," "resembling the sun's heat, with a flowery color." The *batrachis* Athenaïs dedicated to Artemis Brauronia is glossed in the inscription: "a woman's upper garment richly decorated in many colors."[86] The cloak, green variegated with embroidered or painted flowers, depicts the freshness of the blooming fields. When Agoracritus puts it on, he is transformed visually into an embodiment of the green meadow bathed in the warmth of the sun. The donning of the *batrachis* completes the fourth step. The fallen *eiresiônê* of the autumn harvest yields to a symbol of the flourishing prosperity of the spring season, a redundant image for Demos' rejuvenation to his Marthonian self of old.[87]

Demosthenes cries out at Sausage Seller's trumping of Paphlagon: "Hail, glorious victor" (1254). The address, we recall, implies that Sausage Seller has won a victory at Olympia. The games there sought out the best among the good, and their victors had conferred upon them the favor of Zeus. The Athenians rewarded its Olympic victors with *sitêsis,* maintenance with a daily meal for the rest of their lives at the public hearth. Sausage Seller won a victory comparable to that of an Olympic athlete by showing that no one was more detestable. The victor in the contests remains before the audience, still dressed in his tripe-stained clothes, when Demos throws the *batrachis* over him as a sign of his heroism and leads him off to dine at the Prytaneum. We must bear this in mind, for *sitêsis* at the Prytaneum is what Socrates, convicted of corrupting the youth and polluted with foreswearing his citizen's oath, assesses as his worth to Athenians.

Socrates as *Pharmakos*

Todd M. Compton includes Socrates with others who are not poets among his *Victims of the Muses* by defining a poet as "a verbal artist or satirist."[88] His "poets" manifest elements of a *pharmakos* pattern whose name derives from the two *pharmakoi* of the Thargelia. Compton places Socrates among them by seeing his likeness to Aesop, whose life contains seventeen of the twenty-four themes that comprise "the pharmakos tradition" in his description.[89] Socrates' life contains fourteen themes.[90] Compton concludes that "Aesop is the mythological poet-*pharmakos,* and Socrates is the new Aesop. Plato would assimilate Socrates to Aesop chiefly because of the blatant injustice of what amounted to political murder in both cases."[91] The Delphinians executed Aesop on the charge they fabricated of temple robbery *(Life of Aesop* W.127–142). In the *Phaedo,* Plato draws these two avatars of the *pharmakos* pattern together, flushing out, as it were, the subtext and willing his reader to assimilate them to one another: while in prison during the festival of Apollo, Socrates turns at the god's commands the tales of Aesop into song (60c–61b). Compton undoubtedly is correct in seeing the *pharmakos* pattern in the re-presentation of the historical Socrates. Many of his references, however, come from Plato's *Apology of Socrates,* which offers its own clues to Socrates as *pharmakos.* To offset the prosecutor's penalty of death, Socrates ponders as his due reward *sitêsis* (free meals) at the Prytaneum, the highest honor bestowed by Athenians upon conspicuous benefactors (36e–37a). The poor and ugly men who would benefit the city as its *pharmakoi* during the Thargelia dined there before they performed their service to the city of ridding it of the pollution accrued during the last year. In his final speech, Socrates muses about "chancing upon Palamedes and Ajax, son of Telamon, and anyone else of the ancients who died on account of an unjust judgment/trial" (40b). These are forceful clues to seeing Socrates as a *pharmakos,* and they come during the initial stages of Plato's defense, while the *Phaedo* belongs to a later time of reflection and perhaps of upheaval surrounding the publication of Polycrates' *Prosecution of Socrates* sometime after 394 BCE. We will, of course, return to Socrates' *pharmakos.*

CHAPTER 3

Aristophanes' Ready Victim

The Satan expelled is that one who foments and exasperates mimetic rivalries to the point of transforming the community into a furnace of scandals. The Satan who expels is this same furnace when it reaches a point of incandescence sufficient to set off the single victim mechanism. In order to prevent the destruction of his kingdom, Satan makes out of his disorder itself, at its highest heat, a means of expelling himself.

—RENÉ GIRARD, *I See Satan Fall Like Lightning*

When the Athenians returned to their city after the retreat of the Persians in 479 BCE to find its walls, temples, and buildings razed, they wanted what any Greek would want: walls. Not all desire is mimetic.[1] A hungry or thirsty person is not imitating the desire of another for food or drink. Thus protected by city walls, Greeks could negotiate or endure or sally forth; otherwise, they were exposed. Tension with Sparta, whose military might and village life negated the need for walls, dominated the first months of the return (Thuc. 1.90–93). The Athenian Themistocles went to Sparta as an ambassador. There he prevaricated and postponed discussions with the authorities while, at his prompting, Athenians back home frantically threw up walls from whatever stone and rubble were at hand.

There is no mimesis in these early actions with the Spartans but the human need for security.

Although born of a distinguished family, Themistocles did not enjoy the traditional support for his career but relied on his own intelligence and, as Thucydides observes, a remarkable ability to foresee the course of events (1.138.3). During his archonship (493–492 BCE), he persuaded Athenians to develop the Piraeus by enclosing its three natural harbors with walls (Thuc. 1.93.3). Even before the return of the Persians, he seems to have realized that the future for Athenians lay in ships. According to Thucydides (1.93.3), he was the first to envision Athens as a sea power, and for this insight the available model was the Persians.[2] In essence, Persians showed him what was to be desired: naval superiority. Relying upon Athenian triremes, Themistocles manipulated the Greeks to resist the Persians at Salamis and defeat their navy. After the war, the fleet brought Athenians the hegemony of an alliance of eastern Mediterranean cities and islands formed to drive out the Persians and seek reparations. Imitative desire appears to have continued to motivate the league's early policies under its foremost general, Cimon, whose exploits drove out Persians and replaced their dominance with Athenian.[3] In time, differences of ethnicity and morality between the Athenians and their Persian models wore away. Athenians reduced allies to subjects, and the league to a tyranny. The Athenian empire and the glories of classical Athens realized the acquisitive desire in mimesis of the largest tyranny of the then-known world.

In effect, Athenian society underwent crisis that lasted throughout their history, from the assumption of leadership against the Persians in 478 BCE through their defeat at the hands of the Peloponnesians in 404 and into the fourth century. The empire taxed the institutions of what began as a traditional *polis* with an influx of innovations and challenges. The world of Athenians simply changed and kept on changing, not always for the better, but always breaking down fixed and received ways of thought and living. New products spilled into the city, while foreigners brought exotic outlooks on the gods, the world, and, in particular, education to the hearth of Athenians. The attraction and repulsion aroused by their views comes out in Aristophanes' *Clouds*. Strepsiades eagerly seeks the powers of the new-wave rhetoric taught by Sophists to elude his debts and then shrinks in horror when that same rhetoric corrupts his son. This comedy first (423 BCE) associated

Socrates with the crisis in belief in the gods and the stability of language and contributed to that τύχη ("chance") that identifies Socrates as victim (Pl. *Ep.* 325b). The Sophists' teachings met with such acceptance, however, because the atmosphere created by the seizing of an empire and the launching of a war in its defense had instilled desire and readiness and greed.

◆　◆　◆

Socrates first appears as a hoplite soldier during the siege (432–430 BCE) of the rebel Corinthian colony, Potidaea. The references come years after the events in Plato's account of Alcibiades' encomium of Socrates in the *Symposium.* Alcibiades praises Socrates for his endurance (219e–220b). He never appeared drunk from the soldiers' heavy drinking. In the dreadful Chalcidicean winter, when everyone huddled in huts, wrapped in felt and the hides of sheep, Socrates strolled about outside in his cloak and bare feet. Later, in the retreat from Delium (424 BCE), Alcibiades adds, Socrates walked so boldly and fearlessly that he forfended attack and rescued himself as well as his companion, the general Laches (*Sym.* 221a; *La.* 181b).

Socrates' robust health and strangeness were surely well known to Athenians even before his display as a hoplite. Talk in the city after Potidaea probably inspired the comic poet Eupolis to focus some of his wit upon the local oddity in 427 BCE. On the other hand, that Eupolis could refer to Socrates in such a public and topical medium as comedy guarantees people knew (of) him. The *Taxiarchoi* (*Commanders of Companies*) depicts the Athenian general Phormio trying to make a soldier out of the cowardly Dionysus. At some point, as the fragment attests, Eupolis refers to Socrates as "a babbling beggar who ponders everything except provisions for his plate."[4] Socrates could not have been a beggar, since he could still afford a few years later at Delium the bronze weaponry of a hoplite with the status of a citizen they confer. Evidently, despite his wealth, Socrates dressed like a beggar and looked as though he went hungry. Also apparent to the observer was his garrulousness.

In 424 the theater world at Athens must have been abuzz. Two comedians were planning plays about Socrates. Once Eupolis had introduced Socrates as a subject of ridicule, Ameipsias and Aristophanes in obvious mimetic rivalry had to outdo one another in depicting him. Ameipsias produced *Connus,* named apparently from Socrates' music teacher, and Aristophanes offered *Clouds,* whose title he drew from its choristers of clouds. Both plays have

left anecdotes about their performance. Ameipsias is said to have brought
Socrates on stage wearing his customary *tribôn,* a threadbare cloak of a beggar. Socrates stood up in Aristophanes' audience when foreigners wondered
who this Socrates was.[5] Neither story is necessarily historical, but the first
adds to Socrates' image as different from that of the ordinary beggar, not to
mention from the citizen clad properly in the *himation,* who would never
be the subject of comedy. The second exemplifies the doubleness that characterizes the man in reception. T. B. L. Webster has him rise to confirm "his
likeness to the action," while K. J. Dover, commentator on *Clouds,* proposes
"the opposite reason, to imply 'do I look like the sort of man who's playing
the fool on stage?'"[6] Little can be said of Socrates that cannot be doubled in
this way. Thus Diogenes Laertius remarks that "comic poets, while ridiculing
him, praise him unbeknownst to themselves" (2.27).

Athenians twice preferred Ameipsias' Socrates to Aristophanes', granting
Cratinus first prize, and him the second. Aristophanes had to settle for last
place. A displeased Aristophanes complained that he was treated unworthily
(*Nub.* 525–555) and set out to rewrite his play. He never finished, and the
revised *Clouds,* while never performed, is extant in its entirety. Ameipsias'
Connus exists in fragments, the longest of which describes Socrates:

> Socrates, you have come, best among few men and silliest among many,
> also to us. You are a robust one. Where did you get that cloak?
> . . . . . . [a lost line referring to his bare feet]
> This poor condition has proven to be a slight to the cobblers.
> This one, however, though poor, never has endured to pander. (fr. 9)

Socrates' excellence in small companies and silliness in large ones must
refer to what Eupolis deems "babbling." His philosophical talk charmed the
few wealthy and educated Athenians, but it mystified and angered ordinary
men in the streets. The argument that wickedness is caused by ignorance
could have hardly struck the average man as anything but utter nonsense.[7]
Socrates is recognizable in his bare feet and refusal to act like a normal beggar. His insult to the sandal makers foreshadows the resentment his uniqueness aroused. The fragments of Eupolis' and Ameipsias' plays are crucial
in that they offer information about Socrates written before the *Clouds.*

They give external signs of what Socrates looked and acted like and how he affected people.

Martha Nussbaum contends that Aristophanes represents Socrates as he was in the 420s and not as a representative of the Sophists.[8] The latter generally were wealthy and well turned out and taught by exposition. Aristophanes' Socrates, however, is recognizably the same man as that of Ameipsias. He is "a priest of the subtlest babble" (*Nub.* 358) who goes about barefoot (103, 364), foregoes dinner (175), ponders nonsense like the distance of a flea's leap (144–152), becomes lost in thought (225, 228–234), displays endurance throughout the play, and considers the process of education to be analogous to initiation in the mysteries (254–274).[9] Socrates heads an establishment dedicated to thinking, the Phrontisterion (94) (Thinkery), in which dwell "nit-picking thinkers" (101), his associates, Chaerephon, Anti-Right, and students.[10] The Phrontisterion is the antithesis of the *gymnasion,* bastion of the old education where blooming youths race beneath sacred olives (1001–1008). Closed off from the sunlight, it sequesters pale and sickly students who glue their faces to the courtyard in contemplation of the ground and raise their butts to the sky to study the heavens (186–194). Their teacher resides above them, suspended in a basket and removed in lofty thoughts. Nussbaum remarks: "[Socrates'] initial appearance dangling in a basket (223–225) indicates his remoteness from the interlocutor, his detachment from such 'earthly' matters as moral habituation and the management of the passions."[11] Socrates the teacher midwifes (136) the thoughts of his students. He encourages Strepsiades to "think through one of your own troubles" (695) and then, through the painful process of lying in bedclothes infested with biting bedbugs, to "ponder and consider and, waxing wise, spin about in every way" (700–702). "And when you fall into perplexity (*aporia*), leap quickly to another thought of wit" (702–705). The process, Strepsiades realizes, brings it about that "you will know yourself—how stupid and thick you are" (842). "In short, the procedure and its characteristic effects are those of the Socratic elenchus."[12]

Unlike the elenchus of the Platonic Socrates that holds out the prospect of healing, that of the Aristophanes is purely negative.[13] His Socrates begins with what the student believes and, by questions, strips him of his belief and the understanding of the world conveyed by his belief:

STREPSIADES: Well, the thunderbolt whence it is brought blazing with
  fire, teach me this. It strikes and burns us and singes all that is living,
  for Zeus clearly hurls this at those who swear falsely.
SOCRATES: You fool, smelling of hoary Kronos and born before the moon,
  how is it if he strikes perjurers, he didn't burn Simon?
(*Nub.* 395–399)

Strepsiades cannot answer and loses his belief in Zeus as not only the god of
the thunderbolt but also the divine avenger of perjury, resulting in license to
forswear without fear of penalty. Such is the effect of the elenchus. In return
for what he takes away, Socrates offers nothing, for his gods, Void, Vortex,
and Tongue, mimic in their formlessness the nebulosity of his teaching that
holds no true wisdom or enduring insights into the good.

Socrates insists on knowing "clearly" and "correctly" (*Nub.* 250) in a
purely intellectual pursuit that calls into question all conventional wisdom,
the *nomoi* of received wisdom. He displays no concern whether his students
are prepared for the assault of the elenchus or for what they do with what they
have learned in his Phrontisterion. His associate, Anti-Right, offers the way
of nature (*physis*), the opposite of convention (*nomos*). His elenchus reduces
Right, who represents the old way (*nomos*) of education through athletics
and music to perplexity and flight. Anti-Right promotes for Pheidippides
the way of *physis,* which allows one to indulge one's desires and, if caught,
to talk oneself out of trouble. He advises Pheidippides, Strepsiades' son, in a
way of life that skips across the morality of conventional men:

> *You strayed, you had sex, you did a man's woman, you got caught,*
> *you're dead, since you don't know how to talk. Stick with me.*
> *Enjoy your nature, cavort, laugh, consider nothing disgraceful.*
> *If you're apprehended in a man's bed, you will refer him to Zeus*
> *who was overcome by sex and women.*
> *How can you, a mere mortal, be stronger than a god?* (1076–1082)

Pheidippides comes to the Phrontisterion a self-absorbed teenager,
spoiled by his mother's aristocratic aspirations and consumed by his passion
for horses. He cares not a jot for his father or the expense caused by his hip-
pomania and thinks little of breaking his oath to aid his father with his debt.

For his part, Socrates cares no more about the suitability of his students or whether they have the background in propriety and honesty to endure the assaults of the elenchus. Pheidippides listens to Anti-Right and, entering the Phrontisterion, learns the ways of rhetoric. On his return, he rebuffs his father's creditors and then, indulging himself, turns his skills upon his father. Having no curbs in place before he learned the ways of Tongue, he has no way to direct his knowledge. He convinces his father of the rightness of his beating the old man in return for his father's treatment of him in his early years. Pheidippides, then, turns his faculties upon the goal of beating his mother. This goes too far, and Strepsiades awakens what good remains in him.

Clouds ends with Strepsiades' setting fire to the roof of the Phrontisterion. His act, W. Robert Connor points out, recalls the razing and burning of the house of murderers, tyrants, and traitors, a punishment intended to remove the miscreant and his immediate family from society in an effort to forestall the wrath of the gods.[14] At the same time, the bones of the offender's ancestors were exhumed and cast beyond the borders. Like these criminals, Socrates has contaminated the whole community with a pollution that can only be purged by cauterization. In doing so, however, Strepsiades, it seems, causes far worse contamination. So much of his world has been overthrown. He has lost himself, his belief in the gods of his city, and his son to Socrates' teaching. The last words that Pheidippides says, "Be crazy with yourself here and blather on," are the actor's exit line (*Nub.* 1475). Dover contends that Pheidippides enters Strepsiades' house, but Nussbaum points out that "the *entautha* ["here"] of line 1475 suggests the reading, 'You stay *here* and talk foolishness with yourself' . . . . 'I'll go where I can talk to wise men.'"[15] Pheidippides enters the Phrontisterion. Nussbaum continues, "At line 1505 an unnamed student of Socrates shouts that he is dying in the flames." Aristophanes' original audience would surely have recognized the voice of the actor playing Pheidippides and would be able to determine whether the student was Pheidippides. In trying to put his world to rights, does Strepsiades kill his son? An audience angered at being reminded of the destruction of their Ionian kinsmen's city in Phrynicus' *Capture of Miletus* (492 BCE) and shocked at Phaedra's seduction of her stepson in Euripides' first *Hippolytus* (a few years before 428 BCE) may have shown its displeasure by voting the author last place.[16] Even so, whoever the student is who perishes, the loss of the young man underlines the danger of what is taught in the Phrontisterion.

"Aristophanes' portrait [of Socrates depicts] the success of the elenctic attack on *nomos*. This, the play claims, is what Socrates really succeeds in teaching; this is how a pupil really sees and interprets Socratic teaching—especially a pupil of the sort he would carelessly pick, a man more dedicated to pleasure than to virtue."[17] Socrates attracts and is attracted to the young; he grants them access to his way of questioning everything. He is dangerous with his lack of concern about where his questioning leads and what it does to them. Aristophanes replaced the oddball Socrates of Eupolis and Ameipsias with the head of a think tank that teaches the undoing of conventional wisdom and morality, that offers nothing in return by way of wisdom or insight into the good, and cares nothing of the effects for his teaching upon his students. Signs that merely express difference in appearance and behavior in Eupolis and Ameipsias characterize in *Clouds* responsibility for the corruption of the youth in the person of Pheidippides and for the new wave of thinking about gods. He is a danger to society by corrupting its youth and undermining their faith in society and their commitment and loyalty to it.

◆　◆　◆

The charges alleged against Socrates by his past accusers he imagines as given in a sworn declaration before a magistrate. "Socrates is guilty of investigating what lies beneath the earth and in the heavens, for making the lesser argument the greater and teaching others these same things" (Pl. *Apol.* 19b). Plato refers to the Socrates of Aristophanes' *Clouds*. In the *Apology of Socrates*, his Socrates recalls to his jurors how "you even yourselves have seen in the comedy of Aristophanes a certain Socrates being carried about and claiming that he was walking on air and uttering much other nonsense" (19c). The continued impact of *Clouds* after 423 BCE is implied. Yet no evidence exists for the deleterious effects of the *Clouds* upon Socrates for the period between the production of the play and the dramatic time of the *Apology* (399). In the interim, Aristophanes mentioned Socrates in two plays that are extant. In *Birds* (414 BCE), he notes how some were "playing the Socrates" (*esôkratoun*), a reference to his sordid and Spartan-like physical appearance which his second reference, "Socrates unwashed" (1554), specifies. In *Frogs* (405 BCE), he warns the young from his idle chatter that neglects tragedy and deems "wasting time on idle words and scratching up nonsense" the action of a crazy man (1491–1492). Thus Aristophanes joins the comic poets

Callias and Telecleides (D.L. 2.18) in deeming Socrates "a pretentious intellectual,"[18] but Aristophanes does not recall the threat he devised in *Clouds*.
Nonetheless, many accept Plato's statement as historical. Yet the appearance
of historicity does not guarantee factuality, and in the absence of outside
evidence, whether the *Clouds* continued to plague Socrates, as Plato implies,
cannot be proven. Even were it historical, Plato need not have included it
in *Apology of Socrates*. So the question shifts to how the influence of *Clouds*
benefits Plato. Why did Plato refer to it in *Apology*? What does it do in his
story of Socrates?

At six years of age in 423 BCE, Plato was too young to be taken to the
theater and, if he had been taken, surely too innocent to appreciate the attack
of the *Clouds*. He must have read the play in the revised version. When Plato
came to defend Socrates with his *Apology of Socrates,* Socrates was dead.
Plato, in reflecting upon Socrates, used *Clouds* to conjure an image and voice
for Socrates, the one portrayed by the play's most striking scene, the crazy
man who babbles nonsense swinging in a basket. The scene depicts Socrates
as an investigator of nature, which allows Socrates of the *Apology* the spe-
cious defense: "You never heard me speaking of such things" (19c–d). The
Socrates of the physical sciences draws attention away from Aristophanes'
other Socrates, who taught students the destructive argumentation of the
elenchus. Those in the circle would glean more in Aristophanes' *Clouds* than
this, for the elenchus resembles that of the Platonic Socrates, which Plato
criticizes in *Protagoras* and *Republic*.[19] Plato recalls the *Clouds* because it gives
him a view of Socrates as the corruptor of the youth and the destroyer of
traditional morality and belief in the gods. The differences in appearance,
mannerisms, and teachings that mark the Aristophanic Socrates as a threat
to society Plato saw as signs of victimage.[20] Plato's description of Socrates in
Symposium comes after reflection on his life and death. He has Alcibiades
admit that "in the hardships Socrates surpassed not only me but even all the
others, when they were cut off, as often happens on campaigns, and forced to
go without food" (219e). "The soldiers looked askance at him, thinking that
he held them in contempt" (220b). Dover observes:

> If we accept the evidence of Pl. *Sym.* 219 E ff., he must have been talked
> about after his remarkable behaviour at Poteidaia, as a man of extraordi-
> nary toughness. His bearing on the retreat from Delion ... is likely to have

spread his reputation further, but not necessarily for his own good; human nature being what it is, our reaction to those who look much braver than we feel in a headlong retreat is not always generous admiration.[21]

Dover does not consider Socrates a victim, but he aptly describes Plato's subtext of victimage. Already by his late thirties, it seems, Socrates' robustness and manner were attracting the attention of Athenians. They saw him as different, not like them in a way they felt belittled them. In his talk, he acts as his own sacrificial crisis, breaking down the differences that construct society and leaving his interlocutors uneasy, uncertain, and exposed. He is different, and difference has already by 423 invited the suspicions and resentment of Athenians. When in the course of the crisis the community sought its cause, Socrates stood out, as he always had, as different and a ready victim—his τύχη, his bad luck. And if anything can be said with historical confidence of Socrates, he was never a man of the many, even when with them on campaign or in flight. Socrates' victimage is Plato's crisis with Socrates.

◆ ◆ ◆

Whereas Plato does not accept Socrates' guilt as corruptor of the youth (*Apol.* 33d–34b) or responsibility for the crisis affecting Athenian society, Aristophanes wrote *Clouds,* both versions,[22] for an audience willing to consider Socrates guilty of the crisis in the house of Strepsiades and, by inference at least, the city of Athens. Socrates undoubtedly undermines Strepsiades' morality—rather, he further corrupts him by supplying a rationale with his attacks on traditional religion and morality—for Strepsiades arrives at the Phrontisterion already a welcher in intent (*Nub.* 112–118). But Aristophanes also depicts Socrates as contributing through his death to what resolution of the crisis in Strepsiades' household that proves possible for Strepsiades. In this, I see his Socrates acting like the Satan of René Girard's reading of Jesus' question: "How can Satan cast out Satan?" (*Mk.* 3.23). No claim resides in this thesis that Aristophanes knew the books of the Old Testament, and he could not have known those of the New. The victimage mechanism as a formative device functions throughout the hominization of humankind. It belonged to the victimary culture of Athenians and, as their language (*langue*), helped shape how they thought and what they said (*parole*). Aristophanes, conditioned by his desire to imitate the Socrates that he imagines his audience conjures, reproduces the face put on that mechanism without knowing his name, Satan, or his walking grounds, Judeo-Christian scriptures. His shock over failing to take first prize (*Nub.* 518–525) could have been founded in part, an unconscious part to be sure, on the certainty derived from his sense of the justly persecuted victim.

For Girard, the biblical Satan is the name placed upon the mimetic mechanism. Satan is the "ruler of the world," ὁ ἄρχων τοῦ κόσμου (*Jn.* 12.31) because the world is under his tutelage that foments the rivalry that spawns crisis and then provides the victim that resolves conflict and restores harmony and order until he again wants to play his game. "[Satan] may sound like a very progressive and likeable educator," and those who listen to him "may feel initially . . . 'liberated.'"[23] Aristophanes' Socrates is hardly likable but progressive, but the resemblance with Satan goes deeper. Satan seduces his followers into violating and ignoring prohibitions. He applauds the idea that "prohibitions are of no use and that transgressing them contains no danger."[24] He presents himself as a model to be imitated and works through henchmen to extend his influence. Anti-Right's rallying of Pheidippides to act with freedom and license toward others and their women comes to mind. Unfettered by restraint, Satan is easily imitated. Yet, prohibitions function to forestall and curb the outbreak of mimetic rivalry—not mimetic desire, which is healthy and necessary to become human. In their absence, desire soon becomes acquisitive, and rivalry breaks out, and men are back to facing one another on opposite sides of the river bank. Suddenly, Satan the model is now the rival, the scandal before acquiring the object. Many Satans, many rivals, coalesce into one, Satan qua victim. "He is a principle of order as much as disorder."[25] To tease his domain with crisis, to take it to the brink of destruction, and then to haul it back bodily by providing the restoration of harmony and peace through the single victim mechanism that he incarnates expresses what Jesus means, in Girard's reading, by Satan casting out Satan. This is Satan's modus operandi, and, I believe, Aristophanes has reproduced it in the m. o. of his Socrates. In framing the Aristophanic Socrates, Satan makes a Socrates sufficiently dangerous for Plato to strain the longevity of the jurors to import him into his *Apology of Socrates*. Whether or not the jurors saw Socrates swinging in the air twenty-five years ago, Plato says they did (19c). The Platonic Socrates asserts that the Socrates of Aristophanes aroused the slander that formed his past accusers. One of Satan's names is *Diabolos,* Slanderer.

• • •

To listen to Satan is tantamount for Girard to listening to "a very progressive and likeable educator." We feel "liberated," but "Satan deprives us of everything that protects us from rivalistic imitation."[26] Strepsiades arrives at Socrates' Phrontisterion already fascinated by its resident professor's Anti-Right. His determination to defraud his creditors by imitating Socrates has freed him from the anxiety of his account books that kept him tossing and turning (*Nub.* 36: *strephei*) all night and, incidentally, gave him his name. He proves to be an inept pupil, as he himself feared (129–130); yet, as he asserts with confidence (484), he remembers what profits him. Such is the case in his tutelage under Socrates. He learns that Zeus no longer sanctions oaths and consequently does not punish perjurers. He catches onto the subtleties of gender in nouns whose obscurities he later uses to mock his creditors. He imitates his master's disregard for the *nomoi,* the customs that guide and curb behavior, the exchange of money in this instance. When his first creditor challenges him to an oath, he readily complies. Since the gods do not exist to oversee oaths, he is free to say what he likes. He treats his second creditor as he likes, subjecting an Athenian citizen to the goad that equates the man to a recalcitrant animal. Both encounters verge on violence, and since his first creditor will bring a suit and the second intimates an indictment for *hubris,* both promise further violence in the courts.

Satanic Socrates works through surrogates. Right is so incompetent that, were it not too clever, we could imagine his role as a shill to drive students like Pheidippides to his accomplice. Right simply declares his form of education as if longtime practice suffices in itself. He undermines his cautions against pederasty among the boys by his attraction to their bodies (*Nub.* 966, 973–974, 977–978). He offers nothing positive in his schooling except its physical conditioning but expounds through prohibitions and their reverse, deprivation and moderation. Boys shall not mutter a sound, walk out of formation, jazz up their father's music, go about with thighs uncovered, anoint themselves below the navel, eat freely at dinner, titter and giggle, or cross their legs (964–983). They must avoid the agora and the bordello and what goes on in such places. Moderation is demanded, for through moderation Peleus won the goddess Thetis as his bride (1067). But Right lacks arguments for what he says and can only vomit on the ideas of others (907): he represents the unexamined life of the fundamentalist stuck in mind-closed acceptance of the past whose virtues, though limited, have been lost amid the certainty of his stance. He cannot ward off Anti-Right's counterpunching (1038–1042). Moderation may have won Peleus a goddess, but that same moderation between the sheets lost her. "A woman likes to be handled roughly" (1070). Flinging his cloak to the audience like a deserter, Right flees to join the buggered, who constitute the majority of Athenians.

Although "the sybaritic, self-indulgent sophist" is unlike the "restrained, serene, contemplative sophist," Anti-Right must be played by the same actor who plays Socrates to underline their similarity.[27] Nussbaum's vivid description of their differences joins the pair as sophists: "the play argues that these differences conceal a more basic sameness: an underlying intellectualism that dedicates itself to exposing the inadequacies of traditional moral justification, and argues that what cannot justify itself has no reason for being."[28] Anti-Right wants to persuade Pheidippides to his Lesser Argument. While Socrates seduces by his sophistries, Anti-Right acts directly upon Pheidippides. "He will persuade you," Right warns Pheidippides, "against your will to believe everything disgraceful noble, and everything noble disgraceful" (Ar. *Nub.* 1020–1021). Upon the loss of these differences ensues the obliteration of all prohibitions and inhibitions. "Consider, young man, how it is with moderation. Think about all the pleasures you'll miss out on" (1071–1072). Anti-Right follows with the sexual and sensual pleasures of the symposium: "boys, women, drinking games, dips and sauces, wine, and laughter" (1073). With the latter, he urges Pheidippides to give into mocking and jeering laughter without fear of reprisals.[29] "What's life without this?"—namely, shaming others by laughing at them with impunity—he asks (1074). Then he turns to the "necessities of *physis*," "nature," but for him slang for penis.[30] "You made a mistake, you had sex, you did a man's woman, you got caught, and you're dead, because you can't speak" (1076–1077). Stick with me, "indulge your nature, cavort, laugh, and consider nothing shameful" (1078). Should you get caught, just refer them to Zeus." Anti-Right encourages Pheidippides to stop at nothing, enjoy, skirt and break the rules, but he does not espouse anarchy or destruction of the rules themselves. Zeus still has his place—that is, his use. Like his master, Anti-Right does not want to destroy society, as he needs it for a playground for his games of arousing mimetic rivalries.

Strepsiades retrieves his son from the Phrontisterion, assured by Socrates that "he has learned" *that* argument (*Nub.* 1150). Pheidippides gives a brief demonstration of his prowess, and father and son retire to the house for a feast. They are interrupted by the creditors, but after Strepsiades has rebuffed them and returned to the house, it begins. He requests his son sing some oldies for him. Pheidippides refuses with the arrogance of the youth that he has learned from Anti-Right that he can vent at will. His father, placating him, asks for one of the new numbers. Pheidippides responds with lines from Euripides' *Aeolus* about the worst kind of incest, that between siblings of the same mother. Strepsiades, fed up with the impudence, attacks his son with foul and shameless insults. Words lead to blows, and the son leaps upon his father and starts pounding him (1375–1376). The father's pride in his son and pleasure in watching him perform breaks suddenly into mimetic rivalry over the best music, which escalates to violence in the absence of social and familial restraints on their behavior. Strepsiades bursts into the street, calling for witnesses, preparing to take his son to court. Family ties have been wiped away, and now it is an issue of *hubris* between strangers. But Pheidippides admits his actions with the same insouciance that Anti-Right exhibited in being called a buggerer (909–911). The pupil imitates his teacher. He glories as did his teacher in monstrosity, and both think their behavior worthy of a shower of roses. Pheidippides then mounts his case, bolstered by the authority of Socrates (1432), for why the son should beat up his father. The thought is unthinkable, the deed undoable among any Greeks and could only be contemplated in the atmosphere of shameless comedy. But Strepsiades, still fascinated by the speech peddled in the Phrontisterion, considers the case has merit (1437–1439). He wavers until his son threatens to turn his lesser argument on his mother:

> What if with the weaker argument
> I shall defeat you by contending that
> it is right to beat my mother. (1444–1446)

At this, Strepsiades comes out of bewitchment with arguments and, repulsed, sees clearly the causes of the crisis, the son that stands, rather, who speaks, at his expense before him, and Socrates and his lesser argument:

> What else? If you do that,
> nothing will stop me from throwing

> *you into the pit where we throw the bodies of traitors,*
> *you and with you Socrates*
> *and the weaker argument.* (1447–1451)

The seeds sown by Satan and his surrogate have attained fruition. The community of Strepsiades' household has been reduced to chaos of violence by the obliteration of the prohibitions that were laid down to distinguish father from old man, and son from young man. Strepsiades forthwith blames the Clouds for not telling him, a poor, geriatric bumpkin, about what congress with Socrates entailed, but they reject his accusations:

> *You yourself are responsible for this.*
> *You twisted yourself up in this abominable behavior.* (1454–1455)

Strepsiades' victories over his creditors came at the expense of the rules and divine sanctions that regulate the exchange of money. He was riding high when the Clouds warned of trouble coming his way:

> *Such is the passion for the vulgar.*
> *The old man conceived a passion*
> *and desire to cheat on what he borrowed.*
> *Today for certain the old man*
> *will receive trouble that will make*
> *this wise guy, in return for the mischief he began,*
> *receive suddenly something bad.* (1303–1309)

The Clouds have admonished Strepsiades before. They assured him ominously that he would get what he wants, for he desired "nothing great" (435). They remark that he will regret what he is doing in sending Pheidippides into the Phrontisterion (1113). This behavior challenges a simple reading of the Clouds as nebulous patrons of the Phrontisterion. Socrates may claim them as "our divinities" (253) and hold them as the patrons of his Phrontisterion (315–333). But the Clouds are the children of Ocean (277), an ancient deity of the physical world. They are old ones of nature and the outside and the ancient virtues that life in the outside supported. Despite his ignominious defeat, the Clouds praise Right and his tale of the life of

old (1024–1029) but say nothing to the victorious Anti-Right. Charles
Segal explains their nature:

> The Clouds can speak the windy language of the sophist and sharpster if
> called upon to do so. But their native tongue is the pastoral mode (275ff.),
> and this they share with the Just Argument's clean and sweet promises
> of whispering platans, clear complexion, broad shoulders, and so on.
> (1005–1014)[31]

Their forewarnings of Strepsiades are not out of character, for the Clouds
throughout espouse the traditional values that Strepsiades has forgotten in
trying to give his creditors the slip (434). They are believed to promote the
Phrontisterion's obliteration of taboos, interdictions, and prohibitions that
support moral order and society. Through their warnings, however, they
prove to be "agents of divine justice" of gods who support the sanctity of
oaths and mutual responsibility.[32] The gods, specifically Hermes, aid Strepsiades in razing the Phrontisterion and removing Socrates. The convention for
the comic chorus is that after the parabasis it should "degenerate into the
hero's claque."[33] But Clouds "become whatever they want" (348), as Socrates
says, and they become champions of the old ways from those of the new, for
in this way they bring Strepsiades to his senses.

Strepsiades courted Satan, and the Satanic Socrates responds by corrupting his household with mimetic rivalry. Strepsiades could repay his debts;
the failure to do so, he realizes (*Nub.* 1463–1464), is the cause of all that has
gone wrong. He calls to his "most beloved son" to aid him. The connotations
of love in his address, *philate,* are born of obligation,[34] but Pheidippides has
been corrupted so that his obligations turn now to his teachers: "No, I would
not do injustice to my teachers" (1467). Dover comments:

> Pheidippides . . . is shocked at the suggestion that he should violate the
> relationship between teacher and pupil. This is true to life; Pheidippides
> . . . is not abjuring the use of the terms δίκαιον [just] and ἄδικον [unjust]
> (cf. 1332, 1371) but changing their application. It is natural enough that a
> young man should feel himself bound more closely to his intellectual lib-
> erator than to his father.[35]

Satan indeed comes across as Girard's liberating don who captures the son from his family. Strepsiades next appeals to his son to feel awe for Zeus Patroös (1468). *Patröos,* "of one's father," is not a cult title for Zeus among Athenians, but Dover speculates: "πατρῷος could be interpreted as 'whose province is the relationship between fathers and children.'"[36] Pheidippides replies that Zeus does not exist; there is only Vortex who has driven out Zeus (1470–1471). He has gone over to Socrates and Anti-Right. Whereas I hesitated earlier about his death, it is assured that Strepsiades loses his son to his "intellectual liberator" forever.

Pheidippides, disgusted with his father's folly and prating about clay pots, exits to the Phrontisterion. Left alone, Strepsiades sees the light and with true belief accuses Socrates of his madness in rejecting the gods. He consults the nearby herm, avatar of the Hermes he once scorned, and takes the god's advice: Eschew legal fabrications. Burn down the house immediately (*Nub.* 1481–1484). He calls for his slaves, and together they dislodge and burn the roof and send it tumbling upon those within. Strepsiades treats the house as that of perpetrators of heinous crimes whose existence contaminates the city with pollution that must be cauterized by razing their abode.[37] Yet he is not a righteous servant of the gods but is himself infected with Satan's contagion of mimesis. When the students ask why he is burning the house and who he is, he replies that "he is discoursing subtleties with the beams of the house," and he is "the one whose cloak you all took" (1496, 1498). He quotes the second thing Socrates said to him (225) in answer to Socrates' question, "You there, what are you doing on the roof? I am walking on air and thinking about the sun" (1503). Strepsiades imitates the man who replaced him in his son's affection, which, in turn, drives him to imitate Satan: he becomes an *anthropoktonos* like Satan (*Jn.* 8.44), the murderer of his son.

Socrates' last words, "I shall be choked" (*Nub.* 1504), evince acceptance. He dies as Satan's instrument in ending the mimetic contagion of Strepsiades' household. But the power of Aristophanes' Socratic Satan to arouse accusations against the living Socrates did not end with an afternoon's entertainment in 423 BCE—at least, not as far as Plato was concerned. Plato alleges that the spectators left the theater persuaded in the truth of Aristophanes' Socrates, and that they spread the word, infecting the youth and replicating in them their own true belief in this empty portrait of Socrates. Across the years these accusers grew in numbers, until by 399 they had become a symphony. Socrates denies the truth of the Aristophanic Socrates: he knows nothing about natural science and does not teach or collect fees (19d). Nonetheless, Athenians consider him as a source of what is wrong. They are mired in crisis, which confronts its citizens with many scandals. Socrates, however, embodies the one that is shared and has been shared by many. "There is a mimetic competition of scandals" among Athenians, "which continues until the moment when the most polarizing scandal remains alone on the stage. This is when the whole community is mobilized against one scandal and the same individual."[38] This is what Meletus seeks, what the Platonic Socrates most fears (*Apol.* 18b), and what Plato knows happened.

CHAPTER 4

Foundation Murder

As regards Socrates, whom the community—unwilling to soil its hands by contact with an impious creature—asked to do away with himself, Plato's sympathy is every bit as suspect as Sophocles' sympathy for his pharmakos-hero.

—RENÉ GIRARD, *Violence and the Sacred*

L ike other Greeks, Athenians valorized themselves through the τιμή paid them by others. *Tîmê,* the value placed upon or respect given to someone, is usually translated as "honor." The more a man was valued because of his deeds in the fighting, the more he was honored by the community with gifts and prizes of war. Although times had changed appearances, Athenians of Socrates' day still lived by the values of the Homeric warrior's competitive culture.[1] Failure in any form for whatever reason brought a loss of face before others, for such men valued the opinion of others about themselves above all else. In Girardian terms, they let the model define what was to be esteemed, including their estimation of their own value (*tîmê*). Homer's Agamemnon cannot continue after he has lost his prize to Apollo's priest because others have their prizes. He must be given a new one at once and acts upon his acquisitive desire to threaten to take those of Ajax or Idomeneus.

Barry S. Strauss points out that the "the shame of failure . . . created a strong incentive to find someone else to blame."[2] Agamemnon could not blame the god Apollo, who took his prize, so he would blame Ajax or Achilles, to great loss. Athenians living in 403–399 BCE, the years between the Peloponnesian War and the death of Socrates, had much that they needed to blame somebody else for.

Athenians lost the war because of their own folly, greed, mistakes, and propensity for selfish and toadying leadership. They had been shamed by an opponent they should have withered into defeat. Far worse, they lost their empire. The influx of monies in the form of tribute ceased abruptly, as did the manifold forms of income for Athenians at home. Allies, for example, no longer came hat-in-hand to Athens for business and legal matters. Shopkeepers and innkeepers, speech writers, ship owners and sailors, prostitutes, and even the sausage sellers felt the change. Things were politically peaceful, at least on the surface. The amnesty all citizens swore to maintain kept people from prosecuting one another for actions other than criminal that happened during the civil war (404–403 BCE) (Xen. *HG* 2.4.38). But "political concord did not put an end to personal animosities."[3] N. G. L. Hammond goes on to speak of "hatred and fear of the oligarchy," "courts busy with cases," and "apprehension felt by the poor"; Strauss adds division by "class disputes," disputes over "personal power with little reference to principle," and "personal finance or gain."[4] What happened to them was not the responsibility of one man, not even of any individual leader, much less the *idiôtês* (private person) Socrates, who, nonetheless, complied when the democracy called upon him for military service. Yet most Athenians believed in the victimage process and accepted its fundamental misunderstanding that a single victim should be held responsible. Anytus, Meletus, and Lycus were able to convince the majority of Athenians in the jury on that one day in 399 BCE that not only was there such a man, but they knew who he was. A scenario is not difficult to imagine.

Lampadas, a wealthy aristocratic hippomaniac, has recently bought a new steed. Agathocles, his neighbor, has expressed no interest in horses but desires to live like Lampadas. So he wants a horse of his own, but none is available. He tries to buy Lampadas' horse, but Lampadas declines the offer. His refusal becomes a scandal, a stumbling block before the good life Agathocles imagines is Lampadas'. Meanwhile, Lampadas, at first puzzled, now becomes threatened by Agathocles' repeated offers to purchase the horse. This makes him want the horse more and stirs his animosity toward Agathocles. Soon they forget about the horse in their quarreling with one another. They are on the verge of their verbal violence becoming physical when they see Socrates walking by with those rich metics from the Piraeus. This Socrates guy, they say, claims to be poor and dresses in threadbare rags, but he associates with the rich. He must be rich. Hey, he must be hiding his money from the city—no supporting a trireme or a tragic chorus for him. No, he uses his money to buy up all the horses, which is causing us to fight over this horse. So Agathocles and Lampadas report Socrates as a delinquent to the city. They feel better, and whatever happens to Socrates he deserves: he's ugly—his τύχη.

Since before Aristophanes' *Clouds,* Socrates had been marked publicly by signs of victimage both in his person and his way of life. Athenians saw him associating with the very wealthy aristocrats, among whom were the enemies of the democracy, Alcibiades, Critias, and Charmides. Socrates made no secret of his criticisms of governmental institutions, especially the lottery, a fundamental principle of democracy. However little he resembled sophists, he sounded like them to the undiscriminating many,[5] and everyone knows that sophists were atheists who challenged their religion and traditions. Anytus and his fellows brought charges of impiety against Socrates for corrupting the youth of the *polis* with his talk and beliefs about the gods, the same charges brought against the Aristophanic Socrates. Socrates did not prepare a speech; according to Hermogenes, a youthful Socratic present at his death, he said that "he had spent his life living justly and avoiding injustice which he thought constituted a very fine preparation for defense" (Xen. *Mem.* 4.8.4). He adopted an arrogant and/or magnificent tone; both connotations belong to *megalêgoria,* "speaking big," that Xenophon found consistent throughout writers of apologies (*Sym.* 1). (*Megalêgoria* more often denotes arrogant and proud speech, but always with the connotation that "big speaking," if warranted, becomes magnificent speech. Jonas Salk's declaration in November 1953 that "I will be personally responsible for the vaccine" is such a moment.)[6] Anytus, carrying a majority of sixty votes, won a verdict of guilty that Socrates was, as his prosecutor Meletus asserts, the only Athenian who corrupts the youth (25a). Anytus proposed death, surely expecting Socrates to go into exile. Socrates, however, counters with a monetary fine. In voting over the penalty, more Athenians cast their ballot for death, rejecting the monetary fine guaranteed by Socrates' friends. Socrates refused to leave Athens for exile. A month later he was executed.

Plato and other of Socrates' friends left Athens for Megara, where Plato wrote his *Apology of Socrates.*[7] Anytus had exploited the victimary impulses among Athenians. His success confirms what the Athenians' behavior during the war had repeatedly illustrated: they could be seduced by the voice of just about any authority that manipulated their scandalized desires. Despite their democracy, or rather despite the praise of democracy that later folk of all sorts have lavished upon it, in its Athenian form, democracy without Periclean leadership was little better than mob rule—and that little was too often lost to emotions of crisis. Plato set out to defend himself by showing the dysfunctionality of the democracy. He creates of Socrates a *pharmakos* by attaching Apollo's *paradeigma* (23a: model) to Aristophanes' Satanized Socrates. The Socrates of Plato's *Apology* is not the defendant of 399: that Socrates has already been condemned and executed. The Socrates of the *Apology* is a twofold victim. On the one hand, he is the victim of his persecutors, who, acting as *hoi boulomenoi,*[8] defended the community in their own interest by playing to the crowd and mob of jurors to whom they appealed. On the other hand, Plato victimizes a Socrates by offering him as the innocent who undoes the mimetic mechanism of the single victim that destroyed the living Socrates and reveals its fundamental error: the victim cannot be responsible for the social crisis, and his persecutors are the ones who are guilty in acting so. Together, these Socrateses comprise the figure of the *pharmakos* and Plato's *Apology,* the condemnation of the demos.

Plato's Drama of Socrates' Death

Plato's *Apology of Socrates* belongs to Plato's enactment of Socrates' death played out over the *Euthyphro, Apology of Socrates, Crito,* and *Phaedo.* No one can say with exactitude when he wrote the other dialogues, but they come after the composition of the *Apology of Socrates* and frame it into a story that retraces Girard's mimetic mechanism to its end in heroization. The *Euthyphro* begins as act 1, the quest for the one who cares for Athenians. The *Apology of Socrates* comprises act 2, which I divide into five scenes—scene 1: "Awakening the Stones"; scene 2: "Slander, Denial, Mission"; scene 3:

"Resistance to Victimization"; scene 4: "Reaction to Rejection"; and scene 5: "The Good Death." The *Crito* provides act 3, "Scapegoat," while act 4, "The Philosopher's Death," consists of the *Phaedo*.

Act 1. Euthyphro: *The Quest Begins*

Two characters often identify and first debate in the prologue of a tragedy or comedy the play's central action. In Sophocles' *Antigone,* Antigone and Ismene confront Creon's exposure of their brother Polyneices' corpse, while in Aristophanes' play *Knights,* the slaves Demosthenes and Nicias ponder how to deal with Demos' dominance by the Paphlagonian. In the prologue of the *Euthyphro* (2a–3e), Socrates and Euthyphro first evaluate Meletus' indictment of Socrates for impiety. Socrates has just come from a discussion with Theaetetus about knowledge (*Tht.* 210d). He meets Euthyphro before the Porch of the King, which houses the offices of the archon, who inherited the religious duties of the Mycenaean king.[9] This magistrate will soon award Meletus a hearing of his charge before a jury of Athenians. Neither Euthyphro nor Socrates knows Meletus, but Socrates provides a description of the man: "he has long, lanky hair, a scraggly beard and a hooked nose" (*Euthphr.* 2b). Plato's readers surely knew what Socrates looked like. I let K. W. C. Guthrie put his description beside Socrates' description of Meletus.

> In appearance Socrates was universally admitted to be extraordinarily ugly, but it was the kind of ugliness which fascinates. His chief features were a broad, flat and turned-up nose, prominent staring eyes, thick fleshy lips and a paunch, or, as he phrases it himself in Xenophon's *Symposium* (2.18): "a stomach rather too large for convenience."[10]

"The physical description of a person," Debra Nails points out, is "rare" in the dialogues, which puts the reader on alert.[11] Meletus' appearance is that of a pretty boy; lovers of youths in refined pederastic circles would find him attractive.[12] Plato makes much of the contrast between Socrates' external ugliness and the inner beauty of his *psychê,* especially Alcibiades' encomium of Socrates in the *Symposium.* In the context of the indictment, however, Socrates' features not only underscore the aberration of the man from the norm that is a Meletus or a Euthyphro; by being different, they also substantiate for

Athenians, directed by their ideology of physical beauty as an expression of a man's nobility and excellence, the charges brought against him.[13] The Samians, for instance, on seeing Aesop, make fun of his appearance and wonder how "any good can come from this piece of rot" until he reminds them not to look at the cup but at the quality of the wine therein (*Life of Aesop* W 87 Perry). Paul Zanker traces the prototype for this "form of social discrimination and moral condemnation" to Homer's Thersites.[14] But the vignette of Thersites is more than a model; it retraces Girard's mimetic mechanism.

Agamemnon's proclamation that his assault on Troy has failed and his dismissal of the men plunges the army into sacrificial crisis. Discipline lost to the desire to go home, elite and masses charge the ships. Odysseus, upbraiding each man according to his status, has barely restored order when Thersites stands up in council. Bowlegged and lame in one foot below, his head pointed with a tuft of wiry hair, Thersites is the ugliest man who came to Troy (Hom. *Il.* 2.216). Yet he not only dares to upbraid Agamemnon for greed; he twice uses Achilles' very words.[15] Thersites' participation in the debate challenges more than Agamemnon's leadership. His ugliness undermines the privilege and the status of princes evinced by their physical beauty. By his quotations, Thersites asserts to be the same as Achilles. Hierarchy and degree are imperiled. The Argives, disappointed and thwarted, could easily succumb to a renewed blow dealt to the social order and military discipline. Violence, instead, re-erects order. Odysseus struck "Thersites with the scepter on his back and shoulders, and he doubled over in pain, and a fulsome tear fell from him" (2.265–266) and cast "this worthless reviler from assembly" (275). Thersites has obliterated the distinctions of physical beauty and social station that structure the army and induced a sacrificial crisis for which his appearance makes him the ready victim.[16] His expulsion restores order and hierarchy. Much of the historical Socrates has been lost to myth, a process that formed him, along with Thersites and Aesop, into a figure like the *pharmakos*.

The prologue introduces two questions that become programmatic for the Platonic Socrates: Who cares for the Athenians? Who has the knowledge to care properly? They are essentially one question, for no one without the proper knowledge can care properly.

Meletus thrusts himself before the magistrate and a jury as one possessed of the necessary knowledge. Socrates imagines him as a good gardener caring for the young plants by weeding out those who corrupt them (*Euthphr.* 2d–e). His image comes from the Athenians' belief in their autochthony, their birth from the earth (*chthon-*) itself (*aut-*).[17] Hence, Aeschylus speaks in *Eumenides* of their tutelary deity, Athena, as a gardener (911). Socrates is not being completely ironical since he accepts the premise of protecting the young from corruption. But his designation of Meletus as "young" sounds a tone of disbelief if not irony. "It is no mean thing for one so young to have come to the knowledge of such an important matter, for, as he says, he knows how the young are being corrupted and who are the ones corrupting them" (2c). Knowledge derives for Socrates from personal examination and reflection over time. Meletus' youth raises suspicions about him that wait for examination in act 2. Yet the quest has been laid down, and the search begun, for the caretaker with the knowledge of the sickness that affects Athenians and whose care will benefit them. The remaining action of act 1 demonstrates Socrates as such a person.

Euthyphro has arrived before King Archon to lodge a lawsuit against his father for murder. He prides himself—his "use to others" (*Euthphr.* 4e)—on knowing accurately "about matters of the gods" (5a). With a fundamentalist's certainty, he declares that the pollution of murder remains to contaminate those who come near it, whether the doer of the deed is a stranger or one's father. He seeks the court to pronounce the issue moot because of the passage of time—the incident happened five years before—or to assume the burden of the pollution. Euthyphro, Socrates claims now ironically, must possess marvelous knowledge of the gods and piety to prosecute his father for murder and asks to become his student. It is the familiar ploy of the elenchus that Socrates sets up the interlocutor as the model whose wisdom in a matter of a virtue he desires to learn. The question-and-answer session that follows soon identifies Euthyphro's knowledge as that of the ordinary Athenian, the body of ideas and beliefs forged by the poets and handed down by tradition. Unreflective reliance upon the declarations of the poets constitutes for Plato a primary cause of the crisis among Athenians. Socrates prompts Euthyphro to commit himself with statements in the attempt to define piety and then shows him how his statements contradict themselves, leaving him aware of his ignorance and on the threshold of his own inquiry. The process strips Euthyphro of his confidence and, hence, his understanding of his use to others, a necessary virtue for an Athenian.[18] Many in his position, forgetting the subject under discussion, become angry at Socrates as what begins with mimetic desire turns acquisitive and moves toward rivalry. "Straight Thinker" Euthyphro, however, merely wonders how their words go in circles around him and attributes the effect to Socrates without rancor (11b). Socrates has reduced him to perplexity, healing him of the doctrinaire certainty that caused his family so much upset (4de), so that now he declares of piety:

> I say this to you simply, that if someone knows what is pleasing to the gods both to say and to do, by praying and sacrificing, these things are holy and such things preserve private families and the commonwealths of cities. (14b)

Euthyphro has not been cured of his reliance on common beliefs. He still believes what his culture tells him is pleasing to the gods and how to enter into exchange with them. But he has lost the dangerous edge of certainty in his notions of the gods that threatened his household (4d) and sends Meletus scurrying to the city as if to his mother to punish the naughty. What knowledge Socrates has in healing or treating Euthyphro is mainly left implied. He does admit that he does not believe in what the poets say about the quarrels and wars of the gods and, therefore, rejects his city's religious beliefs. He also rejects its system of sacrifice whether understood as therapy, service, or commerce, and thus, by implication, positions himself outside his society's practices of victimage. Laszlo Versényi surmises Socrates' unexpressed belief that gods in their perfection cannot be influenced and cannot influence human beings.[19] For all of this, Meletus correctly indicts Socrates as the innovator of new (ideas about) gods and, since the youth inevitably listen to him, their corruptor. Socrates plays in act 1 the roles of Meletus' corruptor and Euthyphro's healer. Plato *pharmakeus* (sorcerer/pharmacist) dispenses through his human drug (*pharmakos*) the *pharmakon* of his discourse, the elenchus, that is both poison and cure.

Act 2. *Plato's* Apology of Socrates

It is generally agreed that Plato wrote his *Apology of Socrates*[20] and that it is intended to defend Socrates. After that, all is up for grabs, including crucially how he intended to defend Socrates. The date of its composition cannot be stated with certainty. At best, it may be placed within the first ten years after Socrates' death.[21] I have already committed to Mario Montuori's opinion that Plato wrote it shortly after the trial when he and other Socratics were in a place of safety with Euclides in Megara.[22] To contend as I do that Plato used his defense of Socrates not to replicate Socrates' own defense but for his own purpose of defending himself and the others and that he substantially modified Socrates by presenting the miasma, object of blame, as the object of praise, I must challenge the historical interpretation of the work. Setting Megara aside for the moment, therefore, we turn to the dominant reading of the work—namely, that Plato in *Apology of Socrates* more or less truthfully reports Socrates' speech in his defense. The view has many proponents committed to its ultimate motivation, the desire to know Socrates as opposed to knowing early Plato. Let us review the arguments for the historicity of Plato's *Apology*—that is, its truthfulness to Socrates' unattested speech—as presented by Thomas C. Brickhouse and Nicholas D. Smith.

Brickhouse and Smith accept the *Apology* as "essentially accurate in tone and substance (if not in every detail) to what Socrates said" and hence consider the work to be "essentially revealing about the thought of the historical Socrates."[23] They cite scholars who accept the historicity of the *Apology of Socrates*.[24] It is a long, impressive list, but far more believed that the Earth was the center of the universe. They point first to Plato's presence at the trial (34a, 38b), which they understand as a confirmation of Plato's firsthand knowledge and authority as a witness.[25] Plato also mentions himself in *Phaedo*: "Plato," Phaedo remarks, "was sick, I think" (59b). Scholars have interpreted these notices autobiographically, wondering in the case of 59b whether Plato was actually sick. John Burnet responds in the same vein: "[Plato] must have known whether he was ill or not."[26] True, but it does not follow that Phaedo was equally well informed, and he, not Plato, is the speaker of 59b. Plato is the narrator, and as narrator he is not restrained by historical fact. For the purpose of the story, Plato the narrator can have Phaedo say whatever he likes. Phaedo's "I think" and Plato's illness add detail to each figure qua character. The function and contribution of the characters may be analyzed in literary terms for literary effects but not historically because of the lack of corroborating or disconfirming evidence. The fact or nature of Plato's illness lies outside the text, does not bear on it beyond its inferable function to explain the character Plato's absence, and is of no further matter for it.

A similar but more critical misreading surrounds Plato's mention of his presence at Socrates' trial. His appearance has the same kind of literary and textual referentiality. Socrates has just invited those who think that he did them harm in their younger days to come forward to accuse him and seek their revenge (33d). "There can be no difficulty about this," he adds. "There are many of them here whom I see." Plato the narrator's mention of Plato the character's presence shows Plato as one of Socrates' students who does not accuse him and, later, as one of them who helps provide the thirty-minae fine. This Plato, like that of *Phaedo,* belongs to the text. We cannot go behind or through it to get to the real Plato, and then into the real Plato to his intentions. (Besides, it is arbitrary to use Plato's presence as the proof of accuracy without denying accuracy to the *Phaedo* because of his expressed absence.) Plato's use of himself as a character has no import on the accuracy of his text in a modern historical sense.

Brickhouse and Smith next point to the uniqueness of the *Apology* in that it is a series of three speeches with a dialogic interlude only in the first. The form of the apology itself dictates a speech, but the third, with its prophesying (39c), rather than supporting the historicity of Plato's *Apology of Socrates* by its irregularity, should presumably give a pause to the notion of the work as even a defense, much less a defense actually delivered. At any rate, I show below that the first speech is a polyphonic text, a dialogue of twenty voices, each competing to define Socrates. That is, the main speech of the *Apology of Socrates* is a dialogue spoken by one voice. Socrates plays the rhapsode to enact the polyphony in the way of another rhapsode's performance, that of Patrick Stewart's *A Christmas Carol.*[27] The second speech is the offering of a counterpenalty normal in form, not substance, while the third is mythmaking on the *kalos thanatos,* the beautiful death. What Socrates said is not known. Surely the uniqueness argument cuts both ways, eliminating itself as proof of historical accuracy.

Brickhouse and Smith's argument relies heavily upon the assumption that Plato wanted to be faithful to his Socratic originals, man and speeches. Plato, they contend, feared the knowledge of the trial possessed by his readers and blanched before their censures, should they apprehend him in not reporting accurately or nearly so. They admit an element of distortion that cannot be ascertained that derives from "Plato's apologetic intention."[28] Plato, in their opinion, however, did not follow Socratic literature, the *Sokratikoi logoi,* in portraying an idealized Socrates or philosophical life. They suggest such writing, usually thought to begin with, if not shortly before, Socrates' death, may not yet have existed. And even if it did exist, it has no bearing on the *Apology.* True.

The opposite of accurate for Brickhouse and Smith is fictional. They admit that "fiction creates a reality of its own, and that reality—if not in itself incoherent—must be understood and evaluated in its own right."[29] The issue with fiction is not whether the events depicted actually happened or happened as said. We have arrived at the rub. The issue comes down to "the degree that Plato's audience expected historical accuracy."[30] Scholars working in the accuracy mode see Socrates as the speaker and Plato as his more than less faithful amanuensis. It is on the assumption that the audience, for what Plato wrote about Socrates, wanted a high degree—rather, demanded a high degree—of accuracy because of their "great deal of knowledge about the context of Socrates' trial," on which Brickhouse and Smith rest their case for Plato's accuracy.[31] They want to know, and they are not alone, what happened with Socrates and the trial, and to whatever extent the *Apology of Socrates* is fiction; that goal, so desired, escapes their grasp. There is no way to ascertain Plato's faithfulness, and however faithful he is to his idea of Socrates' speech, Xenophon's *Apology of Socrates* is faithful to Xenophon's idea and is a different speech. We can no longer simply prefer Plato's for, pace the usual interpretation, the presence of Plato qua character does not grant the narrator Plato authority.[32]

Evaluation of Plato's *Apology of Socrates* through the opposition of accuracy/fiction does not reflect the assumptions of readers in early-fourth-century Athens. Greeks remained disinterested long after the time of these events in the details of a life; they neither documented births and deaths nor conceived of the concept as such.[33] They would expect a speaker at a trial or writer of a speech delivered at a trial to publish the most persuasive case possible with a judicious, but hardly historically accurate, use of the facts. They expected Cicero's dust, and that surely was part of the fun.[34] At the time, they valued a man's life for its typicality. But Plato's *Apology of Socrates* can, while fictionalized, remain accurate to Plato's vision of the trial and Socrates. That is, Plato did not intend to resurrect the failed speech that culminated in the conviction of the most just man he knew for impiety. That was the past. Socrates' memory would be better served by presenting him in another way and, more to the point, it would serve Plato in Megara, who had his own troubles from his association with Socrates to contend with. To give up the accuracy model for the *Apology,* I realize, is to forsake the *locus classicus* for the "real" Socrates and his thought, a sacrifice scholars and many others are not likely to offer. But the accuracy versus fiction opposition is anachronistic and wrong. The *Apology of Socrates* is not fiction for not reproducing Socrates' failed speech. It is accurate for presenting Plato's defense of Socrates through his, not Socrates', words and opinions. From this perspective, instead of examining the *Apology* as if it were a fossil of a lost speech, we explore the living conception of Plato's vision of Socrates. And it is this vision, not Socrates' or Xenophon's of Socrates, that conjures the Socrates we all want to know.

Soon after the Athenian demos executed Socrates, Plato and "some other Socratics" quit Athens for haven in Megara. They left out of fear of "the savagery of the tyrants." Athens at the time was under the rule of the demos, so these "tyrants" were surely, as Montuori suggests, the leading politicians of the democracy.[35] Engaged in the personal and vengeful politics of the times, they wielded whatever authority they mustered from their charisma with the demos and common interests with friends for their benefit and the profit of their faction, and in competition against others like them. Strauss has traced at least six competing factions in the years 403–395.[36] When Anytus, son of Euonymon, indicted Socrates, he must have thought he had found a ready symbol of the all that the demos hated. He could strike a blow covertly at the oligarchs protected by the amnesty and gain favor with the demos by dispatching from the city that garrulous and contentious busybody of the streets and gymnasia. Socrates made no bones of his dislike of the democratic constitution and his disgust for its leaders.[37] Aelian, writing in the third century CE, sums up Socrates' vulnerability as a target: "Socrates was not pleased with the constitution of the Athenians, for he saw the democracy as tyrannical and monarchial" (*VH* 3.17). Besides, Socrates was well known to associate with the hated Critias, monster among the Thirty Tyrants, and the turncoat Alcibiades, whose son during these years attracted prosecutions for the animosity still smoldering toward his dead father. Anytus secured Socrates' conviction, but even before then his plan had been unraveling and continued to fray. Socrates not only presented himself to the King Archon for arraignment, but he also came to the trial and defended himself. Then, instead of taking advantage of the month's delay before execution, he sat content in a prison whose confinement could easily have been breached by his friends. These friends, many of them present at his trial and death, are surely some of the Socratics who fled to Megara. Socrates' death besmirched the restored democracy's claims to being a merciful and constitutional form of governance that had forgotten all but criminal infractions of the past years. The prosecution played on the resentment of many toward Socrates. Yet, had no charges been brought, Socrates likely would have played out his life in his usual way, and Athens would not have been affected. In any case, there seems to have been no immediate impact, and the stories of the demos' regret and stoning of Anytus should be evaluated as stories, not happenings.[38] But at the time, the anger and frustration of the leaders toward Socrates was real and could easily have spilled over to these friends of his, the young men of aristocratic and wealthy families who had the money and connections to spirit him away at any time during the proceedings. They at least knew that that was the gentlemanly and expected way of doing things. Montuori points out that "Plato gives us clear evidence of the reasons why the democrats were so hostile to the disciples of Socrates at the time of his death and as a consequence of that death" in the *Crito*. Crito is speaking:

> I am ashamed of myself over you and what has happened to you. The whole thing appears to have been handled with utmost cowardice on our part: the appearance in court for the trial when it was possible not to go there, the contest itself and how it came out, and, as if the pièce de résistance of this folly, people think that we let it all get away from us because of some flaw or cowardice on our part in that we did not save you or you save yourself which could have been done if there had been a shred of good in us. (45e–46a)[39]

Socrates drew blame for defending himself in a nonstandard way. His youthful followers "were blamed because 'the case came before the courts when it might have been avoided' and above all because they had not helped Socrates to escape."[40] As Crito explains, "I seem to many who do not know you and me well that, although capable of saving you if I wanted to spend the money, I cared not at all" (*Cri.* 44c). Montuori summarizes:

It is precisely these reasons for the hostility of the democrats toward the memory of Socrates and towards his disciples, the former for not knowing how to defend himself, and the latter for not having saved him from death, that induced Plato to take a resolute stand and begin his literary career.[41]

The Socratics massed in Euclides' house were bound by a mutual fear and fragmented by a personal (view of) Socrates:

> It is not likely however that there was agreement between Socrates' follow-ers, since the defence [sic] of the Master and therefore their own, implied a particular way of interpreting his teaching and example. It is quite likely that there was vigorous and substantial disagreement over the meaning of Socrates' discourse between Plato the aristocrat and Aeschines the plebe-ian; between Antisthenes the cynic and the refined Aristippus; between the Pythagoreans of Thebes and Euclid of Megara. We are entitled to imagine this in view of the jealousy and dislike which, so it is said, they felt for each other.[42]

But Socrates had exposed them all to the same contagion that claimed his life. Socrates aside now, they could be prosecuted for having been corrupted by his teaching and for polluting the welfare and prosperity of all Athenians. The Athenians among the group surely wanted to return to Athens. While a common defense flew in the face of each one's separate vision of Socrates, their way home came by defending themselves, and that entailed defending Socrates. Lysias had already composed an apology, which Socrates lived to repudiate.[43] Xenophon's *Apology of Socrates* was in the future; at this time, he was campaigning with the Spartan general Thibron in Caria. Other con-temporary apologies, which Xenophon says were written (*Sym.* 1), are lost, overshadowed perhaps by Plato's. That house in Megara must have been a hotbed of recriminations and acquisitive desire—"Each one of them claimed to be the heir of the Master"[44]—to seize Socrates and possess the object through writing the defense of Socrates. Amid that rivalry, then, Plato wrote his *Apology of Socrates.* And so it began, and as it turned out, Socrates' death proved to be the founding murder of Plato's philosophy and its project, the development of a form of government (*politeia*) for the just city.

Plato begins his *Apology of Socrates* with Socrates addressing his jurors, whom he insults by referring to them as "Athenian men" and not the customary and respectful "Athenian judges":

> How you were affected, Athenian men, by my prosecutors I don't know. As it is, I myself nearly forgot myself because of them, so persuasively were they speaking. And yet, they have said just about nothing true. I especially marveled at one of the many things they lied about, this part in which they kept saying that you should be on your guard against me since I was clever at speaking. That they are not ashamed that immediately they will be refuted by me in practice, since I do not appear in any way clever at speaking, this seemed to me to be the most shameful thing of theirs. (17ab)

Stewart plays the rhapsode to enact with voice and gesture Charles Dickens' *A Christmas Carol.* He invokes the characters of Scrooge, Marley, the Christmas ghosts, and the others. Dickens gave each character its own name, personality, and part in the story, and Stewart imparts to each its own voice or, at least, distinguishing intonation. Neither Dickens nor Stewart appears in the story. Plato begins his *Apology of Socrates* with Socrates alluding to the jurors who will speak later and voicing two characters: the prosecutors who tell lies and Socrates, who nearly forgets Socrates. We could, therefore, if we wished, posit a fourth part, the Socrates who, like the one listening to a funeral oration (Pl. *Menex.* 235ac), comes into being when Socrates forgets himself. The *Apology,* at least the formal defense of 17a–35d, is not a speech by a single voice but a performance by a single voice of twenty parts. In other words, it is a polyphonic drama in which twenty voices debate and discuss the question raised by the one voice of the character Socrates in his opening remarks. Socrates says, "I almost forgot myself," which Burnet glosses with, "I all but forgot who I was."[45] Socrates returns to himself to distinguish himself from the role of clever speaker cast for him by his prosecutors to assert himself as no clever speaker. The question becomes "Who is Socrates?" Plato begins the related *Gorgias,* part of the heroization stage of the victimage process, with the question "Who is Gorgias?" which sets off an apology of Socrates in a different form. The *Apology of Socrates* is unique not for being a speech but for being a dialogue in dramatic form enacted by one voice. Like other dialogues, it probes for knowledge and understanding of, namely, who is Socrates. One voice is that of a Socrates, but it is only one of twenty in search of Socrates: present accusers, Socrates, past accusers, a comic poet who can include Callias, Ameipsias, Eupolis, and Telecleides as all satirized Socrates in the comic theater, Aristophanes, Callias son of Hipponicus, someone who rejoins, Chaerephon, the god in Delphi, those Athenians crying out in censure of the god's assessment of Socrates, those Athenians crying out in approval of the god's assessment of Socrates, Chaerephon's brother, those Athenians examined by Socrates, those Athenians examined by the youth imitating Socrates, Meletus, those Athenians crying out in support of Meletus, those Athenians crying out in support of Socrates, the jurors who voted for Socrates and the jurors who voted against Socrates, and, at last, Socrates the prophet.

SCENE I. AWAKENING THE STONES: PLATO'S *APOLOGY OF SOCRATES* (17D–19A). The venue is one of the courts of the demos, most likely that of the Heliaia which housed the hearing of indictments for impiety.[46] The Heliaia was located in the agora, perhaps in its southwestern section, and was capable of seating 500 jurors. They now sit as the representatives of the demos charged with administrating its supervision of religious matters. King Archon, so named from his inheritance of the religious province of the ancient kings, presided as judge. He approved that the charges against Socrates merited a trial, but he did not expound upon the law or advise the jury. The jurors themselves expressed directly their approval or disapproval of the claims of the parties. Since the demos never instituted an office of public prosecutor, prosecution depended upon volunteers among the citizenry who stood to profit if successful or suffer a fine for losing with less than 20 percent of the jurors. Socrates' present prosecutors spoke first and so are the first to say who he is. Lycon was a coeval and probably at least known to him. He is a politician and, in the separation of responsibilities (23e), speaks concerning Socrates' injustices toward the orators. Socrates ignores him. He knew Anytus, wealthy son of a self-made man, before the trial (Pl. *Men.* 89c–90b).[47] Anytus, the force behind the prosecution, accordingly speaks for the politicians whom Socrates and his youthful friends so offended. Socrates mentions him four times (23e, 29c, 30c, 31a), but he dwells upon Meletus. Meletus' father was a tragic poet, and so his speaking on behalf of the poets lent the always desirable motive of revenge to his indictment of Socrates (Pl. *Euthphr.* 2b, 12e).[48] All that is known of Meletus is that he is young (26e). A subtext, however, lies latent, for which we must skip ahead in Plato's development of Socrates. In the *Euthyphro,* as we have seen, Plato puts before his reader what Meletus looks like, so that the reader can contrast him in the theater of his mind with Socrates during their elenchus over who cares for Athenians.[49] Meletus owes his prominence in *Apology* not to his father's craft or his role in the troika of prosecutors, but to his appearance and name. He is good-looking, someone who would attract the interest of a lover of youths, as opposed to the ugliness of Socrates,[50] while his name is formed, or can be so understood, on the root *mel-,* which designates "care" and makes of Meletus, presumptively, "He Who Cares."

Socrates' truth about himself starts with a battery of rhetorical topoi common to Attic orators. Lysias, for example, denied being clever at speaking; Isaeus pleaded for pardon for his manner of speaking; and Aeschines cautioned jurors against making an uproar.[51] Socrates proves himself familiar with forensic diction, but he incorporates the language of the court to say things unfamiliar to the court. He claims to tell the truth (17b). Apparently, he does not understand that speaking at the court is aimed at persuading the jurors. When he says, "I am simply a stranger to the manner of speech here" (17d), he refers not to a facility with words but to an utterly different conception of the juror's *aretê*—namely, attendance to whether he speaks justly or not (18a). Although not a foreigner, Socrates is a foreigner to his city's judicial system. From the outset, Plato locates Socrates in liminality characteristic of the *pharmakos,* placing him in limbo between citizen and foreigner.

Plato further develops Socrates' liminality by opposing him to past accusers. These are the many Athenians who have long been accusing Socrates informally of not believing in the gods. Their voices are anonymous and elusive; they say nothing true, they cannot be brought to account in the court or to a cross-examination, and they firmly believe what they know to be true. They say that Socrates "is some kind of wise guy, a thinker of things above and investigator of all things below the earth, and maker of the stronger argument from the weaker" (17b). Such a person, everyone knows, describes the atheist who does not worship the gods of the fatherland or accept their role in the lives of men and undermines the foundations of morality and trust with his speech. Socrates denies the truth in this "talk" that he likens to slops poured over Athenians in their sleep.[52] He traces it back to the Socrates of a comic poet who, at this point, can be any of several but proves to be the Aristophanic Socrates. Accepting him as their model of the atheist while ignoring the mirth of the theater, these Athenians engage in rivalry with Socrates through their envy and misrepresent him through their slander (18d). They pour the dregs of their mimesis over the young and impressionable:

> These accusers are many who have accused me for a long time now and, moreover, they said this stuff to you at an age when you would most readily and deeply believe them, some of you being boys and teenagers, simply accusing me by default in the absence of a defender. (18c)

Nothing opposes the falsehoods of the past accusers. They are like a plague of mimesis that turns out mimeos of Socratic accusers who deeply believe in the justice of their condemnation of him. The young are "incapable of resisting the violent contagion that affects them all when a mimetic snowballing comes within their range, or rather when they come within range of this snowballing, and are swept along by it."[53] Girard here speaks of the crowd that welcomes Jesus into Jerusalem and "suddenly turns against him, and its hostility becomes so contagious that it spreads to the most diverse individuals."[54] Even Peter, the rock of the church, succumbs. Athenians, of course, did not always have Socrates on their minds. They endured the struggles and competitions and rivalries that pit them against one another and, in their zero-sum system, create far more frustrated and envious losers. Throughout, however, remained the common target made available from the differences in appearance, manner, and speech: Socrates. Athens in 399 BCE was a powder keg of mimetic desires and thwarted acquisitive desires that we can only surmise from its recent past: a lost war, failure of its democracy, an experiment in oligarchy gone horribly wrong, and a restored democracy tentatively struggling to retrieve the golden days of the early Peloponnesian War. Among the jurors who sat before Socrates were many of his past accusers, men convinced that he was a demon of impiety and betrayer of the fatherland and personally somehow—exactly how matters not—the cause of their own suffering. The trial was to be the detonator and Socrates the victim of the powder. His present accusers "were relying upon" (19b) the fact that his jurors' ears had long been filled with vigorous and persuasive accusation of Socrates.

Some four centuries later, Flavius Philostratus recorded in his biography of Apollonius of Tyana (d. ca. 98 CE) the miracle that the Neopythagorean wise man had performed in Ephesus (*VA* 4.10). Girard waxes with particular brilliance in his discussion of this miracle as an example of "mimetic escalation" that closely resembles the escalation story of Jesus and the stoning of the adulterous woman (*Jn.* 8.3–11).[55] The same independence of the sources that makes Philostratus' story relevant to that of John renders it relevant to Plato's story of Socrates' past accusers in how the continuum of the mimetic mechanism claims its victims in the same way in unrelated incidents.

The people of Ephesus, beleaguered by a sickness (*nosos*) summon Apollonius to be the physician of their disease (*pathos*). Before Apollonius arrived at the city, he must have realized that the plague belonged not to the realm of unmanageable biological agents but "internal tensions that could be discharged on what we now call a *scapegoat*."[56] On arriving at Ephesus, Apollonius announced, "Today, I will put a stop to the sickness," and gathered all the people to the theater. I follow Girard in quoting T. C. Conybeare's translation in the Loeb Classical Library:[57]

> And there [in the theater] he saw what seemed an old mendicant artfully blinking his eyes as if blind, and he carried a wallet and a crust of bread in it; and he was clad in rags and was very squalid of countenance. Apollonius therefore ranged the Ephesians around him and said: "Pick up as many stones as you can and hurl them at this enemy of the gods." Now the Ephesians wondered what he meant, and were shocked at the idea of murdering a stranger so manifestly miserable; for he was begging and praying them to take mercy upon him. Nevertheless Apollonius insisted and egged on the Ephesians to launch themselves on him and not let him go. And as soon as some of them began to take shots and hit him with their stones, the beggar who had seemed to blink and be blind, gave them all a sudden glance and showed that his eyes were full of fire. Then the Ephesians recognised that he was a demon, and they stoned him so thoroughly that their stones were heaped into a great cairn around him.

Girard observes that Apollonius "has to take great pains and work insidiously like the very devil that he is" to conceal the mimetic nature of his remedy. An old man, by all appearances a beggar like Odysseus, was before them. Apollonius must rouse his audience (they *are* in a theater) so that, without betraying his tactic, he can get one among them to throw the first stone. According to Girard, this person is critical to initiating a stoning. Jesus famously defuses such mimetic contagion coming against the woman taken in adultery by requiring the first stoner to be without sin: "Let him who is without sin be the first to throw a stone at her" (*Jn.* 8.7). Hearing this, the crowd fails to mobilize and disperses. But Apollonius urges his audience: "Pick up as many stones as you can and hurl them at this enemy of the gods." The Ephesians, failing to react to his demonization of the old man, demur at murdering one so wretched. Apollonius presses them, for he needs that first stone. "Why is it the most difficult to throw?" Girard asks before answering, "Because it is the only one without a model."[58] Then the Ephesians, accepting their leader's declaration that the old man is truly a demon, mobilize into a mob with a unified and righteous violence that purges their malaise far better than any tragedy.[59] Meletus must get one Athenian to throw the first stone. His task calls for more words than Apollonius' but is the same one—namely, turning a crowd into a mob driven by contagious imitation. The groundwork is there thanks to the past accusers. All that is needed is the spark. As for ignition, Meletus' task is easier than Apollonius'. The trial ends in the casting of its own kind of stones, bronze ballots that are solid for acquittal or hollowed for condemnation. It is difficult to imagine that Meletus ever worried about getting the minimum voters to avoid a fine.

SCENE 2. SLANDER, DENIAL, AND MISSION: PLATO'S *APOLOGY OF SOCRATES* (19B–24B). The victimary process moves into its second act when the community, beset with plague or other ruin undermining its stability, consults the god. The god responds with an oracle whose usually riddling language must be interpreted. In Plato's *Apology*, the crisis consists of the assault upon traditional morality and beliefs in the role of the gods in the universe launched by teachers of rhetoric and investigators into the physical universe. Their activities imperil the community's sense of its place in the world and its citizens' place in the community, both shaken already by the failure in Sicily, the loss of the war, the treachery of Alcibiades, loss of the democracy to Critias and the other oligarchs, and the struggle for its restoration. The moment is ripe in the victimary process for Athenians to approach the god for a remedy for their cultural malaise. Instead, Socrates' prosecutors take it upon themselves as *hoi boulomenoi,* men willing to stand up for the *polis'* interests, to declare the source of pollution and to initiate a court proceeding to find a remedy. Yet, the oracle belongs to the mythmaking of the *pharmakos,* and the mythmaking dictates its presence. It comes not as a public but as a personal inquiry to Delphi by Chaerephon, a friend from Socrates' youth. "At some time or other, Chaerephon went to Delphi and dared to consult the oracle over this—now as I said, do not make a uproar, men—for he asked whether any one was wiser than I" (21a). As often remarked, everything about Socrates that ensues in Plato's project begins with this oracle. "It is impossible to doubt the facts," H. W. Parke and D. E. W. Wormell declare, "difficult though they are to explain. In the *Apology* Socrates makes his whole manner of life hinge on this oracle."[60] They go on to state the cardinal issue with the existence of the oracle:

> Unless one is to regard this account in the *Apology* as either a piece of fiction written by Plato, or a piece of humbug perpetrated by Socrates himself, the oracle must have been given as described and must have had a determining effect on Socrates' life.[61]

Socrates' assurance to the men of the jury, "I shall tell you the whole truth" (Pl. *Apol.* 20d), appears to leave no room, short of deeming Plato a liar, to doubt its veracity. Brickhouse and Smith rightly judge that "it is most unlikely that he [Socrates] would resort to mere irony on a matter of such substance to his defense."[62] Socrates tells the truth forthrightly (his truth is not humbug) *but* as a character in Plato's *Apology.* He speaks with a character's voice, and what he says holds true to influence the life of that character in Plato's *Apology.* Socrates does not speak with the narrator Plato's voice. This distinction opens the possibility that the oracle has been fabricated by the author.[63] Yes, it is invented by Plato, a bitter pill to swallow and a contention in the judgment of many worthy of transport to Van Dieman's land, but it is not as falsehood opposed to truth in the way of the modern opposition of fictional/historical.

"'The story' I will tell you—whatever I say—is 'not mine,'[64] but I will refer to a speaker trustworthy to you" (20e). It is through the eighth voice, that of Chaerephon, that the oracle and its answer to the question of who is Socrates enters Socrates' defense in Plato's *Apology.* Plato, speaking through Socrates who speaks for Chaerephon, frames the reception of the oracle in terms of the personality of Socrates' lifelong companion.[65] Debra Nails describes him as "evidently a tall and very thin man of pallid complexion, perhaps resembling a corpse (half-dead at *Clouds* 502, jaundiced and hovering silently at *Wasps* 1413, arising from the underworld at *Birds* 1562)."[66] Clearly a favored target of ridicule for the comic poet, he was "impetuous," Socrates says, "for whatever he got worked up about" (21a). Socrates invites the men of the jury to recall the man as if they may judge the likelihood of the story and calls forth the deceased Chaerephon's brother, the twelfth voice who would have in an actual trial immediately borne witness that the story is Chaerephon's, not Socrates' (21a).

Most striking about the story is its element of daring. "Chaerephon went to Delphi and dared to inquire" (21a). What is daring about Chaerephon's inquiry? Greeks of modest means and station asked personal questions; their inquiries were the bread and butter of the oracle.[67] But Chaerephon risks the god's long-standing ire over hubris and rejection by the oracle of the inquirer who preens himself upon being magnificent. Gyges, ruler of Lydia, expected to be called the happiest man, only to receive the response: Aglaos of Psophis, "the poorest of the Arcadians [who was] already advanced in years and had never left the boundaries of his little plot, content with the rewards of his tiny farm."[68] Anacharis, famous for wisdom, expected the oracle to confirm his reputation; he was told: "Myson of Oeta, born in Chen, is fit with a more prudent mind than you."[69] The pattern of these stories, which also underlies Herodotus' story of Croesus and Solon (1.29–33), is the oracle's preference for the humble over the ostentatious and prideful. Chaerephon is saved from the god's rebuke by asking a negative question about someone else. Chaerephon asks, "Is anyone wiser?" which awaits a "no," and he receives, "No one is wiser." Socrates protects himself by shifting, as Melanippe in Euripides' play of that name, what he says to another. Socrates lacks, however, the wisdom Chaerephon implies by his question. He knows he knows nothing and, in the immediate aftermath of learning of the oracle, (21b-d) does the god's job for him in admonishing himself by pointing out that he has no wisdom worthy of the name, except that of knowing he knows nothing worthy of the name.

Plato sets Chaerephon's story in the wider frame of the moralizing oracle that chastises the lofty for their pride. This type of oracle was well known in the sixth century and, from Herodotus' story of Croesus and Solon, in the fifth.[70] Plato wrote Chaerephon's story for readers who would know the kind of oracle he elicited and the god's usual reaction. They would receive Plato's oracle, not as fiction and fable, but as new expression of something that they had heard before and recognized. In terms that are over a century old, Plato is saying something new about Socrates. He is not acting like a modern liar but like an ancient compelled neither by the drive to get "it" right nor to say "it" as no one has said it before. The oracle still remains the beginning of Socrates' life, but that life now belongs to Plato.

How god and his oracle defend Socrates begins in scene 1. Both recognize Socrates as someone apart from other men for his *sophia*. Questions follow. What may we readers conclude about the god? What does Socrates conclude about the oracle? How do both god and oracle defend Socrates?

Burnet observes of Chaerephon's question, "It is certain that this would not impress the Athenian public favourably, and it may fairly be urged that Plato would not have repeated it if Socrates had not said it."[71] His second thought fails to support the oracle's historicity since Plato refers to Chaerephon qua character, but the first pertains since we have a context. We know Athenian attitudes toward those who stand out from the flock in any way. A. W. Gomme states that "it is always dangerous to generalize about a people, but no body of men has ever been so *conscious* of envy and its workings as the Greeks."[72] The innate envy of the Greeks and Athenians derives from their "social system where a man's own situation is appraised and experienced as satisfying or dissatisfying by comparing it with another's."[73] Socrates foresees the envious reaction to what he is about to say. Just before giving the words of the oracle, Socrates demands of his audience:

> Do not make a uproar at me, Athenian men, not even if I seem to say something big to you. (20e)

> As I kept saying, do not make an uproar, men. (21a)

Athenian juries express themselves vocally without fear of reprimand. *Thorybos*, "uproar," denotes a noisy demonstration and interruption that can be either applause or scorn. Socrates requests that Athenians listen quietly, should he speak in his usual way that many have heard in the agora (17c). In fact, they cry out, not at his language, but what he says when he asserts his special relationship with the god Apollo (20e, 21a). To his words that "no one is wiser," some break forth in celebration, but far more surely shout in censure. Pericles addressed the same sorts of Athenians in his funeral oration over the dead of the first year of the Peloponnesian war:

> The knowledgeable and receptive listener would perhaps consider less what was being revealed in comparison with what he wants to hear or knows to be true, while the inexperienced out of envy would consider that some things were being exaggerated, if he hears something beyond his natural abilities. Praises spoken of other men are endurable up to the point that each man thinks that he unaided is capable of doing something of what he has heard.[74]

The same kind of Athenians are sitting on the benches of Socrates' courtroom. Socrates, we are to imagine with Plato, distinguished himself among all others for his *sophia,* and the god has recognized that with his favor. In John Huston's film version of Rudyard Kipling's *The Man Who Would Be King,* Danny Dravot, a sergeant in the British army, passes himself as a god in Kafiristan.[75] He is surrounded by thousands of men dressed in white shirts who accept his divinity as a descendant of Alexander. But when he is bitten and seen to bleed, they realize that he is no different, mortal like them, and their white shirts blend them visibly into a vengeful, murderous mob. Such feelings attend the Athenian reaction to Socrates' claim with no less, as it turns out, seething resentment.

Socrates accepts the truth of the god's statement but, uncertain of its meaning, sets out to investigate it (21b). He seeks someone wiser with whom he can confront the oracle and its response. Greeks generally distinguished between the infallible god and the unreliability of his servants, so Socrates does not act impiously. Neither does he act as simplistically as he purports. He goes around to the various groups of men in the city who are reputed for their wisdom, politicians, poets, craftsmen, and asks them a question. It usually prompts a definition of a moral quality like courage or piety. He follows with a series of questions whose truth is obvious and cannot be denied without seeming foolish. After a while, he gathers together the implications of the interlocutor's positive responses and shows that his original statement is contradictory and must be rejected. He leaves the interlocutor in perplexity; he is willing to resume the questioning but almost never to rescue his victim with knowledge. This process, repeated over the years, created the elenchus, ostensibly an examination but in practice a refutation.[76] Plato has devised for him questions that aim from the outset at refuting his respondent's position. Socrates always contends his own ignorance. After so many exchanges, he would seem to have learned something; yet he professes ignorance—many think insincerely and so ironically. Irony, however, averts violence from Socrates by reducing him to the same perplexity as his interlocutors and lifting discussion above the conflict inherent in the contest.[77] For the victims of his painful incising, however, he more often arouses distaste, ill will, and anger, all of which leads to the creation of scandals. Socrates builds the impression of knowing the answer to the topic under discussion through his skill in demolishing the respondent's position. His respondent, stripped of his long-held beliefs, desires that knowledge which he is certain Socrates possesses. Socrates denies his desire and stands in the way of obtaining it. Thwarted acquisitive desire breeds frustration and stumbling blocks. Many such experiences generate many scandals, each with Socrates at its epicenter and each fueling an explosion. Scandals "secrete increasing quantities of envy, jealousy, resentment, hatred—all the poisons most harmful not only for the initial antagonists but also for those who become fascinated by their rivalistic desires."[78] Without access to his wisdom, his rivals fabricate a substitute by appealing to the usual slanders "of all who pursue wisdom," the same ones that were brought against the Aristophanic Socrates (23d). From conflict that began with a discussion of one of the virtues, for example, scandalized men move to accusing Socrates of being an atheist and corrupting the youth. In time, their many scandals snowball into one, and the mass turns on him.

The same charges brought against the Aristophanic Socrates adhere to the Platonic. The difference between them lies in the motive that has aroused them. The Aristophanic Socrates teaches for profit (*Nub.* 1146). The Platonic has so devoted himself to his investigation that he has been kept from serving the city and the interests of his household and has been plunged into poverty (23b). His investigation, then, accounts for his marginality, an investigation that began with the god and becomes the subject of his service to the god (23b).

Through examining others who think they are wise but are not, Socrates has arrived at his interpretation of the oracle. By "No man is wiser," the god

intends for Socrates to be a *paradeigma,* the model for human knowledge—
that it is worthy of nothing (23a). Whenever he comes upon someone who
thinks he knows something and does not, he "comes to the god's aid" (23b) by
showing that person that he knows nothing. The god's purpose for Socrates
lies in waking "men out of their dogmatic slumbers into genuine intellectual
curiosity."[79] A man cannot begin to pursue true knowledge until he has been
disabused of the false. Socrates goes around, therefore, questioning men "in
accordance with the god" (22a) and in his service (23b). Since he considers
"the god's business to be of the utmost importance" (21e), he perseveres like
Heracles. Whereas Heracles served a mortal, Socrates undergoes his "wandering" and Heraclean "toils" in demonstrating the irrefutability of his oracle
for a god (22a). It is a painful process that has aroused hatred and enmity
against him that must be endured just as Heracles suffered for both his deeds
of good and evil. Euripides (ca. 417 BCE) probed the essence of Heracles'
suffering through the hero's confrontation with the weapons that killed his
children and wife:

> *Oh, the bitter companionship of these weapons.*
> *I am lost whether to keep them or throw them away.*
> *They keep falling against my chest, saying: "With us you killed*
> *your children and wife. In us you have*
> *the killers of your children." Shall I carry them*
> *at my elbows? What can I say? But stripped of them,*
> *in whose company I accomplished the most glorious deeds in Greece,*
> *shall I throw myself down before my enemies and die in disgrace?*
> *They must not be abandoned. With misery (athliôs), they must be preserved.*
> (*HF* 1377–1385)

The adverb *athliôs* conjures the twelve *athla,* or contests, whose completion
conferred immortality upon Heracles. The weapons do more than symbolize; they embody the cost of those deeds, their magnificence and their monstrosity. Socrates reprises the sufferings of Heracles. He carries a burden, the
oracle as he interprets it, that drives him to wander in poverty among men
in service to the god. His Heraclean *ponoi* (toils) are examinations that offer
Athenians the opportunity to pursue true knowledge. He is repaid with the
misery of being hated and slandered.

Socrates owns to the pleasures of watching men squirm under cross-examination (23c). The young men of the very wealthy with time on their hands enjoy the spectacle and frequently imitate him. For these youth, he provides a model of amusement, but their elders, stymied by their questions, become angry at him and accuse him of being "most polluted" for corrupting their youth (23c). It is the same charge brought against the Aristophanic Socrates, but the Platonic Socrates' corruption comes as part and parcel with his service to the god. The oracle defends Socrates in Plato's *Apology* by identifying the convicted and executed miasma as a new Heracles in service to the god whose *ponoi* bring about a new understanding of human wisdom and fulfill the god's command, *gnôthi seauton,* "know thyself." In time, Socrates' service develops into the quest for a new kind of Athenian. For now, he is god's servant who is rejected by his people because of their ignorance over what he brings.

SCENE 3. RESISTING VICTIMIZATION (24B–35D). What Girard says of Guillaume de Machaut's *Judgment of the King of Navarre* in its treatment of the Jews pertains to the drama of Plato's *Apology* before us:

> The text we are reading has its roots in a real persecution described from the perspective of the persecutors. The perspective is inevitably deceptive since the persecutors are convinced that their violence is justified; they consider themselves judges, and therefore they must have guilty victims, yet their perspective is to some degree reliable, for the certainty of being right encourages them to hide nothing of their massacres.[80]

Neither can the historicity of Meletus' prosecution nor his conviction in his judgment of Socrates' actions be denied. We do not have Meletus' speech. By extrapolating from Socrates' cross-examination of Meletus, however, we may conclude that it highlighted Girard's three signs of persecution from *The Scapegoat*.[81] The crimes with which Meletus accuses Socrates destroy the hierarchies of family and city. The victim "belongs to a class that is particularly susceptible to persecution."[82] Socrates' class consists of poor, ugly, and deformed men whom the city uses as *pharmakoi*. They care for Athenians in that they offer themselves as victims to relieve the pollution accrued over the year. In Plato's drama, Socrates stands as *pharmakos* before the throng of Athenians. The scene conjures the Thargelia, which, in turn, implies that Socrates should just pack it in and go beyond the borders. Instead, he asks Meletus a question.

"Who makes the youth better?" (24d). Meletus is nonplussed, freezing before Socrates' question. He shows by his silence, Socrates points out, that he has never cared about or given thought to the youth. Meletus cannot know who corrupts them without first knowing who improves them. Prodded, Meletus blurts out "the laws," thus failing to answer the question. Not what, Socrates replies, but who? Looking out at the jurors, Meletus manages them, and then the council members and assembly members. So far Meletus reflects how education and moral and proper behavior are inculcated in the youth. Members of the community reinforce the beliefs and customs that acculturate the youth by dispensing praise and shame. But then Meletus moves from prosecutor to persecutor when, with certainty he has already shown is baseless, he replies, "Yes, I say this most vehemently," to Socrates' question, "I alone corrupt the youth. Are you saying this?" (25a). Without hesitation, Meletus seeks to divide the community into all against one. The rally of the persecutor could not be more naively stated.

Meletus is bound by the certitude of Socrates' guilt. He accepts the common view of Socrates as an atheistic natural scientist and readily confuses him with Anaxagoras (26d). He comes before the jury armed with prejudices and convictions that "they" are all alike. He need not listen to what this one has to say; nothing he says will wipe away his guilt. He indicts Socrates for not worshipping the city's gods but strange new ones instead (24b). Socrates appeals for clarification on how he corrupts the youth:

> I am not able to understand whether you are saying that I teach the youth that gods exist (so I am not totally atheistic and am not guilty in this way), just not the gods whom the city believes in, and this is what you charge me with, or are you saying that I do not believe in gods at all, and I teach this to others?
>
> I say this, that you do not believe in gods at all. (26c)

Meletus has opened himself to contradiction from which his indictment cannot recover. He fails to appreciate Socrates' shift in the meaning of *nomizein theous* from "to worship gods" to "to believe gods exist" with the addition of the infinitive "to be," *nomizein einai theous.* Socrates' first question begins the wedge between Meletus and logical credibility: "Is there any man who believes that there are human things but does not believe there are humans?" (27b). The jurors cry out (27b), more surely in support of Meletus now caught in Socrates' sophistry than for Socrates and his arguments. Socrates reduces Meletus' indictment to joking and making riddles about serious things by an arrogant, unrestrained, and foolish youth (27a). To do so, he ignores the serious charge of impiety. But, we must remember, that the charge of impiety has already killed Socrates. Plato goes after the implications of Meletus' indictment, for it is not foolish and arrogant but cleverly designed to elicit strength from the mimetic contagion surrounding Socrates. As Socrates says, *pollê apechtheia,* "much hatred" among many directed at him, and the slander and envy of many will destroy him, not Meletus (28a). These forces are the work of the Aristophanic Satan, the Socrates who prefigures in many ways the Platonic. The Satanic Socrates is the Socrates that men resent and hate because of their conviction that atheists destroy the morality and belief in gods that bind the family and polis. The constitution of the *polis* rests upon the efficacy of rituals and sacrifice. Those who reject the gods lack commitment to the city and to its laws and customs that support its hierarchies and enable its communal life. Meletus does not come after Socrates with logic but with the firm belief that many share that he threatens the Athenian way of life. The crisis makes the persecutor, and the persecutor looks for the first stone. He indicts Socrates on a charge of impiety and asks a penalty of death. The mimetic contagion on which he relies will do the rest for him.

Plato begins his second defense of Socrates, object of hatred, with a programmatic quotation: "Are you not ashamed, Socrates, of pursuing such a pursuit from which you run the risk of dying?" (28b). The activities of Socrates the busybody (31c) are well known. What Plato needs in defending him is to redefine their meaning. Socrates wandered about Athens, he has said, toiling like Heracles, an ambivalent figure, benefactor and perpetrator.[83] Many, the majority of Athenians, did not appreciate Socrates' efforts, and judging him impious at his trial, condemned him to death. More of them rejected his counterpenalty. Those encounters with Athenians made Socrates a *pharmakos* qua poison. The *pharmakos* is the human equivalent to the *pharmakon,* the inanimate drug that belonged for Greeks to a realm of uncertainty that they conjoined to the mysterious and sacred and that modern science partitions into primary and secondary effects. Aspirin, one of the most widely used and abused drugs, may relieve pain and ache, but it also causes tinnitus, nausea, and intestinal irritation. The latter are not "secondary" effects but effects that are not desired. Events rendered Socrates qua *pharmakos* the cause of undesired effects in the body politic. Plato must show Socrates qua *pharmakos* as the cure for the body politic. To do this, he brings out from the importuning of the busybody the ministrations of the servant of the god to the *psychai* of Athenians. His Socrates is an Apollonian soldier who maintains his post of philosophizing and questioning himself and others in the face of the specter of death (28e). He is the gift of god who is like a gadfly arousing the sluggish horse of a city from its sleep (30e). The gadfly bothers, but its sting awakens the horse; the gift reprises the first gift, that of Zeus' Pandora to Epimetheus, a gift of evil, a gift of good (Hes. *WD* 83–89). Both are doubled images, neither all *kalon* or *kakon*. The earlier Socrates (19a–23b) probed the meaning of the oracle. This Socrates is the instrument of the god whose message of care for the soul brings to those who listen a better life. Now Socrates traverses the streets and gymnasia of Athens encouraging Athenians to take care of their *psychai* (29d, 30a):

> Are you not ashamed that you care that your wealth be as great as possible and your reputation and prestige and you do not care or concern yourself that wisdom, and truth, and how your *psyche* be as best as possible? (29d)

> I go around doing nothing else than persuading both the younger and older of you not to take care of your bodies and wealth before nor as enthusiastically as your *psychê*—that it be as best as possible. (31a)

Should he come upon someone who disagrees and says that he cares, Socrates declares, "I will not let him go immediately, but I will question, cross-examine, and refute him" (29e).

Athenians probably understood by *psychê* something between the Homeric shade that goes to the underworld at death and a person's character or center of thought and deliberation. They likely would not agree with

Socrates' view that it is the "true self," apart from the body, and that "life can only be lived well if the *psyche* is in command of (ἄρχει) the body," and that *psychê* "meant purely and simply the intelligence, which in a properly ordered life is in complete control of the senses and emotions."[84] On the other hand, they would have thought him daft to think they would give up the pursuit of wealth, reputation, and prestige. These were the prizes of their way of life, the contest system absorbed from Homer and encountered at every juncture in their lives. Wealth validated one's prominence and worth and provided the means to attain greater wealth and higher prestige. Reputation and prestige were sweet to have and sweeter because they came at another's expense in the contest system all played as a zero-sum game.[85] The lust for victory and crushing one's enemies weaken the hold of prohibitions on the competitors who feared shame more than moral condemnation.[86] Athenians lived the life of mimetic rivalry, where his inferior was to be dishonored and his superior envied. The object was easily lost in the heat of their rivalry and lust for domination. That they should turn from the competition to look within for wisdom was tantamount to becoming different persons. This, of course, is what Socrates calls upon them to do: to forsake the contest for a life that is true to one's wisdom and to truth. What Socrates brings with his mission is a message of a life that is better by being nonmimetic in its truth to the individual's sense of self and in its wisdom. These he gains through his own pondering and discussing with others. The result is not a public person in the sense of standing before the people in the assembly. Unwillingness to pander to the desires of the people makes for a short life. But it does not make a man so private that he refuses all service to the community. It makes an individual who is in touch with his *psychê*, which is in control of him wherever he is. Plato illustrates such a man with Socrates at the trial of the generals and the summoning of Leon.

Sometime during the oppression of the Thirty Tyrants (404–403 BCE), Socrates found himself on the west side of the agora in the Tholos. The Tholos was a rotunda where the presidents of the council met that the Thirty had taken over for its headquarters. They had summoned Socrates and four others to escort Leon, a honest man who had injured no one (Xen. *HG* 2.3.39), from his home in Salamis to Athens, where he was to be executed (32cd). "When we came out from the Tholus, the four went to Salamis and escorted Leon, and I went on home" (32d). The Thirty wanted to make as many imitators of themselves as possible to spread the responsibility for their outrages. At great danger, Socrates had no difficulty resisting this kind of mimetic behavior.

In late Pyanepsion (October) of 406 BCE, Socrates was near the Tholos in the Bouleuterion. At that time, he was one of the fifty-man panel of presidents of the council conducting the debate over the generals of the Arginusae Islands near Lesbos. Six of the ten returned to Athens after giving Athenians a stunning victory over a superior Peloponnesian fleet. On their arrival, they were charged with not picking up the dead and with abandoning to the sea the nearly one thousand men who were shipwrecked.[87] The generals appealed to the intervention of a terrible storm that prevented the rescue. Many spoke to the issue, and the generals seemed to be prevailing when debate was suspended after it had become too dark for hands to be seen for a vote. Deliberations were subsequently postponed for three days so that Athenians could celebrate the Apaturia. The Apaturia was a festival whose roots lay in the tribes of Ionians of old.[88] Families from across Attica gathered to conduct their business and to feast and catch up with the year's developments. During the Apaturia of 406, minds and hearts turned to one catastrophic blow, the loss of so many of their relatives to the generals' negligence. Some appeared among them wearing the black of mourning and having their heads closely cut in grief. Anger was ignited, and resentment instilled across Attica, for kinship spread widely and deeply among Athenians.

Socrates was again in the Bouleuterion when the council resumed the issue of the generals. Callixeinus, a member of the council, began by saying that they had all heard the charges and the defendants' rebuttal earlier. He moved that "all Athenians vote by tribes" (Xen. *HG* 1.7.9). His proposal, patently illegal, contravened the recognized prohibition on joint trials as well as established judicial procedures. Euryptolemus' challenge to its legality, however, met with the cry from the throng: "A terrible thing it is if someone will not allow the people to do whatever it wishes" (1.7.12). A motion to judge Euryptolemus and others of his ilk by the same vote as the generals moved the crowd to cry out their approval in an uproar (1.7.13). "The uniformity of reactions" gathered all Athenians into a mimetic snowballing.[89] Athenians condensed six generals into one, redirecting toward a single target the violence they felt toward the objects of the many personal scandals affecting them at this late stage of the war. "These reactions stem from the prevailing power of the social body, or in other words mimetic contagion."[90] George Grote (1859), whose narrative of these events still holds, explains Callixeinus' motive:

> The unparalleled burst of mournful and vindictive feeling at the festival of the Apaturia, extending by contagion from the relatives of the deceased to many other citizens—and the probability thus created that the coming assembly would sanction the most violent measures against the generals—probably emboldened Kallixenus to propose, and prompted the senate to adopt, this deplorable resolution.[91]

Subsequent events amount in Grote's description to tracing the process of mimetic contagion. The resentment of the relatives infects others, who, in turn, imitate their feelings toward the generals. A wave builds, and Callixeinus throws the first stone with his motion. The presidents refuse to put his proposal to the vote. Threatened with inclusion in the charges with the generals, they relent, and the process takes over. Athenians converge upon the generals, six now reduced to a single victim, better to focus their vengeance, and vote for condemnation. Execution by hemlock follows swiftly. Grote allows the reader to feel the resentment. He finds in the generals' behavior reasons for their condemnation: they should not have delegated the rescue; the storm was not so serious that it prevented another commander from moving his fleet out of the area; the honor of seamen, if aroused by committed leadership, would have undertaken a rescue attempt. He does not exonerate the Athenians for disregarding their constitution and habits of lawful behavior, but he allows:

> Both the one [constitution] and the other [habits] strenuously forbade the deed; nor could the Athenians ever have so dishonored themselves, if they had not, under a momentary ferocious excitement, risen in insurrection not less against the forms of their own democracy, than against the most sacred restraints of their habitual constitutional morality[92]

Mimetic contagion, once focused, moved instantly to effect the mimetic mechanism. Athenians strike almost unanimously against the generals as scapegoat for their grief. Only Socrates remained outside of the violence, both that violence that swept Athenians toward the hemlock and that in the crescendo of Grote's narrative:

> The single obstinate prytanis, whose refusal no menace could subdue, was a man whose name we read with peculiar interest, and in whom an impregnable adherence to law and duty was only one among other titles to reverence. It was the philosopher Sokratês; on this trying occasion, once throughout a life of seventy years, discharging a political office, among the fifty senators taken by lot from the tribe Antiochis. Sokratês could not be induced to withdraw his protest, so that the question was ultimately put by the remaining prytanes without his concurrence. It should be observed that his resistance did not imply any opinion as to the guilt or innocence of the generals, but applied simply to the illegal and unconstitutional proposition now submitted for determining their fate, a proposition, which he must already have opposed once before, in his capacity of member of the senate.[93]

Socrates is outside the issue of the generals, but he is not obstinate. He is obedient to his oath as a president and the laws of the city. But his obedience draws from a deeper well of commitment than law-abiding. Socrates remains at his station as Apollo's soldier. His care of his *psychê* combats mimetic rivalry at its source, the desire to be like others. It has rendered him alike to his own self and so free of the mimetic behavior of other Athenians. As a result, he resists the anger and desires that overwhelmed them and let loose victimization. He would have not acted otherwise had there been no laws. That conviction leads me to believe that the Platonic Socrates imitates no one, and as an imitator of no one, Plato's Socrates can only be mythic—this at a time when the man seems his most historical.

"Get behind me, Satan, for you do not think the things of God but of man" (*Mk.* 8.33). Thus Jesus reproves Peter for refusing him his lot as Messiah of suffering, death, and resurrection. Peter, held by the tradition of the Messiah as king and savior, is not prepared for Jesus' transformation, and he becomes a stumbling block to the new order.[94] The moment is yet to happen in this form, but in another it occupies the substance of the conclusion Plato gave to Socrates' defense (34b–35d).

"I am not born from a oak or a rock," Socrates reminds Athenians, "I have relatives and three sons, one a teenager and the others little boys, but nevertheless, I shall not bring any of them up here and beg and plead with you to acquit me" (34d). He has recalled those defendants on even lesser charges who "beg and plea with the judges amid many tears and bring their children up here so as to be most pitiable" (34c). Socrates speaks out against such behavior with self-assurance, even willfulness (37a: *apauthadizomenos*) that is comparable to Jesus' uncompromising rebuke of Peter. Each rejects the model before him absolutely and without doubt for the same reason, to maintain their purpose for which each has come. That purpose and their identities would be lost otherwise to mimetic rivalry. Both bring a new model for men to imitate—one that, lacking the power to ignite mimetic desire, is free of violence. Jesus invites others "to imitate . . . his own *desire*, the spirit that directs him toward the goal on which his intention is fixed: to resemble God the Father as much as possible."[95] Socrates, the warrior of Apollo, calls for men to know themselves, to take care of their souls, that they be as best as possible. There can be no model or rival in this inward journey, and hence no impetus to mimetic rivalry.

Intertextuality of this sort, nonchronological between authors who have no contact, leads me not merely to accept Girard's hypothesis; it convinces me that I am not applying a method to texts but using text to reveal things fundamental.

Socrates has ended his defense. The pebbles have been given, the tally taken, and the verdict rendered (36c). He now faces the jurors; he is condemned of impiety and corrupting the youth of the Athenians, and they are charged with judging the acceptability of his counterpenalty (*antitimêsis*).

SCENE 4. REACTION TO REJECTION OF HIS MISSION (35E–38B). Socrates harbors no anger over the verdict of condemnation. Chortling over having escaped Meletus, however, he admits to surprise at the narrowness of the vote. Uplifted, it seems, by a near acquittal (36a), he turns to the next stage in the proceedings. The procedure under which Socrates was being tried did not prescribe a penalty for conviction. The court chose between options offered by the parties.[96] Meletus proposed a *timesis* of death that expected a counterpenalty of exile. Brought to this juncture by the jury's decision, Socrates asks himself: "ἐγὼ δὲ δὴ τίνος ὑμῖν ἀντιτιμήσομαι, ὦ ἄνδρες Ἀθηναῖοι" (36b) (Well. But what shall I, on my part, O Athenians, award myself?).[97] The question stops him, and he slips into a reverie comparable to his absence in thought at Potidaea (Pl. *Sym.* 220cd) and on the way to Antiphon's party (*Sym.* 174d–175b) to contemplate his question before the jurors:

> Is it not clear that I shall propose something worthy of me? What am I worthy of suffering or paying because I was not at rest during my life? (36b)

This Socrates, we recall, is the second voice in the polyphony of Plato's *Apology of Socrates* that endeavors to define Socrates. It is the voice of the man himself who truly believes that he benefits Athenians. Therefore, it should be of no surprise that this voice ignores the topical meaning of "penalty" for the root meaning of *tim-*, "worth, respect." [98] This is to say, Plato shifts the meaning of *antitimēsomai* from the derived, "I shall propose a penalty to counter another," to "I shall estimate my worth as a reward for my deeds." Thomas G. West explains:

> The Greek word for "propose as (one's) desert" is *timasthai,* whose root meaning is simply "estimate or value at a certain publicly recognized price," or "honor or reward [someone with something]" (cf. *timê,* "honor" or "price"). By extension the word came to be used in court to mean "assess the punishment due." But Socrates insists upon using the word in its original, nonjudicial sense, whereby it may refer to the worth or value of a man, good or bad. When Socrates says, "What shall I propose [as my punishment]?" he is also saying, "What [good or bad thing] do I deserve?" or "How shall I honor myself?"[99]

Again we see that there is little or nothing about Socrates that is not doubled.

The jurors wait for him to propose "exile"; then they can collect their jury pay of two obols and leave. What most are thinking may be gleaned from what Socrates says next, beginning with: "I did not remain at leisure throughout my life" (36b). Few jurors and the Athenians they represent would agree with him. He shuns by choice the activities pursued by citizens: "money-making, household managements, generalships, leadership of the assembly and other public offices, clubs, and factions" (36c). He considers himself "too good" (36c) for the life of an Athenian. He claims to be of no "use" in those pursuits. Athenians would agree that he is "useless" in their opinion—namely, because he has withdrawn from public life and makes no contribution to the "center," the community clustered around the agora. Some of the jurors perhaps heard Pericles in 431, but everyone would hold to his particular censure of the useless man:

> There resides in the same men the care of private business and public affairs, while the rest, directed toward their own activities, can understand public business adequately. We alone consider one who takes no part in such matters, not as abstaining from public life, but as being of no use whatsoever. (Thuc. 2.40.2)

Socrates busies himself by accosting Athenians individually about caring for themselves and the city. He says he's "busy" (31c: *polypragmonô*); they say he's "meddling" in their business, another meaning of *polypragmonô*. He calls his encounters *diatribai* ("conversations") but more likely most jurors considered them "wastes of time," also a meaning of *diatribai* (37c). To him, they are a "great benefaction" (36c). To the Athenian in the street who surely did not invite a demonstration of his ignorance, or think that he needed to be prompted to tend to himself, thought them "too overbearing and too hateful" (37d), "overbearing" for having him bear down on them with questions that never seem answerable and "hateful" for subjecting them to his superiority. He denies it, but he does lord over them the way he does the wretched defendants trying to save their lives (37a). How can they share his conviction that he does no harm willingly (37a)? In fact, they believe what is said of him in what he calls "great slanders" (37b: *megalas diabolas*). Neither are they convinced that he could not remain quiet; surely he is speaking with his usual ironic insincerity when he says that to do so would be to disobey the god (37e–38a).

So Clay rightly remarks that "the majority of the jury . . . took his irony as insincere and, indeed, as an offensive assertion of superiority."[100] For his part, however, as Socrates accepts himself as Apollo's *paradeigma* he speaks of his superiority, not ironically but truthfully. He is too good for the normal intercourse of the *polis*, he actually cares for Athenians as the gift of the god, and his benefactions to them has left him a poor man (36d). Socrates earlier offered his "ten-thousand fold poverty" as proof of his "service to the god" (23b). He sees his actions as a benefaction and asks "what befits a poor benefactor who needs to have leisure time to exhort you?":

> Is there anything more fitting, Athenian men, than such a man be fed at
> the Prytaneum, much more than if someone of you has won the horse race
> at Olympia, or the two- or four-horse chariot race. That man makes you
> seem to be *eudaimones,* while I make you *eudaimones.* He does not need
> the support, while I do. If I am bound to propose my worth according to
> what is just, I propose this, sustenance in the Prytaneum. (36de)

The miasma deems himself worthy of dining beside the victorious athlete!
This he proposes as a proper penalty to counter the death asked by his prosecutor? To be treated as a benefactor of the *polis*? Well, Xenophon said he
spoke big (*Apol.* 1). West expresses the outrage of many jurors and readers.
"In order to appreciate the impious arrogance of this claim, it must be understood that the prytaneum was the ancient common hearth of the city, the
vital symbol of its sacred center. . . . Socrates treats the sanctified hearth of the
city as a kind of free eating place for the deserving poor."[101] But that is exactly
what the Prytaneum is, for the *pharmakoi* were surely fed there.[102] Socrates
deems himself worthy of dining as the city's guest at its hearth with both
benefactors, the lofty and the lowly. What does this proposal add to Plato's
characterization of Socrates as a *pharmakos* figure?

We must first note that in pondering his question, Socrates does not
doubt his value and worth to Athenians. He may be talking to the jurors, but
he has withdrawn into his mind. The cost of his efforts, his poverty, dominate
his thoughts. From poverty and reduced circumstances his mind flips to the
fat cat aristocrat who eats gratis at the Prytaneum because he can afford horses.
An underlying sameness and an evident difference immediately surface.

During the last hours of the games, the Olympic victor received his
crown of wild olive before the temple of Zeus. Wreathes were laid out on a
tripod covered with bronze and later with silver and gold. The herald cried
out the victor's name, his city, and his father's name. Before Zeus, who wears
the crown of victory over his father and predecessor, Cronus, the Hellano-
dikes placed the wreath upon the head of the god's mortal surrogate, endow-
ing him with the god's favor in the form of *kudos,* mana of victory.[103] Socrates'
probing of the meaning of Apollo's oracles through toils worthy of Heracles
have conferred upon him a mission. Through the god's intervention, he has
come to consider himself Apollo's gift to Athenians and *paradeigma* for
human wisdom. These boons, conferred upon him by the god, empower

him in a way comparable to the god's *kudos*. As for the difference, Socrates is outside the Prytaneum, and the victor is inside.

To understand the basis for the proposal, we must bring the victor outside the Prytaneum. We see that the victor endowed with *kudos* when *outside* the Prytaneum comes under suspicion of seizing a tyranny; he escapes that pollution and becomes a hero only with his installation *inside* the Prytaneum. By requesting *sitêsis,* Socrates asks the *polis* to welcome him into its family at the communal hearth so that the Prytaneum may fulfill its functions of purifying the miasma for him as well as for the victor and utilizing the favor (*kudos*) conferred by Apollo for the benefit of the city by bringing him, an individual who stands out from the others, back into the citizenry with them. It is the proposal of Socrates' dreamlike state, one that is impossible for Plato's Socrates.

In her study of the social functions of the victory ode, Leslie Kurke regards "epinikian *kudos*"—that is, *kudos* gained by victory (*nikê*) in the Panhellenic Games at Olympia, Delphi, Corinth, and Nemea—"as the civic adaptation of its Homeric precursor":

> The athlete, like the Homeric hero, is endowed by the gods with *kudos* that ensures his victory. This talismanic force lingers with the victor, haloing him with dangerous power. The civic community replaces the Homeric sovereign as the beneficiary of the victor's *kudos,* which, when shared with the city, contributes to its supremacy.[104]

Long mistranslated as "glory," Emile Benveniste restored the power of *kudos* to "a magic power that is irresistible."[105] Conferred by the gods at their will, *kudos* renders success secure for its recipient. "It acts like a *talisman* of supremacy. . . . or the bestowal of *kûdos* by the god procures an instantaneous and irresistible advantage, rather like a magic power."[106] Mortals recognize its advent by the abrupt intrusion of the divine into their world. Eumelus' chariot, leading Diomedes' team in the race at the funeral games for Patroclus, suddenly crashes, and Antilochus perceives the intervention of Athena, who "has roused speed in Diomedes' horses and put *kudos* in him" (Hom. *Il.* 23.406) and leaves off pursuing Diomedes. The ground sizzles from the strike of lightning, and Nestor cries out to Diomedes, "Zeus, son of Cronus, bestows *kudos* on Hector today" (*Il.* 8.141) and urges that they give up the chase.

The advent of the god's *kudos* elevates Diomedes and Hector above the others. Yet there is a danger to heroic *kudos,* which Homer lets be seen: Antilochus gives up the quest for victory in the funeral games, and Nestor in the battle before Troy. The heroes accept defeat, erasing their identity as heroes. Granted that these are small incidents, but they indicate the threat: *kudos* has the effect of wiping away the differences that constitute the human condition—that is, *kudos* inspires sacrificial crises—for obliterating hierarchies is the essence of such a crisis. The god's *kudos* marginalizes the victor. As long as he remains in the god's sanctuary, this power is contained like radioactive waste in a storage facility. When he leaves for home, he takes with him a force that, by its origin from the god, imperils the structures of the human condition. For when gods come into the world, Demeter to Eleusis or Dionysus to Thebes, the world of humans is forever changed. Herodotus tells how Cylon, victor in a foot race in the Olympic Games of perhaps 640 BCE, "preened himself on seizing a tyranny" on the presumption that his victory would draw followers from the populace (Hdt. 5.71). Gathering friends and with the support of his father-in-law, tyrant of Megara, Cylon seized the acropolis at Athens, where his attempt at a coup fell apart.[107] The victor's fellow citizens not only envy his success but, ever suspicious of aristocrats like Cylon, they await, on tenterhooks, to see whether he will incorporate his *kudos* for the benefaction of the city or exploit it for a tyranny, the nadir of political bestiality. This dynamic plays out in the opening lines of Pindar's *Olympian Ode* 5:

> *Accept with laughing heart, daughter of Oceanus,*
> *the sweet pinnacle of lofty accomplishments and crowns at Olympia*
> *and the gifts of Psaumis and his chariot with feet untiring.*
> *He exalted your city, Camarina, provider of the people,*
> *and honored her twice six altars at the greatest feasts of the gods*
> *with sacrifices and five days of competitions*
> *in horses and mules and the single-running steed.*
> *He won and dedicated to you luxurious* kudos *and extolled by the herald's cry*
> *his father, Akron, and his newly-founded city.* (1–8)

Psaumis' victory in the mule race at Olympia came at great expense for him and his household. But it also infused both with the *kudos* of Zeus. Unlike the Homeric warrior, however, the aristocratic athlete lives in a *polis* where he at best shares ruling power with citizens of less wealth and prestige but no less envy and rivalry. With his song of welcome, Pindar soothes their fears and diffuses tensions and endeavors to reintegrate the victor into the community. Psaumis' victory redounds to the glory of his city, and the whole community shares in and benefits from it.[108] Psaumis dedicates his crown of ivy and adorns his city with feasts on the meat of sacrifices, showering Camarinians with Zeus' *kudos* from Olympia.

The dynamics of the equestrian contests limited competition to the very wealthy among the citizenry, the aristocrats. These were men locked in competition with themselves within the city and usually allied with their kind in other cities. Their loyalty traditionally was directed more toward their families and class than the community, and there remained the chance that any one of them, given the opportunity, might seek absolute rule for himself—that is, a tyranny. Victory in the Olympic Games had been associated with tyranny in Athenian political life since the mid-seventh century with Cylon. In the next century, the Athenian tyrant, Pisistratus, so valued success in the four-horse chariot race that he restored a bitter enemy to Attica because the latter had the herald announce his victory in the name of Pisistratus.[109] A man became a tyrant by overthrowing existing governmental structures and establishing himself as an autocrat. Tyrants were a phase in the history of Greek cities, particularly those moving toward democratic rule. They were often accepted for the stability they imposed, but the tyrant was a loner. He drew nothing from the center of the city, and he gave nothing in return.[110] He was outside the hierarchy that defined the human condition, a liminal figure simultaneously above and below ordinary man, as Jean-Pierre Vernant explains:

> The wayward, solitary path along which the tyrant, rejecting the beaten track and the posted route, ventures, exiles him far from the city of men, with its regulated forms of exchange and reciprocal contacts, relegating him to an isolation comparable both to that of a god, who is too far above men to come down to their level, and to that of a wild beast, so dominated by its appetites that it can brook no restraint. The tyrant despises the rules that control the ordering of the social fabric and, through its regularly woven mesh, determine the position of each individual in relation to all the rest, in other words—to put it more crudely, as Plato does—he is

perfectly prepared to kill his father, sleep with his mother, and devour the flesh of his own children.[111]

Kurke points out that "athletic victory and tyranny form a natural contrast because the former is the product of *megaloprepeia* ["the lavish public expenditure of wealth by those who can afford it" (167)], the latter its frequently suspected goal."[112] The victor, it is feared, will use his wealth to influence citizens and his talisman to seize power over them. In *Pythian Ode* 11, Pindar addresses this fear directly in the first person he uses for general truths:[113]

> May I love honors from the gods but be eager for what I can gain in my own strength. I find in the affairs of the city that the middle flourishes with greater happiness. I blame the life of tyrannies. I strain myself after achievements common to others. (50–54)

The poet declares that this family of aristocrats has no ambitions for rule in the city despite its past victories at Olympian and Delphi in the equestrian games (46–50). They reject designs on a tyranny and prefer to live a life that abjures the competition for achievements beyond the ordinary.[114]

The god's *kudos* has marginalized the Olympic victor. Outside the Prytaneum, he is in effect *miaros,* "tainted," with excessive ambition in the envious eyes of others. Athenians install him, as they did their newborns in the festival Amphidromia at the family hearth, as a family member of the city at the city's hearth in the Prytaneum.[115] The Athenians do not invite him to the Prytaneum primarily to reward him. They invite him to civilize him, to forestall his using his *kudos* for himself and to appropriate it for their own benefit.

Socrates eschews the path taken by Athenians in favor of that pointed out by Apollo. He is a liminal figure: too good to participate in the city's affairs (36c) at its center in the agora and useless, were he to try (31d), and both the god's gift and a "gadfly" (30e), a lowly insect. His poverty, like the victor's wealth, removes him from the others. He cares for Athenians in ways that they reject, which has rendered him *miarôtatos,* "most polluted" (23d). What does this portrait suggest? A self-willed outsider wielding power over others without regard, as they see him, for their welfare. Although strange at first to imagine, Plato sets up Socrates as a tyrant—that is, the single man with the power of the god, like Pisistratus with Athena, to instruct and show the Athenians what is good for them.[116] It is the autocracy of Socrates' mission, that he alone knows the way to the good, that casts him in the mold, not the sandals, of a tyrant. Socrates inflicts his care upon Athenians no less than the tyrant his. Athenians may benefit, but neither Socrates nor tyrant dispenses that care altruistically. Each offers it for his own gain. Their goals differ of course, Socrates' Apollo's service, the tyrant's his own profit. Although an immense difference, it is also a superficial difference, one that obfuscates the underlying continuum: the individual who seeks power over the group. To yield to Socrates, as to yield to the tyrant, destroys life as lived by the Athenians. Thus Aristophanes warns against "sitting with Socrates and prating" (*Ra.* 1491–1492).

Socrates sees in his dream his Socrates installed in the Prytaneum as the benefactor and gift of Apollo. His poverty improves Athenians by its cause, caring for their souls, more than the victor's wealth. Thus Socrates' poverty is the complement of the hero's feasts and games. These are short-lasting goods that seem to make Athenians *eudaimones,* but it is the happiness of a full stomach and a moment's entertainment. Socrates' gift of *eudaimonia* creates a *daimon,* a spirit in a man, that is good (*eu-*) and directs him toward knowledge of self and an inner prosperity that stays with him for a lifetime.

This is Socrates the character, the second voice, who defines himself as a benefactor. *Sitêsis* for this Socrates does not express arrogance; rather, it appeals to the Prytaneum to carry out its role in civilizing and politicizing the *kudos* of the god granted the individual. On the other hand, Plato's Socrates, the figure created by the polyphony of his *Apology of Socrates,* cannot dine in the Prytaneum. Why? The Olympic victor is a diachronic figure. He is first miasma outside the Prytaneum and then hero inside it, separate roles distinguished by time, space, and appearances. He is one and then the other, and both roles appear different. Socrates is synchronic: whether outside or inside the Prytaneum, he comprises both identities simultaneously, for the cure that he brings Athenians, care for their *psychai,* is the poison that destroys the value of those activities (36b). Socrates would confound his dinner mates in the Prytaneum no less than those who listened to him outside the Prytaneum. In the Homeric eschatology of the average Athenian, the *psychê* does not exist until his bones have been dried out by the funeral fires.[117] How could they respond but with confusion, discomfiture, and anger to the self-proclaimed gift of Apollo, who encourages them to care for their *psychai*? *Sitêsis* is a daydream, and with the statement, "I am not accustomed to thinking that I deserve anything bad" (38b), the dream fades and Socrates awakens to reality and an *antitimesis* of a monetary fine.

What does the proposal of *sitêsis* contribute to Plato's portrait of Socrates? It anticipates Plato's assessment of Socrates in the *Phaedo* as "the bravest and also the wisest and most just man" (118). It implies that the character Socrates, who does not see himself as polluted, accepts the verdict that renders him guilty of impiety. He is who he is now because he pursued the god's identity for him. He has proven that those who pride themselves on their wisdom not only are not wise but fail to realize this. His toils on behalf of the god have, however, brought him to the realization that he is the god's model for human wisdom: he has none and knows that he has none. That knowledge came about through the *kudos* from the god, and he offers it to the *polis* to take to itself by embracing him at the Prytaneum. But there is more. Socrates, while accepting the verdict, does not accept the identity it conveys upon him, for in his view he has done no man an injustice (37ab). The responsibility for the crisis and burden for removing it has been thrust upon him, but he is yet to accept it. He is not yet ready to offer himself as victim for the stability of the Laws (Pl. *Cri.* 54bc).

At the end of scene 3, Socrates emerges from his reflections to propose a fine of one *mna,* a sum worth at the time the wages of 60 days for a skilled workman or 240 for a juryman.[118] He acquiesces to his young friends' sureties for a larger fine of thirty *mnae* (38b). Socrates' proposal of *sitêsis* estimates his worth to himself rather than constituting a legally recognized penalty.[119] Most of scene 3, therefore, and all of scene 4 lie outside the legal background of the defense. They are needed, not by the scenario, but by the text's purpose of revealing what persecutors hide from themselves—namely, the innocence of the victim and their own guilt. They effect the transition of Socrates from criminal to savior, miasma to hero, and from Athens to the world of the dead. Girard calls this phenomenon, a leap that he admits defies rational explanation, "double transference." We have already seen its magic in the transformation of the loathsome seller of sausages into Agoracritus, caretaker of Demos.[120] Oedipus of Sophocles' *Oedipus the Tyrant* helped with understanding the scapegoat. Now Oedipus of his *Oedipus at Colonus* aids in seeing the underlying mythmaking—that is, the transformation of the mimetic mechanism into story—in Plato's treatment of Socrates in transition.

Both figures have come to possess certain knowledge. Socrates knows that he never willingly wronged anyone (37a) and that he cannot forsake the "unexamined life" without disobeying the god (37e–38a). He has gained this knowledge from his "wandering" like Heracles on his labors (22a) and "going about" (30a, 31c) and from his inquiries into Apollo's oracle. Oedipus, who has been taught by wandering (Soph. *OC* 8), states with positive assurance of the future that "I will never leave this seat" (45) once he has entered the shrine of the Eumenides. The certainty of his knowledge grows as it transforms from mere mortal to something approaching the divine. Here it rests upon the knowledge that Apollo once gave him long ago in an oracle that he would find rest in the sanctuary of those dread goddesses (*OC* 88). Both figures state that they will never leave, respectively, Athens and Colonus, but remain to convey a boon upon Athenians. The latter refused Socrates because they failed to find the beauty beneath the ugliness that Oedipus encourages Theseus to search out (*OC* 576–578). Athenians have cast away the *kudos* of Apollo that Socrates offered in his care that they be as best and prudent as possible. Oedipus holds out victory over their future enemies, the Thebans. Both figures conceal their benefit beneath the unpleasing exterior of their appearance. Moreover, both assert their innocence. Socrates is guilty of no offense against anyone, while Oedipus pleas that the parricide and incest were acts that he suffered, not did in full intent, because the former was an act of self-defense and the latter of ignorance (266–267, 960–999). Both figures, finally, are on the cusp of migration. Socrates, rejected by Athenians from his community's hearth, soon will depart to the "happiness of the Blessed" (Pl. *Phd.* 115d). Oedipus, accepted as a citizen among Athenians, will soon enter into the inner sanctum of the dread goddesses. Such similarities result not from coincidence or imitation but from the dynamics of the end stage of the mimetic mechanism. The responsibility of the *pharmakos* derives from his consent, and his innocence condemns his community, lest it recognize the god as its own violence, to reward him as a hero.

SCENE 5. THE GOOD DEATH (38C–42). "For the sake of not much time, Athenian men, you will have the name and be charged with the responsibility

by those who wish to revile the city of having killed Socrates" (38c). This
Socrates, it becomes clear (39d, quoted below), is Apollo's gift endowed with
his *kudos,* while the revilers will upbraid Athenians for not appreciating his
worth and the innocence that the god's *kudos* warrants. Mention of the brev-
ity of time recalls another Socrates, the Satanic Socrates of Aristophanes. At
the beginning (19a) and end (24a) of his defense against his first accusers,
Socrates points to the difficulty of removing in so little time slander that has
become so widespread (24a: *pollên*). The slander tells the story of Aristophanes' Satanic Socrates, who investigates the physical universe, manipulates
and undermines language, and teaches both skills to others. The slander is
the myth of Socrates the atheistic and immoralistic teacher. However he
denies substance to the figure, the majority of jurors and Athenians accept its
truth. They are trapped by its "violent contagion, which is so effective in the
myths that it prevents communities from ever finding out the truth, namely,
the innocence of their victims."[121] The myth of Satanic Socrates sweeps Athenians along, justifying and being justified by their violence toward the one
man they deem harmful to the city's religious and moral fabric. Theirs is the
disillusion of the persecutor.[122] The accusation they bring against Socrates
springs from Satan and, although offering temporary relief, subjects them
again to the mimetic mechanism and its eventual need for another victim.
Through his innocence shown in the Passion, Jesus, Girard explains, "'has
canceled' this accusation; he 'set it aside.' He nails the accusation to the
Cross, which is to say that he reveals its falsity."[123] Jesus demonstrates the
innocence of the victim and puts an end to the mimetic chain ending with
the surrogate victim. Socrates is guilty of speaking and probing his culture;
others are guilty of making his words subversive and harmful. Plato can see
the man's innocence but also the harm that his language can perpetrate (30b).
His Socrates cannot escape the story told of him; it is too persuasive. He
remains mortal and Greek in pronouncing *timôria,* retribution, punishment,
upon those who have killed him (39c–d), but it is retribution that serves the
god's purpose for him and initiates his murder as the foundation of Plato's
philosophy, as we now see.

   At the end, Socrates speaks with the voice of the prophet, since, as is
said, "the soul, escaping the body and drawing nigh its divine nature, gains a
mantic element":[124]

I desire to utter oracles for you, O you who have condemned (ἀπεκτόνατε) me, for I am at that point where men quite often pronounce oracles when- ever they are about to die. I say, you men who have killed (ἀπεκτόνατε) me, that retribution will come to you immediately after my death much harsher, by Zeus, than the one you inflicted in killing me. You have done this now, thinking that you will be released from giving a refutation (*elen- chos*) of your life, but the opposite by far will come your way, I say. Those who refute you will be more numerous. I have been restraining them, and you did not perceive them. They will be harsher in as much as they are younger, and you will be angrier. For if you think, by killing me, you will hold in check someone from reproaching you because you do not live cor- rectly, you are not thinking nobly. That means of escape is not very possible or noble, but that other is both most noble and very easy: not to restrain others but to prepare oneself to be as best as possible. (39cd)

Socrates' words, ἐμὲ ἀπεκτόνατε, at first connote the legal, "you have con- demned me to death." But his true judges, those who acquitted him, dispense justice. What these words denote is legal murder, "you have killed me," for justice does not entail retribution. At the same time, the words impart by the aspect of the verb that establishes a present condition from a past act that he speaks as dead to pronounce upon their victimage culture for its avatars, as Achilles, removed by his slaying of Hector, summarizes the human condi- tion under Zeus (Hom. *Il.* 525–534). The Athenians that Socrates addresses murdered him in the confidence of their legal system and heedless of conse- quences. They wielded the violence of their court, sanctioned by sacrifices and prayers to the gods, without thought of retribution, for they spoke for all Athenians, although not all Athenians concurred with their decision. By victimizing Socrates, they defended their use of the mimetic mechanism to restore order to their community. In return, they must face a phalanx of Socrateses, young and vigorous men who will probe and question them, the only vengeance proper for an innocent, so that they give an account (*elen- chos*) of themselves. They no longer are to avoid giving a payment. They no longer can shroud their murder in silence, for that method has been exposed by the taking of the innocent's life.

This moment in the Athenian court will be replayed centuries later in the Sanhedrin when the prophet Stephen, falsely accused, cries out to his persecutors the tale of their murders:

> Stiff-necked and uncircumcised in hearts and ears, you always oppose the holy spirit, your fathers and so you. Whom of the prophets did your fathers not persecute? They killed the ones who announced beforehand the coming of the Righteous One whose betrayers and murderers you have now become, you who received the law through the directions of the angels and observed it not. (*Acts* 7.51–53)

Girard points out that Stephen reproduces the curses leveled at the Pharisees by Jesus (*Mt.* 23.34–36), to which he adds the murder of Jesus.[125] The Jews in the Sanhedrin can barely listen. They grind their teeth and seethe with anger. When Stephen fell silent, "they cried out in a loud voice and stopped their ears and ran at him in unison. They cast him from the city, and they stoned him to death" (*Acts* 7.57–58). It is hearing their murder spoken aloud, Girard points out, that they cannot tolerate. "How can we miss the point that they kill in order to cast off an intolerable knowledge and that this knowledge is, strangely enough, the knowledge of the murder itself?"[126] Stoning comes to both men, to the one with rocks outside the city thrown by all, to the other with voting pebbles cast in its center by the majority. Both perish to reveal that social harmony founded on the murder of an innocent (respectively, Jesus and Socrates and now Stephen) can no longer function once it has been, and continues to be, exposed. Their deaths mirror one another:

> If the ritual gesture [that killed Stephen] can be to a certain extent deritualized and become spontaneous without really altering its form, we can imagine that such a metamorphosis can also take place in the other direction; the form of the legal execution [that killed Socrates] is nothing more than the ritualization of spontaneous violence. If we look carefully at the martyrdom of Stephen, we inevitably come up against the hypothesis of the founding murder.[127]

So too with Socrates, not the Socrates of the trial but of Plato's *Apology of Socrates*. Stephen appeals to Jesus that "you not put this sin upon them" (*Acts* 7.54). Let the violence perish unimitated. Socrates calls out to Athenians to relinquish the way of restraint—that is, the contest system and its destructive mimesis of envy and shame.[128] Plato's Socrates dies to put even these Athenians on the path toward making themselves as best as possible. For this, they must consider and define the meaning of "best," a search that puts one in mimetic rivalry with oneself—that is, cancels the mechanism. It seems to have led Plato to justice in the city. Socrates did not die to create philosophy, but his death led Plato to its creation.

Socrates' conversation with those jurors, his proper judges, ends Plato's *Apology of Socrates*. He speaks of death, what it may be like, in ways that seem less philosophical than musing. Scholars insist correctly that his word for "converse," *diamythologêsai* (39e), contains no element of telling myths, but his vision of his *elenchus*-filled afterlife appears more mythic than philosophical. But as one disdainful of myths, at least those of tradition, Socrates does qualify and hedge his presentation of death and the afterlife devoted to questioning and cross-examining the great poets of old. Poets are of interest, as they were the earliest fonts of wisdom and Plato's opponents in war of philosophy's against poetry's. James A. Coulter proposes that his eagerness to spend time (41b: *diatribê*) with Palamedes, victim of Odysseus' false accusation, conceals his desire to refute him as a "pretender to wisdom" as part of Plato's criticism of Gorgias' theory of rhetoric.[129] That his *daimonion* has not interfered with his actions at the trial seems to Socrates to be "a great proof" (40c) that those actions and their consequences have proven to be good. His last request to his prosecutors and those jurors who condemned him cannot be irony, although it surely is futile—namely, that they watch over his sons as he did. One thing he says, however, is clear: "it was better that I am dead and released from these doings" (41d). *Ta pragmata,* "things done, deeds," has appeared as "troubles": these are troublesome deeds that he is better shut of. Socrates concedes victimization, but he has yet to accept himself as one worthy of being victimized: he has done no wrong in this view. "I am convinced that I am not guilty toward any human being" (37b).[130] As yet, Socrates is not a proper victim.

Act 3. Scapegoat: Crito

Crito, fellow demesman and old friend, arrives at dawn to the prison where Socrates has been held for the last month. He bears dreadful news. The ship

carrying the sacred embassy has reached Sunion on its voyage from Delos
and should be home today or tomorrow. The scruple that the city stay free
of pollution during its absence forestalled executions until its return, allowing Socrates' friends time with him.[131] Now that respite is coming to an end.
Crito waits for Socrates to awaken. Not for the first time has he wondered
over how easily and calmly Socrates endures his imminent death. Socrates
puts it to his age, but Crito knows that others of his age have been upset and
angry in his situation (*Cri.* 43bc). Socrates' demeanor expresses his acceptance of the rightness of his defense and the decision, although mistaken, of
the jury. He did say one thing at trial, as we have seen, that reveals something
about his inner state: "This is clear to me, that it is better that I die now
and escape troublesome doings" (*Apol.* 41d). *Beltion,* "better," denotes "more
advantageous" and raises the question, "To whom is it more advantageous
that Socrates die?" At the time Plato wrote *Apology* 41d, I assume that he
had yet to compose and perhaps think about the matters that would become
the *Crito.* But in Socrates' rejection of his dear friend's appeal that he escape
prison and avoid death, Plato offers an answer. His answer comes in the form
of Socrates as a proper victim, "proper" for being who he is and "victim" for
what he does in regard to the crisis underlying his friend's appeal. Crito is
an honorable man and ordinary Athenian, and what he says would have the
approval of ordinary Athenians.[132] And that is the crisis, for Crito's appeal
entails preferring one's interests to those of the city by setting aside its court's
decision and invalidating its laws.

  ἀλλ᾽, ὦ δαιμόνιε Σώκρατες, ἔτι καὶ νῦν ἐμοὶ πιθοῦ καὶ σώθητι (*Cri.* 44b).
"Yet, O demonic Socrates, still even now obey me and get to a place of safety."
Socrates' behavior these last weeks has confounded Crito. He reproaches
Socrates by saying that he is "possessed by a *daimon.*" Yet Crito is as worried
about what people will say about him as about losing a friend. "They" will
claim that he was stingy and refused to spend the money to save Socrates,
and that he preferred money to friends (44b). Their ignorance of the situation—namely, Socrates' obstinacy and refusal to leave—notwithstanding,
they will say this because flight is what they expect a man to do. They model
their talk upon what the man of epic, ὁ ἀνὴρ ἀγαθὸς καὶ ἀνδρεῖος, "the good
and manly man" of *aretê* would do.[133] He first appears in epic as the warrior
with the military prowess and power to defend himself and his household,
the counsel to form and execute military tactics, and the capability to help

his friends and harm his enemies. The ethic lost much of its military emphasis but otherwise still functioned as the ideal during the late fifth century.[134]
Crito measures Socrates' interests, as he would his own, against those of the
city according to the epic standard. Should their interests enter into serious
conflict, he would prefer his own without hesitation.[135] Accordingly, Crito
urges Socrates, "who [he points out] has been speaking of caring for *aretê*
through all his life" (45d) to imitate the *agathos,* the man of *aretê.*[136] Such a
man has the resources and gumption to act to save his life, to keep his sons
from becoming orphans, and to avoid the shame of sitting in prison and
doing to oneself what those who desire to ruin him so want (45c).

The *aretê* standard derives ultimately from epic, primarily, from Homer's
Iliad and *Odyssey,* the versions most familiar to Greeks. It was the way warriors and heads of households followed to survive and protect their families
and to gain the honor and immortality in song they craved. It was highly
competitive and mimetic in that the same objects of limited number were
pursued by all, and nothing beyond a certain sense of shame before others
curbed mimetic desire from becoming acquisitive and breaking into violence.
This transition is the story of the *Iliad,* as Gil Baile has shown.[137] Rivalry over
prizes that mark a warrior above the others substitutes for the deeper rivalry
over worth, that of Achilles' natural fighting abilities and unquestioned claim
to honor and that of Agamemnon's authority as king sanctioned by Zeus and
society. The conflict tears apart the army who lacks recourse to settle a quarrel
between men bent on their own superiority. Neither man can yield from the
shame of losing face. Translated into Athenian society of the fifth century,
the ideal of the *anêr agathos* proved utterly destructive and dysfunctional.
The competitive ethic, the contest system discussed earlier, created struggles
over leadership among men locked in mimetic rivalry over every good, men
who maintained their positions of power by flattering the people with public
funds and generous programs, and sought approval not from the "others"
but from their equals, their competitors and enemies. Hardly adequate for
the heroes of epic, the standard of the *anêr agathos* proved disastrous for a
democracy in control of an empire.

Pressured by Crito, Socrates finds himself in the position of his shadow
in Platonic discourse, Alcibiades, as the latter stood on the deck of his ship in
the wake of the *Salaminia.* The Athenians had sent their state ship to escort
him from Sicily, where he shared command of their assault on Syracuse in 415

BCE. His enemies at home intended to try and execute him for his alleged role in the mutilation of the herms on the eve of the expedition. To avoid upsetting the morale of the men, they allowed Alcibiades to follow the *Salaminia* in his own ship. He complied until they approached Thurii in Italy. Then Alcibiades disappeared to reappear in Sparta, where he rendered valuable aid and comfort to his city's enemy.[138] When the forces of law manipulated by his enemies came calling, Alcibiades favored his own interests and escaped, preferring to become a traitor to his country but true to his own benefit, the way of the *anêr agathos*.[139] Socrates now finds himself, as it were, where egoism, personal ambition, and promotion of self cross with the values of the city, its laws, and welfare.

Socrates rejects Crito's urging to imitate the crowd. The many act willy-nilly, doing now good, now harm, because they are in the grip of the received wisdom of the poets. Socrates, it is true, has spoken often of *aretê*, but his is the *aretê* of knowledge, not of the *anêr agathos*. Socrates follows the expert whose knowledge of the skill at hand promotes the health of body and soul. Without the benefit of such knowledge, men risk corrupting both body and soul by depriving them of what makes them healthy (*Cri.* 47c–48b). What is needed is the cure for the selfishness and egoism displayed by Alcibiades, his enemies, and the many who act through traditional values and unexamined beliefs. Only someone who stands free of the infection, who is not affected by the disease that ignorance wreaks on the body and soul can administer the therapy.

Whether Socrates was condemned justly or unjustly matters naught to Crito, who advocates flight with the conviction of an Alcibiades trailing the *Salaminia*. Socrates replies by conjuring a conversation with the Laws of the city for Crito's benefit lest he not understand that Socrates is not refusing to leave but consenting to stay. The Laws declare that they have not wronged him and, I infer, that he has not wronged them because they say he was wronged by men:

> Now as it is, you will depart [for Hades], if you depart, having been done injustice not by us but by men. (*Cri.* 54b)

With this concession, "done injustice . . . by men," the Laws dismiss for Plato the Socrates of the prosecutors and the majority of the jury. Let us stay with him for a moment.

This is the Socrates whom the first and penultimate voices in Plato's polyphony have defined as guilty of impiety and corrupting the youth. They succeeded in victimizing him as the one responsible for the crisis affecting their land. His banishment by hemlock restores communal harmony through focusing the multiple scandals that arise in a time of crisis upon one scandal, thus cleansing the contagion of destructive mimesis. Hence, this Socrates resides fully in the victimary mechanism of Athenian culture. Plato evidently wants nothing to do with him. "Philosophy," Cesáreo Bandera contends, "has no use for a sacred victim. The idea that sacred unanimity is entirely dependent on the elimination of the sacred victim, is profoundly repugnant to Plato and to philosophy in general."[140] Thus Plato chooses to ignore the Socrates of the prosecutors.

What Bandera has discovered in working with Plato's last work, *Laws,* is suggestive for *Crito,* one of his first. Bandera points out that Plato wants to use the sacred as the sanction for his city's laws. The sacred provides a prohibition that almost all citizens shrink from violating. As an example, Plato offers the abhorrence of committing incest because contravening the sacred brings about the destruction not only of the individual but also of his family and city. As constituted in the sacrificial mechanism, however, the sacred is tainted with the crime of the sacrificial victim and its killing. Thus "it is of utmost importance not to look at the victim qua victim. One must avoid even the thought that the victim is being in any way victimized, as we would say today."[141] Beneath victimization, the "comedy" that is the rites of *thusia,* lurks the specter of the murder of a human being.[142] Poets with their wailing and cries of pity for the victim threaten to let the cat out of the bag; their actions conflate the evil of exposure of the murder with their purpose of grief and sympathy. In this, they reflect the ambiguity of the sacred, itself a cure and a poison, boon and curse, good and evil, and are to be banished from the city. Plato needs "to separate the sacred from the killing in order to keep the sacred pure; not—and this is crucial—in order to stop the killing, but in order to do it unambiguously, that is, without fearing for the sacred."[143] To accomplish this,

> paradoxically, he [Plato] must separate the sacred from the killing (or ignore the sacred victim altogether, which is the same thing) for the same reason that the victim had always been considered sacred: to justify the killing, to do the killing and, at the same time, be able to claim innocence.

He would desacralize the killing in order to keep the sacred character of the victimizing process running smooth, free from ambiguity.[144]

This is to say, the sacred without the victim sanctions the laws, and philosophy takes over the role of concealing the murder in the sacrificial mechanism. This, I believe, is what happens in *Crito*. Through the sweet agreement of reasoning together, the Laws victimize Socrates, who has in any case already consented to be victimized.

Socrates asks Crito what they should say to the Laws and the city if they asked:

> Tell me, Socrates, what do you intend to do? By the deed which you are attempting, is there anything other than that you are proposing to destroy us the laws and the whole city as far as it lies within you? Or does it seem to you that a city will continue to exist and not be capsized in which the established judgments have no strength and are made null and void and corrupted by private citizens? (50b)[145]

If Socrates left the city without persuading it and the Laws of the correctness of this action, the city and its laws, the Laws aver, would slip into sacrificial crisis like a ship into the obliterating sea. Here we see Girard's first two stereotypes of persecution: crimes that bring about the loss of differences.[146] Without laws the city will disintegrate into a mimetic competition of individual desires. Athenians lived upon the precipice, ever in danger of sliding into flames of the rivalry among its leaders who, like Alcibiades, preferred their own interests over the welfare of the community. What the Laws need of Socrates is for him to suffer the consequences of an unjust verdict in order to support the system of justice itself against the corrosive and debilitating effects of the contest system. They are persuading him, in effect, to throw the first stone at himself so that his victimization may strengthen the system of laws and courts that will put an end to the single victim mechanism. How do the Laws go about this? by fulfilling Girard's third stereotype: "Sometimes the persecutors choose their victims because they belong to a class that is particularly susceptible to persecution because of the crimes they have committed."[147]

Socrates' life has rendered him the Laws' proper victim because he has remained in Athens all his life, leaving only once for the Isthmus and on military service (*Cri.* 52b). His continued presence implies his acceptance of the city's laws and agreement with their management of its courts. Any citizen who flees a judgment would be liable to charges of disobeying the laws, but Socrates is accountable far beyond all others:

> To these charges, we say that you, Socrates, are liable if you do what you are thinking, and you not the least of Athenians but most of all. And if I should ask, "Why?" Perhaps they would upbraid me justly by saying that especially among Athenians I have agreed on an agreement with them. (*Cri.* 52a)

The Laws victimize Socrates by casting him as the paragon of civic values, or rather of adherence to the values of the city as opposed to his own. He was born, raised, and educated in the city; he married and had children in the city; and he refused to propose exile from the city at his trial. He has, the Laws strangely emphasize, left the city less than "the lame and blind and other cripples" (*Cri.* 53a), a puzzling comparison were it not for the emphasis on Socrates' ugliness among the Socratics and the propensity of such unfortunates to be scapegoated.

The Laws speak as the community to victimize Socrates by giving him the advantage in his death. By dying for them, Socrates dies not for Athenians but for something greater that Plato calls the Laws but constitutes, rather, what laws embody, the stumbling of the mind of mortals toward justice.

And yet, Socrates' behavior cannot be unique. Many Athenians surely spent their lives in the city with the same exceptions as Socrates. Many married and raised families and obeyed the laws. It is true that Socrates was particularly fond of life in the city (Pl. *Phdr.* 230de) as Sophocles' Oedipus was inclined to feel the pain of others (*OT* 58–64). Both propensities opened them to victimization. Still, Socrates has already consented to offer himself before the Laws speak. Indeed, he spent his life in the city but not in the activities of the many, and it is this, not his mere presence, that makes him different. "I am a lover of knowledge," he tells Phaedrus (Pl. *Phdr.* 230d). He has consumed his days in the gymnasia and streets of Athens in pursuit of knowledge through questioning, examining, and refuting himself and "the men in the city" (230d). He has come, he tells Crito, to abide by a set of *logoi,* arguments:

> We must examine whether we are to do this, leave here, or not. Not now
> for the first time but always have I been of the sort to obey nothing among
> what I own except that argument which appears best to me on consider-
> ation. Those arguments which I kept discussing in the past I cannot cast
> out now because this misfortune has come upon me. They appear to me to
> be pretty much as they always have been, and I honor and value the same
> arguments as before. (*Cri.* 46bc)

Socrates identifies himself with these arguments, which he reviews for Crito
(46c–50a). They have spent their lives discussing and refining them. Socrates
cannot turn his back upon them or repudiate what has occupied his life since
youth without becoming a silly child (46cd).[148] Socrates has become one
with the arguments of a lifetime. They and he have become tantamount to
one being, and by being true to them, Socrates imitates himself. Even before
the Laws speak, Socrates has consented to remain out of mimetic rivalry with
his lifelong self by not opposing past arguments with new ones on behalf of
leaving. Socrates consents to being victimized through imitating himself, a
form of mimesis that cannot become rivalistic or acquisitive and thus ends
the mimetic mechanism by stopping it at its font.

The victimary mechanism turns all reciprocal violence upon the victim.
The latter is Other, someone for whatever quality or reason is different from
the rest. In this form, the mechanism necessarily entails murder, for, although
all agree upon the victim's guilt, no one person can be guilty of the crime for
which the victim is killed. The death of Socrates of the prosecutors and jurors
is murder, but in *Phaedo*, Socrates' Socrates dies a philosophical form of the
mechanism that ends in death without violence. In *Crito*, Socrates turns
the mimetic forces that foment reciprocal violence upon himself. The Laws
claim him as their victim through his lifelong allegiance, but he offers himself
as the man of a life of philosophy.

Bandera points out that "Plato cannot have it both ways."[149] That is,
Plato cannot have the power of the sacred to sanction laws without the
sacred victim, for it is the transference of the victim to the sacred that sacral-
izes the killing. No victim, no "sacred taboo-breaker," no sacred.[150] But what
is Socrates if not a sacred breaker of taboos? He bears *kudos* from the god
Apollo and the prosecutors' mark as a saboteur. Philosophy, at least Platonic
philosophy, began when Plato came to write the *Apology of Socrates*. In this,

the death of Socrates as the legalized murder of the Athenian court became the founding murder of Plato's philosophy. The prosecutors' Socrates dies as the victim of the traditional sacrificial mechanism, but Plato turns from that death to a philosophical form at the end of the *Phaedo*. In Socrates' last moments, in a setting removed from the many, the hemlock does not take Socrates' life but gives him an immortality of philosophical discussion.

As it happened, Socrates has participated in philosophical discussions of all sorts throughout the ages and surely will continue to do so.

Act 4. The Philosopher's Death: Phaedo

Socrates' friends can but surrender to their astonishment. They have arrived at the prison on the day Socrates is to die to find him joyous. He explains that the philosopher in him has been rehearsing his death all his life. The philosopher practices withdrawing from the distractions of the body to allow his *psychê* to pursue wisdom.[151] Nothing would be more ridiculous than to lament the day when his soul attains its release and departure for the happiness of the good gods and men better than those living now (*Phd.* 63b, 64a).

In *Apology of Socrates,* Plato likened Socrates' willingness to run the risk of dying in his commitment to the justice of his acts to Achilles' desire to avenge Patroclus at the cost of an early death (*Apol.* 28bd). The death that took Achilles was the warrior's "beautiful death"; it seems to be the impetus behind Plato's conception of the philosopher's death.[152] Death seizes the warrior as a young man cut down in battle, freeing him from the stain of cowardice and bathing him in the luster of his celebrity and *aretê* secure. Death spares him from the ravages of aging and the old man's death that deprive the body of all that is human.[153] The warrior's fellows, considering his body the extension of the living man, fight over it to spare it the dehumanizing mutilation by the enemy and cremate it amid elaborate rituals and funeral games. The *psychê,* a double in appearance of the living body,[154] separates from the body and enters the underworld, where it dwells, mired in the past, in liminality between the life and death of the body that no longer exists. But with the philosopher, the body bears no meaning. Socrates tells Crito to care for his body according to custom (115c), for it will have been vacated. The death that comes to an old man after a lifetime of devotion not only completes the philosopher's work of purifying the soul; it also releases the soul from the body for its migration to a place where it continues the quest for knowledge. There the soul resides in a liminal state between the encumbered vision imposed upon mortals and the immortality and divine wisdom of the gods (66a–67b, 80cd).

Freed from the confines of mortality, Socrates spends his last hours in bringing good news to his companions. He speaks in response to Simmias' and Cebes' concern for the soul's condition, whether it remains intact or is scattered after death, and offers arguments that transform the meaning of death with a message of immortality that lies within their reach as mortal men if they are willing to give themselves to philosophy. His *logos* changes the meaning of death from finality to renewal of the quest for truth, which, in turn, changes the role of the *pharmakon*. The transition launches from Socrates' dismissal of the request from the administer of the *pharmakon* that he not talk, to avoid weakening the efficacy of the *pharmakon* (*Phd.* 63d). The administer, locked in monosemy, understands *pharmakon* as poison. He represents not only the majority of Athenians who have decreed that Socrates drink poison but also the whole of the trial, condemnation, and prison. Socrates dismisses him, "ἔα ... χαίρειν αὐτόν" (63e). "Never mind him," for Socrates has withdrawn to a joy born of looking forward to what is coming. In this, he claims the same kind of freedom as Sophocles' Ajax: "Don't you know that I no longer owe service to the gods" (*Ai.* 589–590). Ajax has resolved to die, which moves him outside the limitations of the human condition and beyond Athena's anger or aid. The *pharmakon* now serves as the soul's cure of its corporeal shackles, a therapy of release and departure from the prison of the body and its hampered vision of the truth. This refines Jacques Derrida's insight, for it is not the *pharmakon* that is transformed:

> The hemlock, that potion which in the *Phaedo* is never called anything but a *pharmakon,* is presented to Socrates as a poison; yet it is transformed, through the effects of the Socratic *logos* and of the philosophical demonstration in the *Phaedo,* into a means of deliverance, a way toward salvation, a cathartic power. The hemlock has an ontological effect: it initiates one into the contemplation of the *eidos* and the immortality of the soul. *That is how Socrates takes it.*[155]

It retains the natural properties to cause death by "a peripheral neuropathy, a toxin-induced condition resembling the Guillain-Barré syndrome, brought about by the alkaloids in *Conium maculatum,* the poison hemlock plant."[156] What changes is the reception of its properties from society's poison to cure its corruption to the individual's elixir to cure his soul from its corruption, the body. The Socrates whom the Athenians banish as *pharmakos* conveys as *pharmakos* upon his community, his new "jurors" (*Phd.* 63e), the benefits of his *logos,* a way to salvation and deliverance from death. He says in effect: Imitate me. I'll show you the way. Probe yourself for knowledge of yourself. Imitating Socrates turns one inward. It cannot be mimetic. It is a journey to knowledge apart from the Satanic mechanism of comparison, envy, and violence. It releases mimesis to its foundational role of building a human being.

Notes

Introduction

1. Miguel de Cervantes Saavedra, *The Ingenious Hidalgo Don Quixote de la Mancha*, trans. John Rutherford (New York: Penguin, 2003), 166.

2. René Girard, *Deceit, Desire and the Novel: Self and Other in Literary Structure*, trans. Yvonne Freccero (Baltimore: Johns Hopkins University Press, 1966), 2–4, where mimetic desire is called triangular desire; René Girard, *Violence and the Sacred*, trans. Patrick Gregory (Baltimore: Johns Hopkins University Press, 1977), 145–147; René Girard, *Things Hidden since the Foundation of the World*, trans. Stephen Bann and Michael Metteer (Stanford, CA: Stanford University Press, 1987), 282–298; Pierpaolo Antonello and João Cezar de Castro Rocha, *Evolution and Conversion: Dialogues on the Origins of Culture* (New York: Continuum International Publishing, 2007), 54–61; Richard J. Golsan, *René Girard and Myth: An Introduction* (New York: Garland Publishing, 1993), 1–13; Michael Kirwan, *Discovering Girard* (Cambridge, MA: Cowley Publications, 2005), 14–23.

3. Cervantes Saavedra, *Don Quixote*, 167.

4. Girard, *Things Hidden*, 15.

5. Harry Sidebottom, *Ancient Warfare: A Very Short Introduction* (Oxford: Oxford University Press, 2004), 56.

6. For Clytemnestra's sexuality, see Wm. Blake Tyrrell, *Amazons: A Study in Athenian Mythmaking* (Baltimore: Johns Hopkins University Press, 1984), 97–100.

7. For the contest system as a zero-sum game, see Alvin W. Gouldner, *Enter Plato:*

Classical Greece and the Origins of Social Theory (New York: Basic Books, 1965), 45–51.

8. This is the "shame culture" of the Homeric hero. See E. R. Dodds, *The Greeks and the Irrational* (Berkeley: University of California Press, 1951), 17–18; W. H. Adkins, *Merit and Responsibility: A Study in Greek Values* (Chicago : University of Chicago Press, 1960), 48–49; Walter Donlan, *The Aristocratic Ideal in Ancient Greece: Attitudes of Superiority from Homer to the End of the Fifth Century b.c.* (Lawrence, KS: Coronado Press, 1980), 1–24.

9. Donlan, *Aristocratic Ideal*, 15–18.

10. Girard, *Evolution and Conversion*, 57.

11. Wm. Blake Tyrrell, "The Unity of Sophocles' *Ajax*," *Arethusa* 16 (1985): 155–185; Frieda S. Brown, *Athenian Myths and Institutions: Words in Action* (New York: Oxford University Press, 1991), 65–72.

12. The elenchus involves refutation, which creates the danger of its descending into a game and an eristic to win the argument rather than attain truth (Plato, *Republic* 539bc); Richard Robinson, *Plato's Earlier Dialectic*, 2d ed. (Oxford: Oxford University Press, 1953), 84–85.

13. For example, W. D. Woodhead, "Gorgias," in *The Collected Dialogues of Plato*, ed. Edith Hamilton and Huntington Cairns (New York: Pantheon Books, 1961), 240, offers "after uttering and listening to such abusive language" adequate but concealing the voice of the participle.

14. Cesáreo Bandera, *The Sacred Game: The Role of the Sacred in the Genesis of Modern Literary Fiction* (University Park: Pennsylvania State University Press, 1994), 62. Bandera points out that "since the poets are ambiguous creatures, living, as they do, in proximity of the sacred, they should be expelled in properly sacrificial manner. First, you consecrate them—anoint them with myrrh and place on their head a garland of wool, as was traditionally done with the sacred victim—then you expel you to protect the community from ambiguous sacred contamination. It was only half a joke."

15. John Wilson, "'The Customary Meanings of Words Were Changed'—Or Were They? A Note on Thucydides 3.82.4," *Classical Quarterly* 32 (1982): 18–20. Wilson corrects the misunderstanding that Thucydides (3.82.4) says that the meanings of words changed. Wilson contends that Thucydides meant that "descriptions which in themselves implied moral blame or some other kind of reprobation—were replaced by 'good,' and vice versa" (18).

16. Polycrates, teacher of rhetoric, published a treatise, *Accusation of Socrates* (Isocrates, *Busiris* 4), around 394 BCE, within the range of the years accepted for the dating of Plato's *Gorgias*. The question arose whether *Gorgias* was written as a response to the *Accusation* and its contention of Socrates as *misodemos* (hating the demos) or provoked the *Accusation*. As usual, enough is known to create the question and not enough to secure a conclusion. The relative chronology of the two works cannot be fixed, and the question remains open. See Dodds, *Greeks and the Irrational*, 28–30.

17. See above, note 2.

18. Girard, *Evolution and Conversion*, 160.

19. Ibid., 162.

20. On date of composition of the *Apology of Socrates*, see W. K. C. Guthrie, *A History of Greek Philosophy*, vol. 4, *Plato—The Man and His Dialogues: Earlier Period* (Cambridge: Cambridge University Press, 1975), 71–72; Thomas Brickhouse and Nicholas D. Smith, *Socrates on Trial* (Princeton: Princeton University Press, 1989), 1–2.

21. Diogenes Laertius 2.10, 106; Mario Montuori, *Socrates: Physiology of a Myth*, trans. J. M. P. and M. Langdale (Amsterdam: J. C. Gieben, 1981), 79–86.

22. Montuori, *Socrates*, 201–212. The Thirty Tyrants were deposed in 404–403 BCE; democracy was restored in late summer 403, and the trial of Socrates occurred in 399. Montuori (202) finds "a definite confirmation of the correctness of this interpretation in Aelian, *Miscellaneous Stories* 3.17: "Socrates was not pleased with the constitution of the Athenians, for he saw the democracy as tyrannical and monarchial."

23. Montuori, *Socrates*, 82.

24. Girard, *Things Hidden*, 438.

Chapter 1. Mimesis, Conflict, and Crisis

1. Gouldner, *Enter Plato*, 56.

2. Aristophanes, *Birds*, 1282; Nan Dunbar, *Aristophanes Birds* (Oxford: Oxford University Press, 1995), 636.

3. Diogones Laertius, 2.123.

4. Charles H. Kahn, "Aeschines on Socratic Eros," in *The Socratic Movement*, ed. Paul A. Vander Waerdt (Cornell, NY: Cornell University Press, 1994), 87–106. For the Socratic writers, see G. C. Field, *Plato and His Contemporaries: A Study in Fourth-Century Life and Thought*, 3rd ed. (London: Methuen, 1967), 133–157.

5. Diskin Clay, "The Origins of the Socratic Dialogue," in *The Socratic Movement*, ed. Paul A. Vander Waerdt (Ithaca, NY: Cornell University Press, 1994), 23–47.

6. Clay, *Origins*, 27.

7. A. Momigliano, *The Development of Greek Biography* (Cambridge, MA: Harvard University, 1971), 46: Socratic writers aimed "towards capturing the potentialities of individual lives."

8. W. K. C. Guthrie, *A History of Greek Philosophy*, vol. 3, *The Fifth-Century Enlightenment* (Cambridge: Cambridge University Press, 1969), 39–57.

9. Girard, *Evolution and Conversion*, 57.

10. Girard, *Evolution and Conversion*, 57.

11. Andrea Wilson Nightingale, *Genres in Dialogue: Plato and the Construct of Philosophy* (Cambridge: Cambridge University Press, 1995), 60; Penelope Murray, *Plato on Poetry:*

Ion; Republic 376e–398b9; Republic 595–608b10 (Cambridge: Cambridge University Press, 1966), 231.

12. Nightingale, *Genres*, 65.

13. Richard Robinson, *Plato's Earlier Dialectic*, 2d ed. (Oxford: Oxford University Press, 1953), 7–19; Brickhouse and Smith, *Socrates on Trial*, 131–136, and *Plato's Socrates* (New York: Oxford University Press, 1994), 5–29; Clay, *Origins*, 180–189.

14. An exception is *Meno* 98b, where Socrates asserts that he knows the difference between correct opinion and knowledge.

15. See also Plato, *Euthyphro* 9d; *Protagoras* 331c; *Republic* 349a.

16. Scholars debate the ability of the elenchus to yield philosophical knowledge rather than to establish inconsistency in the answerer's beliefs. See Brickhouse and Smith, *Socrates on Trial*, 131–132, and *Socrates*, 17–21.

17. Girard, *Things Hidden*, 11: "Competitors are fundamentally those who run or walk together, rivals those who dwell on opposite banks of the same river." Girard plays with the etymology of "rival," from Latin *rivalis*, someone using the same *rivus*, stream.

18. Robinson, *Dialectic*, 8.

19. Ibid., 9.

20. Thrasymachus accuses Socrates of resorting to irony to avoid answering a question (Plato, *Republic* 337a).

21. Robinson (*Dialectic*, 9, 10) refers to the answerer as Socrates' "victim."

22. Robinson, *Dialectic*, 10.

23. Brickhouse and Smith, *Socrates*, 25.

24. For the *pharmakos* in Plato, see Jacques Derrida, "Plato's Pharmacy," in *Dissemination*, trans. Barbara Johnson (Chicago: University of Chicago Press, 1981), 61–171; Todd M. Compton, *Victim of the Muses: Poet as Scapegoat, Warrior, and Hero in Greco-Roman and Indo-European Myth and History* (Washington, DC: Center for Hellenic Studies, 2006; distributed by Harvard University Press), 154–165.

25. A. E. Taylor, *Plato: The Man and His Work* (New York: Meridian Books, 1956), 534.

26. G. S. Kirk, *The Songs of Homer* (Cambridge: Cambridge University Press, 1962), 312–315; Murray, *Plato on Poetry*, 96–97; Andrew Ford, "The Classical Definition of Ῥαψῳδία," *Classical Philology* 83 (1988): 300–307; W. K. C. Guthrie, *A History of Greek Philosophy*, vol. 4, *Plato—The Man and His Dialogues: Earlier Period* (Cambridge: Cambridge University Press, 1975), 200–201.

27. René Girard, *A Theater of Envy: William Shakespeare* (New York: Oxford University Press, 1991), 4.

28. Murray, *Plato on Poetry*, 102.

29. For this distinction in Plato between the productive arts that create visible things and the practical (i.e., active) arts that create invisible things, see Diogenes Laertius 3.84.

30. Peer pressure and the need to attract talent would have compelled the Epidaurians to offer prizes of as comparable as possible value to those given by the Athenians. The prizes given winning rhapsodes are unknown, but the victor in singing with a cithara at Athens, David Young calculates, received amphoras of oil worth the equivalent of 1059 days of full employment for a skilled workman. David C. Young, *The Olympic Myth of Greek Amateur Athletics* (Chicago: Ares, 1985), 122.

31. Murray, *Plato on Poetry*, 103–104.

32. Ibid., 114.

33. Ibid., 115.

34. Ibid., 116.

35. Rosemary Harriott, *Poetry and Criticism before Plato* (London: Methuen, 1969), 82.

36. Debra Nails, *The People of Plato: A Prosopography of Plato and Other Socratics* (Indianapolis: Hackett, 2002), 213–214.

37. Girard, *Evolution and Conversion*, 57.

38. Ibid.

39. Girard, *Theater of Envy*, 164–165.

40. A. W. Gomme, A. Andrewes, and K. J. Dover, *A Historical Commentary on Thucydides*, vol. 4, *Books V 25–VII* (Oxford: Oxford University Press, 1970), 429.

41. Girard, *Evolution and Conversion*, 59.

42. The publication dates of *Gorgias* and *Republic* are unknown, but *Gorgias* is usually placed earlier in the relative chronology of Plato's dialogues (Guthrie, *Earlier Period*, 50).

43. E. R. Dodds, *Plato Gorgias: A Revised Text with Introduction and Commentary* (Oxford: Oxford University Press, 1959), 13, suggests from what Socrates says to Callicles, "Perhaps they [the people] will seize upon you, if you're not careful" (Plato, *Gorgias* 519a), that "a man so ambitious and so dangerously frank about it may well have forfeited his life."

44. Dodds, *Gorgias*, 273–279; L. B. Carter, *The Quiet Athenian* (Oxford: Oxford University Press, 1986), 163–182; Andrea Wilson Nightingale, "Plato's *Gorgias* and Euripides' *Antiope*: A Study in Generic Transformation," *Classical Antiquity* 11 (1992): 121–141.

45. The term "rhetor" (*rhêtôr*, "speaker"), used of Gorgias, indicates "one who knows the theory of rhetoric"; the term is applied more widely to denote "those who practised public speaking, especially in the assembly . . . , and so came to mean virtually 'politician,' as it does at 466 d 1" (Dodds, *Gorgias*, 194).

46. We cannot be certain, since the dramatic date of the *Gorgias* cannot be fixed.

47. Plato, *Hippias Major* 282b; Diodorus Siculus 12.53.1–2.

48. George Kennedy, *The Art of Persuasion in Greece* (Princeton, NJ: Princeton University Press, 1963), 62; W. K. C. Guthrie, *A History of Greek Philosophy*, vol. 3, *The*

Fifth-Century Enlightenment (Cambridge: Cambridge University Press, 1969), 270.

49. Dodds, *Gorgias*, 9.

50. Ibid., 15.

51. Devin Stauffer, *The Unity of Plato's* Gorgias: *Rhetoric, Justice, and the Philosophic Life* (Cambridge, MA: Cambridge University Press, 2006), 18, suggests that it may be a clue to Socrates as *dosis* (gift) since this role for him came about through Chaerephon's question (Plato, *Apology* 20e–21a); hence, the delay could be due to "his activity of dialectical cross-examination" that was "made necessary by the god's answer to Chaerephon's question."

52. Dodds, *Gorgias*, 192, who considers Polus' style "in any case Gorgian to the point of grotesqueness" and a Platonic parody.

53. Plato, *Meno* 73c: *aretê* is nothing other than "being able to lead men."

54. See Plato, *Philebus* 58a: "I [Protarchus] used to listen to Gorgias frequently saying that the power of persuading differs by far from all skills, for it renders all things enslaved beneath it willingly and not through force."

55. George Kimball Plochmann and Franklin E. Robinson, *A Friendly Companion to Plato's* Gorgias (Carbondale: Southern Illinois University Press, 1988), 34, comment on 456a: "again a double irony, for the obvious sarcasm contains the truth that the power of the rhetor is not derived from rational deliberations but is a kind of unexplained force."

56. Harry G. Frankfurt, *On Bullshit* (Princeton, NJ: Princeton University Press, 2005), 53.

57. Ibid., 18–19, 33–40, 46–48, 52–56, 59–60.

58. Ibid., 63.

59. I translate in freer language that, I believe, captures the moment. A less inspired translation of the whole sentence is the following: "It [rhetoric] appears to me, then, Gorgias, to be a certain study, that does not belong to art, but to a soul that is sagacious and manly, and naturally powerful in its intercourse with men" (Henry Cary, *The Works of Plato*, vol. 1, *The Apology of Socrates, Crito, Phaedo, Gorgias, Protagoras, Phaedrus, Theaetetus, Euthyphron, Lysis* [London: George Bell & Sons, 1901], 155).

60. James Davidson, *Courtesans and Fishcakes: The Consuming Passions of Classical Athens* (New York: St. Martin's Press, 1997), 21–22.

61. Ibid., 25–26.

62. Xenophon (*Mem.* 1.3.5) says that Socrates "ate enough for pleasure and was so ready to eat that his desire for bread became his *opson*." Socrates seems to have eaten according to Greek ideology of food, or could it be that the ideology dictates how a myth should eat?

63. Dodds, *Gorgias*, 225. Theophrastus in *Characters* (2.1) defines the *kolax* as "the man aiming at the pleasant so there may be some aid for himself regarding money and the things that may be had through money."

64. Adkins, *Merit and Responsibility*, 30–57, 156–168; Donlan, Aristocratic Ideal, 1–24.

65. Adkins, *Merit and Responsibility*, 230.

66. Girard, *Violence and Sacred*, 57.

67. Herodotus 6.52; Apollodorus, *Library* 2.2.1.

68. Pelias and Neleus: Apollodorus, *Library* 1.9.8–10; Akrisios and Proitos: Apollodorus 2.2.1; Castor and Polydeukes: Apollodorus 3.10.6–7 and 3.11.2.

69. Girard, *Violence and Sacred*, 64.

70. Ibid., 63.

71. Ibid., 62.

72. See Wm. Blake Tyrrell and Larry Joe Bennett, "Sophocles' Enemy Sisters," *Contagion* 15/16 (2008/2009): 1–18.

73. For the "Greek contest system," see Gouldner, *Enter Plato*, 41–74; for a description of aristocratic values, see Donlan, *Aristocratic Ideal*, 1–34.

74. For a survey of the lives of women in Athenian society, see Sue Blundell, *Women in Ancient Greece* (Cambridge MA: Harvard University Press, 1955), 113–149.

75. For the motives impelling funeral legislation, see Robert Garland, "The Well-Ordered Corpse: An Investigation into the Motives behind Greek Funerary Legislation," *Bulletin of the Institute of Classical Studies of the University of London* 36 (1989): 1–15; Richard Seaford, *Reciprocity and Ritual: Homer and Tragedy in the Developing City-State* (Oxford: Oxford University Press, 1994), 78–86.

76. For the Amazon myth, see Tyrrell, *Amazons*, 40–63; for the Persian, see Edith Hall, *Inventing the Barbarian: Greek Self-Definition through Tragedy* (Oxford: Oxford University Press, 1989), 1, 101–159.

77. Girard, *Violence and Sacred*, 50.

78. Plochmann and Robinson, *Friendly Companion*, 112.

79. For the discussion of the fragments of the *Antiope*, see Carter, *Quiet Athenian*, 163–179.

80. Nightingale, *Generic Transformation*, 76, and 67–92 for Plato's use of *Antiope* in *Gorgias*.

Chapter 2. Plato's Victimary Culture

1. Walter Burkert, *Homo Necans: The Anthropology of Ancient Greek Sacrificial Ritual and Myth*, trans. Peter Bing (Berkeley: University of California Press, 1983), 3: "Sacrificial killing is the basic experience of the 'sacred.' *Homo religiosus* acts and attains self awareness as *homo necans*."

2. Karl Meuli in Walter Burkert, *Greek Religion*, trans. J. Raffan (Cambridge, MA: Harvard University Press, 1985), 58.

3. For the rites of *thusia*, see Jean Rudhardt, *Notions fondamentales de la pensée religieuse*

et actes constitutifs du culte dans la Grèce classique (Geneva: Droz, 1958), 257–266; Burkert, *Homo Necans*, 55–57; Wm. Blake Tyrrell and Frieda S. Brown, *Athenian Myths and Institutions: Words in Action* (New York: Oxford University Press, 1991), 73–83.

4. Jean-Louis Durand, "Greek Animals: Toward a Topology of Edible Bodies," in *The Cuisine of Sacrifice among the Greeks*, ed. Marcel Detienne and Jean-Pierre Vernant, trans. Paula Wissing (Chicago: University of Chicago Press, 1989), 104.

5. Marcel Detienne, *Dionysus Slain*, trans. Mireille Muellner and Leonard Muellner (Baltimore: Johns Hopkins University Press, 1979), 75–79.

6. Durand, *Greek Animals*, 91.

7. Ibid.

8. René Girard, *I See Satan Fall Like Lightning*, trans. James G. Williams (Maryknoll, NY: Orbis Books, 2001), 73.

9. Girard, *Violence and Sacred*, 5.

10. Aristophanes (*Clouds* 984) characterized traditional education as old fashioned by saying it was "full of cicadas and Bouphonia."

11. Girard, *Violence and Sacred*, 7.

12. Ludwig Deubner, *Attische Feste* (1932; Hildesheim: Georg Olms, 1966), 158–174; Girard, *Violence and Sacred*, 98, 307; H. W. Parke, *Festivals of the Athenians* (Ithaca, NY: Cornell University Press, 1977), 162–167; Jean-Pierre Vernant, "Théorie générale du sacrifice et mise à mort dans la θυσία grecque," *Le Sacrifice dans l'antiquité, Entretiens sur l'antiquité classique* 27 (1981): 1–21; Burkert, *Homo Necans*,136–143; Erika Simon, *Festivals of Attica: An Archaeological Commentary* (Madison: University of Wisconsin Press, 1983), 8–12.

13. Verlyn Klinkenborg, "If It Weren't for the Ox, We Wouldn't Be Where We Are," *Smithsonian* 24 (1993): 93.

14. Athenians held a court and proceedings for inanimate objects implicated in killing (Pausanias 1.24.4; Aeschines 3.244; Parke, *Festivals*, 163.

15. Girard, *Violence and Sacred*, 43–49, 98.

16. René Girard, "The Plague in Literature and Myth," *Texas Studies in Literature and Language* 15 (1974): 833–845; Girard, *Violence and Sacred*, 76–77.

17. For the sacrifice of Menoeceus, the son of Creon, see Euripides, *Phoenician Women* 911–1018; Helene P. Foley, *Ritual Irony: Poetry and Sacrifice in Euripides* (Ithaca, NY: Cornell University Press, 1985), 106–146.

18. Girard, *Violence and Sacred*, 89–118; Girard, *Satan Fall*, 82–94.

19. For rituals of sacrifice in these myths and, in particular, Euripides' *Iphigenia at Aulis*, see Foley, *Ritual Irony*, 65–102.

20. Euripides, *Erechtheus* fr. 50 (Austin); Apollodorus, *Library* 3.15.4.

21. Philochorus in F. Jacoby, *Die Fragmente der griechischen Historiker*, vol. 3. b. (Leiden:

E. L. Brill, 1954), 328 F 105.

22. René Girard, *The Scapegoat*, trans. Yvonne Freccero (Baltimore: Johns Hopkins University Press, 1986), 24.

23. Let her be sacrificed.

24. *Kupria* in Proclus, *Chrestomathia* 80.42–9.

25. Sean Alexander Gurd, *Iphigenias at Aulis: Textual Multiplicity, Radical Philology* (Ithaca, NY: Cornell University Press, 2005), 17.

26. Ibid.

27. Ibid.

28. Foley, *Ritual Irony*, 99.

29. Nancy Sorkin Rabinowitz, *Anxiety Veiled: Euripides and the Traffic in Women* (Ithaca, NY: Cornell University Press, 1993), 49.

30. What Girard says of Sophocles applies equally to Euripides: "If the tragic poet did away with the lynching of the victim, he himself would be 'lynched'" (*Violence and Sacred* 201).

31. For the festival of the Thargelia and the *pharmakos*, see Jane Ellen Harrison, *Prolegomena to the Study of Greek Religion* (Cambridge: Cambridge University Press, 1903), 94–114; Deubner, *Attische Feste*, 1966, 179–198; Vernant, *Ambiguity and Reversal*, 128–131; Parke, *Festivals*,146–147; Girard, *Violence and Sacred*, 101–131; idem, *The Scapegoat*, trans. Yvonne Freccero (Baltimore: Johns Hopkins University Press, 1986), 25–44; Burkert, *Greek Religion*, 82–84; Dennis D. Hughes, *Human Sacrifice in Ancient Greece* (London: Routledge, 1991), 140–155; Compton, *Victim*, 3–18. Compton (*Victim*, 13–18) provides a list of the themes of the *pharmakos* complex; for those relating to Socrates, see Compton, below, note 89.

32. Helladios in Photius, *Lexicon* 534a: "It was the custom at Athens to lead two *pharmakoi*, one for the men and one for the women, for purification. The one for the men had black figs around his neck, and the other, white figs . . . This purifying averted diseases of plague which began with the Androgeos of Crete. After he was killed illegally at Athens, the Athenians fell sick with plague, and the custom prevailed to purify the city with *pharmakoi*"; Harpocration, *Lexicon of the Ten Orators* s. v. *pharmakos*: "They [Athenians] let out two men at Athens who would be purifications (*kartharsia*) of the city in the Thargelia, one man for the men and one for the women. Pharmakos is a proper name. Pharmakos stole Apollo's sacred drinking bowls; he was caught by Achilles' men and stoned to death. The things done in the Thargelia are an imitation of this event." Athenians caused the pollution not so much by taking Androgeos' life as by staining the earth and angering its deities with blood prematurely and so wrongfully shed (Dodds, *Greeks and Irrational*, 36).

33. Harpocration, *Lexicon of the Ten Orators s. v. pharmakos;* see above, note 31.

34. Parke, *Festivals*, 146.

35. See Stephen G. Miller, *The Prytaneion: Its Function and Architectural Form* (Berkeley:

University of California Press, 1978), 4–24, for the functions of the Prytaneum. *Pharmakoi* were fed at public expense (Scholiast on Aristophanes, *Knights* 1136), and Demos invites Agorakritos, formerly the thoroughly loathsome Sausage Seller, to the Prytaneum, "where that *pharmakos* [Paphlagon] used to sit (1404–1405), but direct evidence of their support in the Prytaneum is lacking.

36. Scholia on Aristophanes, *Frogs* 733; on *Knights* 1136; on Aeschylus, *Seven Against Thebes* 680; Deubner, *Attische Feste*, 184n5; Compton, *Victim*, 4–5.

37. Scholia on Aristophanes, *Knights* 1136c.

38. Girard, *Scapegoat*, 12–24.

39. Hesychius, *Lexicon*, s. v. *kradêsitês* (fig-branch man): "*pharmakos*, the one struck with fig branches"; Hipponax fr. 5 (West): "to purify the city and to strike the [*pharmakos*] with branches"; fr. 6: "striking [him] in a meadow and beating him with branches and squills as though a pharmakos." Tzetzes (*Chiliades* 5.726–737) has the *pharmakos* struck "six times on his penis with squills, wild figs and other wild things."

40. Herman Melville, *Moby Dick or The Whale* (London: Oxford University Press, 1958), 24.

41. Girard, *Violence and Sacred*, 257.

42. Tzetzes, *Chiliades* 56.726–37:

> *The* pharmakos *was an ancient* katharma *(that which is thrown away in cleansing) of this sort.*
> *Should a disaster take hold of the city by divine wrath,*
> *whether it be famine or plague or some other harm,*
> *they led out as if for sacrifice the man uglier than everybody else*
> *for a purification and remedy* (pharmakon) *for the diseased city.*
> *Setting up the sacrifice* (thusia) *in a suitable place,*
> *putting in his hand cheese and barley cakes and figs,*
> *having struck him six times on his penis*
> *with squills, wild figs, and other wild things,*
> *finally they burned him with fire on wild wood*
> *and scattered the ashes into the sea to the wind*
> *for a cleansing of the diseased city, as I said.*

43. See Girard's remarks about "the stoning of the Ephesus beggar" (*Satan Fall*, 74–79). For the question whether *pharmakoi* at Athens were killed, see Hughes, *Human Sacrifice*, 149–155, 164–165.

44. Jan N. Bremmer, "Scapegoat Rituals in Ancient Greece," *Harvard Studies in Classical Philology* 87 (1983): 304.

45. Girard, *Satan Fall*, 72. Compton (*Victim*, 4) speaks of the *pharmakos* as "magic man" or "sacred-man" for the same reason but without explanation.

46. In Larry J. Bennett and Wm. Blake Tyrrell, "Making Sense of Aristophanes' *Knights*," *Arethusa* 23 (1990): 235–254, we called this process the "*pharmakos* complex," which places the emphasis on the whole as opposed to its parts. It now seems better, given

Girard's "mechanism," to see obtaining a *pharmakos* as a process.

47. When an individual's undue prominence posed a threat to everyone in the form of divine vengeance, citizens met in the agora, and anyone named by a majority of the 6,000 present was obliged to withdraw in accord with the citizens' wishes. The man selected by *ostraka* (potsherds) removed the nemesis fomenting among citizens, and his departure, while contaminating him with divine disfavor, conferred upon him the role of communal deliverer. Hence, the victim retained his citizenship and property, and after ten years was allowed to return without prejudice. For ostracism, see N. G. L. Hammond, *A History of Greece to 322 B.C.* (Oxford: Oxford University Press, 1959), 221; D. Kagan, "The Origin and Purposes of Ostracism," *Hesperia* 30 (1961): 393–401; Vernant, *Ambiguity and Reversal*, 133–135; Josiah Ober, *Mass and Elite in Democratic Athens* (Princeton: Princeton University Press, 1989), 73–74.

48. Francis D. Cornford in *The Origin of Attic Comedy*, ed. Theodor H. Gaster (Garden City, NY: Anchor Books, 1961) set the rites of Thargelia in a dramatic fertility ritual to which he believed comedy owed its origin. Presuming the historicity of this paradigm, he attempted to reproduce it in each extant play. This methodology vitiated many of Cornford's insights, since anything short of a match opened it to nitpicking, criticisms of failing to prove the existence of the paradigm, or forcing evidence into a prescribed model. See A. W. Pickard-Cambridge, *Dithyramb, Tragedy and Comedy* (Oxford: Clarendon Press, 1927), 329–349. The steps act as clues for an audience to recall what it already knows. One suffices—and it need not be the same one for everyone—for the process to be recognized.

49. Girard, *Scapegoat*, 14–19, 24–27; Compton, *Victim*, 13–18.

50. Ferdinand de Saussure, *Course in General Linguistics*, trans. W. Baskin (New York: Philosophical Library, 1959), 8–15.

51. Helladius in Photius, *Library* 534a 3; see above, note 31.

52. Antoninus Liberalis, *Metamorphoses* 25: "When plague seized all of Boeotia, and many were dying, the Boeotians dispatched ambassadors to Apollo of Gortyne. The god said to them to propitiate the two infernal deities. He said that they would stop the wrath if two maidens willingly became offerings to the twain [Persephone and Hades]. None of the maidens in the city obeyed the oracle until a hired woman brought the response to the daughters of Orion. When they found out, they were at the loom. They accepted death for the citizens before the common sickness fell upon them and killed them. Calling three times upon the spirits of the earth that they were willing offerings, they struck themselves with the shuttle beside the clavicle and made the gore break forth. Both fell to the ground. Persephone and Hades, taking pity, led stars up out of the earth. These appeared and were brought up to the heavens. All the Boeotians established in Orchomenos in Boeotia a sanctuary for these maidens. And to them each year young men and women carry propitiations."

53. Hellanicus in Jacoby, *Fragmente* 323a Fragment 23: "Codrus receives the kingship from Melanthus and died for his fatherland in the following way. When the Dorians brought war upon the Athenians, the god declared to the Dorians that they would destroy Athens if they did not kill Codrus the king. Codrus, discovering this, dressed

in humble clothes as a woodcutter. Taking an axe, he went toward the fortified camp of the enemy. When two of the enemy encountered him, he struck one and killed him. He was killed by the other who did not know who he was." Hellanicus' account is essentially repeated by the Scholiast to Plato's *Symposium* s.v. Kodros 208d: "The Dorians engaged in war against the Athenians. The god declared in an oracle that the Dorians would seize Athens if they did not murder Codrus the king. Codrus, learning this, dressed in the humble clothes as a woodcutter. He took up a sickle and went toward the fortified camp of the enemy. Two of the enemy approached him. He struck one and knocked him down. Codrus was struck by the other who did not know who he was and died."

54. Pseudo-Callisthenes in Stobaeus, *Florilegium* 3.7.66: "A chasm filled with water appeared in the city of Celaina in Phrygia on account of the wrath of Zeus Idaeus. It drew down into the depths many houses and people with them. Since the community was in danger, Midas the king received an oracle that the earth would close up if he threw the most valuable thing in human existence into the abyss. The people of Celaenas hurled gold, silver, and the women's jewelry into the chasm, but the evil did not stop. Anchurus, Midas' son, reckoning that nothing was more valuable in existence than a human life, giving his father the runaround and bidding farewell to his wife, Timothea, rushed on horseback into the place of the chasm."

55. Aelian, *Miscellaneous Stories*, 12.28: "It is said that Leon's daughters, Praxithea, Theope, and Eubole, were killed for the sake of the city of the Athenians when Leon contributed them to the city according to a Delphic oracle. For it is said that the city would not otherwise be saved unless they were slaughtered/sacrificed [*sphagiastheien* means both]." On the other hand, Erechtheus' giving of his daughter for the victory over the Eleusinians is not an instance of the *pharmakos*, as she does not offer herself willingly (Eur. *Erechth.* fr. 50 (Austin); Aelius Aristides 191 (Dindorff); Apollod. *Bib.* 3.15.4.

56. Helladios in Photius, *Library*, 534a; Harpocration, *Lexicon of the Ten Orators*, s. v. *pharmakos*. See above, note 31.

57. Hellanicus in Jacoby 1954.323a Fragment 23; see above, note 52.

58. Diogenes Laertius, 1.110.

59. Pseudo-Callisthenes in Stobaeus, *Florilegium* 3.7.66; see above, note 53.

60. Antoninus Liberalis, *Metamorphoses* 25; see above, note 51.

61. Pausanias, *Description of Greece* 9.17.1: "When war was about to break out for the Thebans and Heracles against the Orchomeneans, an oracle came to them that victory in the war would be theirs if someone who was most distinguished among the citizens for the reputation of his descent agreed to die by . . . hand. Antiopoinos, most glorious for the renown of his ancestors, did not find pleasant the idea of dying for his country, but it pleased Antiopoinos' daughters. They killed themselves, and are honored for what they did."

62. Sandor Goodhart, "Ληστὰς ἔφασκε: Oedipus and Laius' Many Murderers," *Diacritics* 8 (1978): 58–61; 58: "The oracle in Creon's report, upon which so much depends, speaks distinctly of a multiplicity of murderers." Mark R. Anspach, "Introduction," in René

Girard, *Oedipus Unbound* (Stanford, CA: Stanford University Press, 2004), xx–xxi.

63. The singular *tina*, not in agreement with the plural *tous autoentas*, is more likely to have been altered to the commonplace plural *tinas* than the reverse. Thus *tina* is the "more difficult reading"—that is, harder to understand and so more easily corrupted by *tinas*. The *lectio difficilior* is usually preferred; lack of manuscript authority for *tina*, however, causes concern. For *lectio difficilior*, see Paul Mass, *Textual Criticism*, trans. Barbara Flower (Oxford: Oxford University Press, 1958), 13.

64. Codrus: Hellanicus in Scholia to Plato, *Symposium* s.v. *Kodrus* 208d; see above, note 52. Daughters of Leon: Aelian, *Miscellaneous Stories*, 12.28 (see above, note 54), who does not describe them but they are surely beautiful. Cratinus: Athenaeus, *Deipnosophistai* 602 cd: "Renowned is what happened to Cratinus the Athenian. He was a handsome lad . . . [who] willing gave himself up for the city that nurtured him"; Anchurus: Stobaeus, *Florilegium* 3.7.66; see above, note 53.

65. Girard, *Violence and Sacred*, 77–80.

66. See Vernant, *Ambiguity and Reversal*, 118–125.

67. Goodhard, *Many Murderers*, 62–68.

68. Girard, *Violence and Sacred*, 72.

69. Ibid., 73.

70. See Larry J. Bennett and Wm. Blake Tyrrell, "Making Sense of Aristophanes' *Knights,*" *Arethusa* 23 (1990): 235–254.

71. Alan H. Sommerstein, *Knights* (Warminster, UK: Aris and Phillips, 1981), 47: "It was Demosthenes who had occupied the promontory of Pylos in Messenia and had made all preparations (Thucydides 4.29–30; cf. 4.32.4) to assault the adjacent island of Sphacteria and defeat the Spartan garrison there; but Cleon, who came out with reinforcements and commanded the attack jointly with Demosthenes, gained almost all the glory of the victory."

72. K. J. Dover, *Aristophanes Clouds* (Oxford: Oxford University Press, 1968), 106.

73. Girard, *Violence and Sacred*, 68–77.

74. W. Robert Connor, *The New Politicians of Fifth Century Athens* (Princeton, NJ: Princeton University Press, 1971), 68–75; G. E. M. De Ste. Croix, *The Origins of the Peloponnesian War* (London: Duckworth, 1972), 355–371.

75. Aristophanes, *Knights* 328–329, 384–390, 457–460, 616–623, 683–687, 836–842.

76. Pausanias 9.17.1: "It displeased Antipoinos, for his ancestry was glorious, to die for his country." See above, note 60. Antoninus Liberalis, *Metamorphoses* 25; see above, note 51.

77. Bernard M. W. Knox, "The Date of the *Oedipus Tyrannus* of Sophocles," *American Journal of Philology* 77 (1956): 144–147; Manfred Landfester, *Die Ritter des Aristophanes* (Amsterdam: B. R. Grüner, 1967), 75–78.

78. Pindar, *Olympian Ode* 9.1–4 (Snell); Francis Cornford, "*The Origin of the Olympic*

Games," in Jane Ellen Harrison, *Epilogomena to the Study of Greek Religion and Themis: A Study of the Social Origins of Greek Religion* (New Hyde Park: New York, 1962), 256.

79. Bennett and Tyrrell, *Making Sense*, 252; Carl A. Anderson, "The Gossiping Triremes of Aristophanes' *Knights*, 1300–1315," *Classical Journal* 99 (2003): 1–9.

80. Michael Kirwan, S.J., *Discovering Girard* (Cambridge, MA: Cowley Publications, 2005), 67.

81. Girard, *Things Hidden*, 30.

82. Girard, *Satan Fall*, 72.

83. The character is called Allantopoles in the manuscripts, but the term designates his trade and is not a name. Use of Sausage Seller renders the term a name, so that when we learn the character's actual name, its power as a motif of transition is diminished.

84. The noun *spondai* (libations; peace) is a feminine plural that Aristophanes visualizes as two women whom Demos asks if he can *katatriakontoutisai*. Sommerstein (*Knights*, 219) etymologizes the neologism as "to pierce them (*outasai*) three times (*tria*) with a long pole (*kontos*) from below (*kata-*)," a sign, he says, that Demos' "virility is evidently first-class."

85. Henry George Liddell and Robert Scott, *A Greek-English Lexicon*, revised supplement, rev. Henry Stuart Jones with Roderick McKenzie (Oxford: Clarendon Press, 1996), 311.

86. *Inscriptionae Graecae, consilio et auctoritate Litterarum Borussicae*, vol. 2, *Inscriptiones Atticae aetatis quae est inter Euclidis annum et Augusti tempora*, 2nd ed. (Berlin: Akademie der Wissenschaften, 1873–), 1514.48; E. Abrahams, *Ancient Greek Dress* (Chicago: Argonaut, 1964), 102: "The epithet ποικίλος [*poikilos*], applied to dress, undoubtedly means 'richly decorated,' and the ἀνθινά [*anthina*], 'flowered garments,' frequently mentioned in inscriptions, presumably refers to garments ornamented with floral designs."

87. This reading of the *batrachis* is one of the many insights that my friend, colleague, and coauthor Larry Joe Bennett came up with, but it was special, and I cannot let it go by without recognition. I still see that beautiful man sitting on the floor, having gotten out of his wheelchair on the way to "bottom walk" downstairs, gleefully explaining his gem of an idea to my wife, Mary Ann.

88. Compton, *Victim*, xi, 191n1. For Compton's discussion of Socrates, see *Victim*, 154–165, and "The Trial of the Satirist: Poetic Vitae (Aesop, Archilochus, Homer) as Background for Plato's *Apology*," *American Journal of Philology* 111 (1990): 330–347.

89. Compton, *Victim*, 13–18.

90. Compton (*Victim*, 165) lists these themes (set below in quotation marks) briefly in note 64, which I have elaborated. The numbers in parentheses denote his theme, while those in brackets give an ancient source:

(i) "Ritual pollution" as "criminal impiety" (1a1), the charges brought against Socrates [Pl. *Apol.* 24bc]; (ii) "communal disaster" (2b) in the form of young critics [39cd]; (iii) "oracle" (3), given Chaerephon by Apollo [21a]; (iv) "worst" (4)—namely, ugly (4d) [Pl. *Sym.* 215 ab, e]; poison imagery (4f) [*Phd.* 117b]; (v) "best" (5) as gift of god [Pl. *Apol.* 30d]; "sacred" (5a), divine mission [30a]; (vi) "selection by public meeting" (7), the trial of Socrates; (vii) "exile" (10a), refused [37ce]; (viii) "death" (11), discussed [40c–41a] and achieved [Pl. *Phd.* 118]; (ix) "divine persecutor-patron" (18), Apollo [Pl. *Apol.* 30a]; (x) imprisonment (21), Plato's *Crito;* (xi) "blame poet" (22); "animal fables for blame" (22c), gladfly and horse [Pl. *Apol.* 30e]; (xii) "consecration of the poet" (23a); (xiii) "conflict with political leaders" (24) [Pl. *Ep.* 325b]; (xiv) poet as soldier (26), Potidaea and Delium [Pl. *Apol.* 28e].

91. Compton, *Victim*, 164.

Chapter 3. Aristophanes' Ready Victim

1. Girard, *Evolution and Conversion*, 56.

2. The Athenians' rise to power in the ensuing decades brought them into mimetic rivalry with the Corinthians over commerce with Sicily and points west. The Corinthians did not present a model of an empire.

3. For an account of the Delian League, see John V. A. Fine, *The Ancient Greeks: A Critical History* (Cambridge, MA: Belknap Press of Harvard University Press, 1983), 329–381.

4. Eupolis, *Taxiarchoi*, fr. 357 Edmonds, whose translation I have paraphrased.

5. Ameipsias: Diogenes Laertius, 2.27. Aristophanes: Aelian, *Miscellaneous Stories* 2.13. In "Aristophanes and Socrates on Learning Practical Wisdom," *Yale Classical Studies* 26 (1980): 71, Martha Nussbaum points out that the anecdote implies that "the non-foreigners in the audience were in no perplexity about who Socrates was, or whether the character on stage was he."

6. T. B. L. Webster, *Greek Theater Production* (London: Methuen, 1956), 60; Dover, *Aristophanes*, xxxiii.

7. Pl. *Meno* 77b; *Prot.* 351b. Correct thinking about what is beneficial to the individual leads him to desire what is just; hence, faulty thinking leads to what is harmful and a source of injustice. See Brickhouse and Smith, *Socrates*, 85–92, esp. 92.

8. Nussbaum, "Aristophanes," 43–97.

9. Nussbaum, "Aristophanes," 73n58.

10. Anti-Right is Nussbaum's ("Aristophanes," 50n15) designation of the *hêttôn* (weaker, inferior) *logos*, usually rendered Wrong, of the manuscripts. Similarly, *kreittôn* (stronger, superior), is given as Right. Anti-Right reproduces the action of Hetton "to speak against (anti-) conventions (*nomoi*) and customs" (1104). On the names of these characters, see Dover, *Clouds*, lvii–lviii, who settles on "Right" and "Wrong."

11. Nussbaum, "Aristophanes," 70.

12. Ibid., 74. Nussbaum refers to the description of the elenchus in *Sophist:* "They question a man on these matters where he thinks he is saying something, although he is really saying nothing. And as he is confused, they easily convict his opinions, by bringing

them together and pitting them side by side, and thus showing that they are contrary to each other at the same time in the same respect about the same things" (230b).

13. Nussbaum, "Aristophanes," 76.

14. W. Robert Connor, "The Razing of the House in Greek Society," *Transactions and Proceedings of the American Philological Association* 115 (1985): 86, 88n29.

15. Nussbaum, "Aristophanes," 78.

16. Albin Lesky, *A History of Greek Literature*, trans. James Willis and Cornelis de Heer (New York: Crowell, 1966), 230, 370.

17. Nussbaum, "Aristophanes," 86.

18. Nightingale, *Genres*, 63.

19. Nussbaum, "Aristophanes," 82–88.

20. In *Greek Laughter: A Study of Cultural Psychology from Homer to Early Christianity* (Cambridge: Cambridge University Press, 2008), 255, Stephen Halliwell points out that Plato distinguishes between the nonsense of the comic and "those who over the years have maligned Socrates with real 'malice and denigration' (φθόνῳ καὶ διαβολῇ 18d)."

21. Dover, *Clouds*, li.

22. Ibid., lxxx–xcviii.

23. Girard, *Satan Fall*, 32.

24. Ibid., 33.

25. Ibid., 34.

26. Ibid., 32.

27. Dover, *Clouds*, lxxix.

28. Nussbaum, "Aristophanes," 66–67.

29. Halliwell, *Greek Laughter*, 245–246.

30. Jeffrey Henderson, *The Maculate Muse: Obscene Language in Attic Comedy*, 2nd ed. (New York: Oxford University Press, 1991), 77.

31. Charles Segal, "Aristophanes' Cloud-Chorus," *Arethusa* 2 (1969): 152.

32. A. M. Bowie, *Aristophanes: Myth, Ritual, and Comedy* (Cambridge: Cambridge University Press, 1993), 130.

33. Dover, *Clouds*, lxix.

34. *Philotês* and its derivatives belong to a vocabulary of moral terms that is "strongly permeated by values which are not personal but relational" (Emile Benveniste, *Indo-European Language and Society*, trans. Elizabeth Palmer [London: Faber & Faber, 1973], 278–282).

35. Dover, *Clouds*, 264.

36. Ibid.

37. Connor, *Razing*, 79–102.

38. Girard, *Satan Fall*, 23.

Chapter 4. Foundation Murder

Unless otherwise noted, all in-line references in this chapter are to Plato, *Apologia Socratous* in *Platonis Opera*, vol. 1, edited by John Burnet (Oxford: Oxford University Press, 1900).

1. For shame culture in Homer, see Dodds, *Greeks and the Irrational*, 17–18.

2. Barry S. Strauss, *Athens after the Peloponnesian War: Class Faction and Policy 403–386 B.C.* (Ithaca, NY: Cornell University Press, 1986), 32.

3. Hammond, *History*, 448.

4. Ibid.; Strauss, *Class Faction*, 114.

5. G. B. Kerferd, *The Sophistic Movement* (Cambridge: Cambridge University Press, 1981), 56: "There should be no real doubt that he was so regarded [as a sophist] by his contemporaries."

6. http://en.wikipedia.org/wiki/Jonas_Salk.

7. Montuori, *Socrates*, 79–86.

8. The Athenians did not have a public prosecutor. Any citizen could act on behalf of the city by bringing an indictment as *ho boulomenos*, the one willing. To avoid frivolous indictments, he had to obtain the vote of at least 20 percent of the jurors or be fined.

9. For Plato's *Euthyphro*, see Taylor, *Plato*, 146–156; Guthrie, *Plato*, 101–124; Laszlo Versényi, *Holiness and Justice: An Interpretation of Plato's* Euthyphro (Washington, DC: University Press of America, 1982).

10. W. K. C. Guthrie, *Socrates* (Cambridge: Cambridge University Press, 1971), 66–67.

11. Nails, *People*, 102.

12. Dover, *Clouds*, 78, 80.

13. In *The Mask of Socrates: The Image of the Intellectual in Antiquity*, trans. Alan Shapiro (Berkeley: University of California Press, 1995), 32, Paul Zanker points out that "as in many cultures, the Greeks tended to dismiss the unpopular, the marginalized, and the dissident as physically defective and ugly." Zanker speculates that although Socrates was ugly, he was probably not unique in this regard. "That his unfortunate appearance became such a focus of attention must derive from the offensive nature of his intellectual activities" (34). Zanker speaks of portraits of Socrates, the earliest of which "originated about ten to twenty years after his death" (34).

14. Zanker, *Mask*, 12.

15. "He [Agamemnon] has dishonored me, for he has taken my prize and keeps it, seizing it himself" [Homer, *Iliad*], and "For surely, son of Atreus, you would revile him [Achilles] now for the last time" (2.242–1.232). Thersites recalls Achilles' accusation of Agamemnon for being greedy (1.222–2.225–233) and letting others carry the load (1.163–168–2.229–233), and harming his people (1.231–2.234), and that it would be better to leave for home (1.169–171–2.236–238).

16. Compton, *Victim*, 183: "Thersites, a sort of epic *pharmakos*."

17. Nicole Loraux, *The Children of Athena*, trans. Caroline Levine (Princeton, NJ: Princeton University Press, 1993), 3–21, 37–71.

18. Similarly, Crito laments not being of "use" to Socrates in avoiding the trial and its aftermath (Pl. *Cri.* 46a). As Adkins, *Merit and Responsibility*, 231, observes, "Whether called *agathos polites* or *agathos*, he [the ordinary man] is a self-sufficient unity, able to defend both himself and his friends."

19. Versényi, *Holiness and Justice*, 120–124: "As for the *Euthyphro* itself, and in the context of the other related dialogues' discussion of love and the gods, there is but one conclusion that can be drawn: Whether or not perfect gods exist—whatever such 'existence' might mean in view of the perfection of the gods—they can in no way enter into human affairs. We can no more seek to improve or serve them in any way than they can improve or seek to improve, or love, or concern themselves with us or anything in any way whatsoever" (124).

20. Brickhouse and Smith, *Socrates on Trial*, 1n2, point out that "to the best of our knowledge" only G. A. Ast, *Platons Leben und Schriften* (Leipzig: Weidmann, 1819) and J. Zürcher, *Das Corpus Academicum in neuer Auffassung dargestellt* (Paderborn: J. Schöningh, 1954) "have doubted the authenticity of Plato's *Ap.*"

21. Brickhouse and Smith, *Socrates on Trial*, 1–2.

22. Montuori, *Socrates*, 79–86.

23. Brickhouse and Smith, *Socrates on Trial*, 2.

24. Brickhouse and Smith, *Socrates on Trial*, 3n9. Socrates rebukes Polus for trying to refute him by supplying "many witnesses," as if truth were susceptible to the decisions of a court trial (Plato, *Gorgias* 471e). Also Plato, *Laches* 184d.

25. Brickhouse and Smith, *Socrates on Trial*, 2–3.

26. Burnett, *Phaedo*, 9, on *Phaedo* 59b.

27. Patrick Stewart, *Patrick Stewart Performs Charles Dickens' A Christmas Carol*, Audio CD, 79382-9, Simon & Schuster, 1991.

28. Brickhouse and Smith, *Socrates on Trial*, 4.

29. Ibid., 5.

30. Ibid.

31. Ibid., 6.

32. Ibid., 6n2: "Xenophon's version is explicitly based upon second-hand information, whereas Plato was actually at the trial."

33. For ancient biography, see Janet Fairweather, "Fiction in the Biographies Ancient Writers," *Ancient Society* 5 (1974): 231–242. Zanker, *Masks*, 10, notes that the Greeks sought "the true meaning of a figure" in the body as opposed to the head and used "the portrait statue . . to put on display society's accepted values, through the example of worthy individuals, for a didactic purpose. Personal and biographical details were of lesser importance."

34. In 74 BCE, Cicero successfully defended Aulus Cluentius Habitus against a charge of poisoning. Quintilian (*Institutio Oratio* 2.17.21) records Cicero's boast that "he had poured darkness (*tenebras*) on the eyes of the judges." *Tenebras* has come to be rendered "dust." Athenian audiences in assemblies and the courts certainly had to have enjoyed what one speaker said and looked forward to the rebuttal of the other. In *Phaedrus*, Socrates speaks of the speaker's skill: "Will not skill in doing this [speaking of the just and unjust] make the same case seem to the same people to be just and, whenever they wish, unjust?" (261c).

35. Montuori, *Socrates*, 201–203.

36. Strauss, *Class Faction*, 90–104.

37. Burnet, *Plato's Euthyphro*, 74: "Anytus and his friends were working hard to restore the πάτριος πολιτεία (i.e., the moderate democracy of the days before the Peloponnesian War), and the Socratic criticism must have seemed dangerous to him."

38. Diogenes Laertius preserves the story that the Athenians were so taken by remorse that "they banished the other prosecutors and put Meletus to death" (2.43).

39. Montuori, *Socrates*, 211.

40. Ibid.

41. Ibid., 212.

42. Ibid., 205; Diogenes Laertius, 2.7, 60, 65; 3.35, 36; 6.1, 7; 6.2.26.

43. Cicero, *Orator ad M. Brutum* 1.231; [Plutarch], *Moralia* 836b; Diogenes Laertius 2.40: "'How, Lysias asked, if the speech is a fine one, would it not suit you?' And Socrates replied: 'Would not fine clothes and sandals not suit me?'"

44. Montuori, *Socrates*, 206.

45. Burnet, *Plato's Euthyphro*, 68.

46. Brickhouse and Smith, *Socrates on Trial*, 25.

47. Anytus and Socrates were acquainted. Socrates hints at Anytus' inferiority in comparison with his father (Plato, *Meno* 90a) and prophesizes that his son will turn out a drunkard (Xenophon, *Apology of Socrates* 30).

48. For a biography of Lycon, Anytus, and Meletus, see Nails, *People*, 188–189, 37–38, 202.

49. By providing a description of both Meletus and Socrates, Plato encourages his reader

to watch their drama in "the theatre of the mind," for "the written quotation of any spoken sentence is a very incomplete transcript of what was conveyed by the utterance itself" (O. Taplin, *Greek Tragedy in Action* [Berkeley: University of California Press, 1978], 2, 3).

50. For the points of beauty in a beloved, see K. J. Dover, *Greek Homosexuality* (Cambridge, MA: Harvard University Press, 1978), 68–81.

51. Lysias 19.1–2; Isocrates 10.1; Aeschines 2.24; Brickhouse and Smith, *Socrates on Trial*, 49–53.

52. Burnet, *Plato's Euthyphro*, 77.

53. Girard, *Satan Fall*, 21–22.

54. Ibid., 19.

55. Ibid., 57.

56. Ibid., 52. Girard has in mind "the sacrifices of people called *pharmakoi*" (51, 51n3).

57. F. C. Conybeare, *Philostratus: The Life of Apollonius of Tyana, The Epistles of Apollonius and the Treatise of Eusebius*, 2 vols. (New York: Macmillan, 1912), 362–367.

58. Girard, *Satan Fall*, 56.

59. Ibid., 53.

60. H. W. Parke, and D. E. W. Wormell, *The Delphic Oracle* (Oxford: Blackwell, 1956), 402.

61. Ibid.

62. Brickhouse and Smith, *Socrates on Trial*, 89.

63. So Montuori contends (*Socrates*, 221–222).

64. Socrates is quoting from Euripides' *Melanippe the Philosopher* (fr. 484 Nauk). See also Plato, *Symposium* 177a; Burnet, *Plato's Euthyphro*, 89.

65. For portrait frames, see Clay, *Origins*, 23–31, who asserts that "the frame dialogues (*Phaedo, Theaetetus, Parmenides*, and *Symposium*) give the impression of historical accuracy and present themselves as the scrupulous record of the sources of our knowledge of past events. In them we encounter the sources and guarantors of our knowledge of Socrates." But, as Clay concludes, "when the curtain closes, we realize that it is Plato himself who is the ultimate authority for the Socratic dialogues that are his creations" (29).

66. Nails, *People*, 86.

67. Parke and Wormell, *Oracle*, 393.

68. Ibid., 99: no. 244 (Valerius Maximus 7.1.2).

69. Ibid., 99: no. 245 (Diogenes Laertius, 1.106).

70. Ibid., 385; Herodotus 1.29–33.

Notes
171

71. Burnet, *Plato's Euthyphro*, 90.

72. Gomme, *Ten Years' War*, 103.

73. Gouldner, *Enter Plato*, 56.

74. Thucydides 2.35.2.

75. *The Man Who Would Be King* (1975), directed by John Huston and starring Sean Connery and Michael Caine.

76. Robinson, *Dialectic*, 7–10.

77. Clay, *Origins*, 95: "In Plato's *Apology* and throughout the Socratic dialogues, Socratic irony makes the questions with which Socrates is engaged seem impersonal. What Socratic irony is meant to foster is the search for enlightenment free from both the entanglements of pride and the authority of a dominating philosophical personality in possession of the truth."

78. Girard, *Satan Fall*, 16–17.

79. Robinson, *Dialectic*, 17.

80. Girard, *Scapegoat*, 6.

81. Ibid., 12–23.

82. Ibid., 17.

83. G. S. Kirk, "Methodological Reflections on the Myths of Heracles" in *Il mito greco: Atti del Convegno internazionale (Urbino 7–12 maggio 1973)*, ed. B. Gentili and G. Paioni, 285–297 (Rome: Edizioni dell' Ateneo & Bizzarri, 1977), 286.

84. Guthrie, *Socrates*, 149–150.

85. Gouldner, *Enter Plato*, 45–55.

86. Ibid., 78–96.

87. Xenophon, *History of Greece* 1.6.34–7.35; Diodorus Siculus 13.100–3.2; George Grote, *History of Greece*, vol. 8 (1859; reprint, New York: Harper & Brothers, 1959), 173–210; Hammond, *History*, 415–416.

88. Parke, *Festivals*, 88–92.

89. Girard, *Satan Fall*, 24–25.

90. Ibid., 19.

91. Grote, *History*, 195.

92. Ibid., 203.

93. Ibid., 200–201; Xenophon, *History of Greece* 1.7.14; *Memorabilia* 1.1.18, 4.4.2.

94. James G. Williams, *The Bible, Violence, and the Sacred: Liberation from the Myth of Sanctioned Violence* (New York: HarperCollins, 1991), 189.

95. Girard, *Satan Fall*, 13.

96. Burnet, *Plato's Euthyphro*, 149; A. W. R. Harrison, *Law of Athens* (Oxford: Clarendon Press, 1971), 2.80–82.

97. Henry Cary, *The Works of Plato*, vol. 1, *The Apology of Socrates, Crito, Phaedo, Gorgias, Protagoras, Phaedrus, Theaetetus, Euthyphron, Lysis* (London: George Bell & Sons, 1901), 23.

98. Emile Benveniste, *Indo-European Language*, 340–345.

99. Thomas G. West, *Plato's Apology of Socrates: An Interpretation, with a New Translation* (Ithaca, NY: Cornell University Press, 1979), 64n107.

100. Clay, *Origins*, 94. Clay goes on, however, to state: "But there is another point of view shared by Socrates and the Delphic oracle that contemplates his irony from higher ground and sees it as sincere" (94).

101. West, *Plato's Apology*, 212. Socrates' counterpenalty, its content, and its status as a counterpenalty, have occasioned much discussion. See Brickhouse and Smith, *Socrates on Trial*, 214–221.

102. See chapter 2, note 35.

103. Benveniste, *Indo-European Language*, 346–356; Leslie Kurke, *The Traffic in Praise: Pindar and the Poetics of Social Economy* (Ithaca, NY: Cornell University Press, 1991), 206; Wm. Blake Tyrrell, *Smell of Sweat: Greek Athletics, Olympics, and Culture* (Wauconda, IL: Bolchazy-Carducci Publishers, 2004), 224–225.

104. Kurke, *Traffic in Praise*, 206.

105. Benveniste, *Indo-European Language*, 346.

106. Ibid., 348.

107. Herodotus 5.71; Thucydides 1.126; Plutarch, *Solon* 12; Hammond, *History*, 155–156.

108. Kurke, *Traffic in Praise*, 203–205.

109. A. Andrewes, *The Greek Tyrants* (New York: Harper & Row, 1963), 84, 110.

110. Marcel Detienne, *Dionysus Slain*, trans. Mireille Muellner and Leonard Muellner (Baltimore: Johns Hopkins University Press, 1979), 58–59. See also Vernant, *Ambiguity and Reversal*, 226–227.

111. Vernant, *Ambiguity and Reversal*, 227.

112. Kurke, *Traffic in Praise*, 215.

113. Ibid., 215–216.

114. Ibid., 214–218.

115. The father, carrying the infant, runs around the hearth on the fifth day of the infant's life, ending its marginal state between life and death (Burkert, *Greek Religion*, 255).

116. Pisistratus dressed a tall young woman as Athena and, standing beside her in a chariot, proclaimed through heralds, "O Athenians, receive with good intentions Pisistratus whom Athena herself has honored most among men and leads back home to her

acropolis" (Herodotus 1.60.4–5). For this "ceremony," see W. Robert Connor, "Tribes, Festivals and Processions: Civic Ceremonial and Political Manipulation in Archaic Greece," *Journal of Hellenic Studies* 107 (1987): 42–47.

117. Homer, *Odyssey* 11.215–224; Richard Broxton Onians, *The Origins of European Thought About the Body, the Mind, the Soul, the World, Time and Fate: New Interpretations of Greek, Roman and Kindred Evidence Also of Some Basic Jewish and Christian Beliefs* (Cambridge: Cambridge University Press, 1988), 59–61.

118. Young, *Olympic Myth*, 117.

119. Thus there is, as law dictates, one *antitimesis*, that of a fine, as Brickhouse and Smith, *Socrates on Trial*, 219–212, rightly contend.

120. Girard, *Satan Fall*, 72.

121. Ibid., 138.

122. Girard, *Scapegoat*, 15.

123. Girard, *Satan Fall*, 138. The context is Paul's *Letter to Colossians* (2.14–15) in the translation given in *Satan Falling*: "[Christ has] cancelled the accusation that stands against us with its legal claims. He set it aside, nailing it to the cross. He thus disarmed the principalities and powers and made a public spectacle of them, drawing them along with this triumph" (137).

124. Eustathius, *Commentary to Homer's* Iliad 1089 in Burnet, *Plato's Euthyphro*, 164.

125. Girard, *Things Hidden*, 171.

126. Ibid., 172.

127. Ibid., 173.

128. Gouldner, *Enter Plato*, 53.

129. James A. Coulter, "The Relation of the *Apology of Socrates* to Gorgias' *Defense of Palamedes* and Plato's Critique of Gorgianic Rhetoric," *Harvard Studies in Classical Philology* 68 (1964): 269–303. The quotation is found on page 296.

130. The translation is Burnet's in *Plato's Euthyphro*, 156.

131. Guthrie, *Socrates*, 64–65.

132. Adkins, *Merit and Responsibility*, 230–232.

133. Ibid., 31–38, 156–163.

134. Ibid., 53–71.

135. See Gouldner, *Enter Plato*, 52–55, especially page 54 for dysfunctions inherent in the contest/competitive system.

136. *Agathos* (ἀγαθός) is the adjective of *aretê*. Callicles states boldly, "To suffer this, being done injustice, is not the condition of a man (*anêr*), but of a slave who, when done injustice and smeared with mud, cannot come to his own aid or that of someone for whom he cares" (Plato, *Gorgias* 483ab).

137. Gil Bailie, "Sacrificial Violence in Homer's *Iliad*," in *Curing Violence*, ed. Mark I. Wallace and Theophus H. Smith (Sonoma, CA: Polebridge Press, 1994), 45–70.

138. Thucydides 6.61.4–7; Hammond, *History*, 391.

139. For Alcibiades' reasons for defecting from Athenians, see David Gribble, *Alcibiades and Athens: A Study in Literary Presentation* (Oxford: Oxford University Press, 1999), 55–61, who contends that "the tension which led to Alcibiades' split with the city was between purely personal and civic values" (55).

140. Bandera, *Sacred Game*, 59.

141. Ibid., 52.

142. Ibid., 53–54.

143. Ibid., 59.

144. Ibid.

145. The image of the ship lost at sea comes from *anatetraphthai* (Pl. *Cri.* 50b) from *anatrepô*, "the *vox propria* for the 'capsizing' of a vessel" (Burnet, *Plato's Euthyphro*, 201).

146. Girard, *Scapegoat*, 12–17.

147. Ibid., 17.

148. What Muhammad Ali once said is appropriate: "The man who views the world at 50 the same as he did at 20 has wasted 30 years of his life." http://www.10ktruth.com/the_quotes/ali.htm.

149. Bandera, *Sacred Game*, 61.

150. Ibid., 61.

151. G. M. A. Grube, *Plato's Thought* (Boston: Beacon Hill, 1958), 125: the soul (*psychê*) "does not include anything beyond the reason or intellect." Similarly, Grube, *Plato's Thought*, 327n2: "mind or intelligence."

152. Jean-Pierre Vernant, *Mortals and Immortals: Collected Essays*, ed. Froma I. Zeitlin (Princeton, NJ: Princeton University Press, 1991), 50–74.

153. Vernant, *Mortals and Immortals*, 64.

154. Ibid., 187–189.

155. Derrida, *Pharmacy*, 126–127.

156. Enid Bloch, "Hemlock Poisoning and the Death of Socrates," in *The Trial and Execution of Socrates*, ed. Thomas C. Brickhouse and Nicholas D. Smith (New York: Oxford University Press, 2002), 258.

Bibliography

Abrahams, E. *Ancient Greek Dress*. Chicago: Argonaut, 1964.

Adkins, Arthur W. H. *Merit and Responsibility: A Study in Greek Values*. Chicago: University of Chicago Press, 1960.

Anderson, Carl A. "The Gossiping Triremes of Aristophanes' *Knights*, 1300–1315." *Classical Journal* 99 (2003): 1–9.

Andrewes, A. *The Greek Tyrants*. New York: Harper & Row, 1963.

Anspach, Mark R. "Introduction." In René Girard, *Oedipus Unbound,* edited by Mark. R. Anspach, vii–liv. Stanford, CA: Stanford University Press, 2004.

Bailie, Gil. "Sacrificial Violence in Homer's *Iliad*." In *Curing Violence,* edited by Mark I. Wallace and Theophus H. Smith, 45–70. Sonoma, CA: Polebridge Press, 1994.

Bandera, Cesáreo. *The Sacred Game: The Role of the Sacred in the Genesis of Modern Literary Fiction*. University Park: Pennsylvania State University Press, 1994.

Bennett, Larry J., and Wm. Blake Tyrrell. "Making Sense of Aristophanes' *Knights*." *Arethusa* 23 (1990): 235–254.

Benveniste, Émile. *Indo-European Language and Society*. Translated by Elizabeth Palmer London: Faber & Faber, 1973.

Bloch, Enid. "Hemlock Poisoning and the Death of Socrates." In *The Trial and Execution of Socrates*. Edited by Thomas C. Brickhouse and Nicholas D. Smith, 255–278. New York: Oxford University Press, 2002.

Blundell, Sue. *Women in Ancient Greece.* Cambridge, MA: Harvard University Press, 1955.

Boas, George. "Fact and Legend in the Biography of Plato." *Philosophical Review* 57 (1948): 439–457.

Bowie, A. M. *Aristophanes: Myth, Ritual, and Comedy.* Cambridge, UK: Cambridge University Press, 1993.

Bremmer, Jan N. "Scapegoat Rituals in Ancient Greece." *Harvard Studies in Classical Philology* 87 (1983): 299–320.

Brickhouse, Thomas C., and Nicholas D. Smith. *Plato's Socrates.* New York: Oxford University Press, 1994.

———. *Socrates on Trial.* Princeton: Princeton University Press, 1989.

Burkert, Walter. *Greek Religion.* Translated by J. Raffan. Cambridge, MA: Harvard University Press, 1985.

———. *Homo Necans: The Anthropology of Ancient Greek Sacrificial Ritual and Myth.* Translated by Peter Bing. Berkeley: University of California Press, 1983.

Burnett, John. *Plato's Euthyphro, Apology of Socrates, and Crito.* Oxford: Oxford University Press, 1924.

———. *Plato's Phaedo.* Oxford: Oxford University Press, 1911.

Bury, R. G. *The Symposium of Plato.* 2nd. ed. Cambridge, UK: W. Heffer & Sons, 1932.

Carter, L. B. *The Quiet Athenian.* Oxford: Oxford University Press, 1986.

Cary, Henry. *The Works of Plato.* Vol. 1: *The Apology of Socrates, Crito, Phaedo, Gorgias, Protagoras, Phaedrus, Theaetetus, Euthyphron, Lysis.* London: George Bell & Sons, 1901.

Cervantes Saavedra, Miguel de. *The Ingenious Hidalgo Don Quixote de la Mancha.* New York: Penguin, 2003.

Chroust, Anton-Hermann. *Socrates, Man and Myth: The Two Socratic Apologies of Xenophon.* Notre Dame, IA: University of Notre Dame Press, 1957.

Clay, Diskin. "The Origins of the Socratic Dialogue." In *The Socratic Movement,* edited by Paul A. Vander Waerdt, 23–47. Ithaca, NY: Cornell University Press, 1994.

———. *Platonic Questions: Dialogues with the Silent Philosopher.* University Park, PA: Pennsylvania State University Press, 2000.

Compton, Todd M. "The Trial of the Satirist: Poetic Vitae (Aesop, Archilochus, Homer) as Background for Plato's *Apology.*" *American Journal of Philology* 111 (1990): 330–347.

———. *Victim of the Muses: Poet as Scapegoat, Warrior, and Hero in Greco-Roman and Indo-European Myth and History.* Washington, DC: Harvard University Press, 2006.

Connor, W. Robert. *The New Politicians of Fifth Century Athens.* Princeton, NJ: Princeton University Press, 1971.

———. "The Razing of the House in Greek Society." *Transactions and Proceedings of the American Philological Association* 115 (1985): 79–102.

———. "Tribes, Festivals and Processions: Civic Ceremonial and Political Manipulation in Archaic Greece." *Journal of Hellenic Studies* 107 (1987): 40–50.

Conybeare, F. C. *Philostratus: The Life of Apollonius of Tyana, The Epistles of Apollonius and the Treatise of Eusebius.* 2 vols. London: William Heinemann and New York: Macmillan, 1912.

Cornford, Francis D. *The Origin of Attic Comedy.* 1919. Edited by Theodor H. Gaster. Garden City, NY: Anchor Books, 1961.

———. *The Origin of the Olympic Games.* In *Jane Ellen Harrison. Epilogomena to the Study of Greek Religion and Themis: A Study of the Social Origins of Greek Religion,* 212–259. 1921. New Hyde Park: New York, 1962.

Coulter, James A. "The Relation of the *Apology of Socrates* to Gorgias' *Defense of Palamedes* and Plato's Critique of Gorgianic Rhetoric." *Harvard Studies in Classical Philology* 68 (1964): 269–303.

Davidson, J. F. "The Parodos of the Antigone: A Poetic Study." *Bulletin of the Institute of Classical Studies of the University of London* 30 (1983): 41–51.

Davidson, James. *Courtesans and Fishcakes: The Consuming Passions of Classical Athens.* New York: St. Martin's Press, 1997.

De Ste. Croix, G. E. M. *The Origins of the Peloponnesian War.* London: Duckworth, 1972.

Derrida, Jacques. "Plato's Pharmacy." In *Dissemination,* 61–171. Translated by Barbara Johnson. Chicago: University of Chicago Press, 1981.

Detienne, Marcel. *Dionysus Slain.* Translated by Mireille Muellner and Leonard Muellner. Baltimore: Johns Hopkins University Press, 1979.

Deubner, Ludwig. *Attische Feste.* 1932. Hildesheim, Germany: Georg Oolms, 1966.

Dodds, E. R. *The Greeks and the Irrational.* Berkeley: University of California Press, 1951.

———. *Plato Gorgias: A Revised Text with Introduction and Commentary.* Oxford: Oxford University Press, 1959.

Donlan, Walter. *The Aristocratic Ideal in Ancient Greece: Attitudes of Superiority from Homer to the End of the Fifth Century B.C.* Lawrence, KS: Coronado Press, 1980.

Dover, K. J. *Aristophanes* Clouds. Oxford: Oxford University Press, 1968.

———. *Greek Homosexuality.* Cambridge, MA: Harvard University Press, 1978.

Dunbar, Nan. *Aristophanes* Birds. Oxford: Oxford University Press, 1995.

Durand, Jean-Louis. "Greek Animals: Toward a Topology of Edible Bodies." In *The Cuisine of Sacrifice among the Greeks,* edited by Marcel Detienne and Jean-Pierre Vernant, 87–118. Translated by Paula Wissing. Chicago: University of Chicago Press, 1989.

Edmonds, J. M. *The Fragments of Attic Comedy after Meineke, Bergk, and Kock.* Leiden: E. J. Brill, 1957.

Fairweather, Janet. "Fiction in the Biographies Ancient Writers." *Ancient Society* 5 (1974): 231–242.

Field, G. C. *Plato and His Contemporaries: A Study in Fourth-Century Life and Thought.* 3rd ed. Frome, UK: Methuen, 1967.

Fine, John V. A. *The Ancient Greeks: A Critical History.* Cambridge, MA: Harvard University Press, 1983.

Foley, Helene P. *Ritual Irony: Poetry and Sacrifice in Euripides.* Ithaca, NY: Cornell University Press, 1985.

Fontenrose, J. "The Hero as Athlete." *California Studies in Classical Antiquity* 1 (1968): 73–104.

Ford, Andrew. "The Classical Definition of Ῥαψῳδία." *Classical Philology* 83 (1988): 300–307.

Frankfurt, Harry G. *On Bullshit.* Princeton, NJ: Princeton University Press, 2005.

Gagarin, Michael. "Socrates' *Hubris* and Alcibiades' Failure." *Phoenix* 31 (1977): 22–37.

Garland, Robert. "The Well-Ordered Corpse: An Investigation into the Motives behind Greek Funerary Legislation." *Bulletin of the Institute of Classical Studies of the University of London* 36 (1989): 1–15.

Girard, René. *Deceit, Desire and the Novel: Self and Other in Literary Structure.* Translated by Yvonne Freccero. Baltimore: Johns Hopkins University Press, 1966.

———. *I See Satan Fall Like Lightning.* Translated by James G. Williams. Maryknoll, NY: Orbis Books, 2001.

———. *Oedipus Unbound: Selected Writings on Rivalry and Desire.* Edited with an introduction by Mark R. Anspach. Stanford, CA: Stanford University Press, 2004.

———. "The Plague in Literature and Myth." *Texas Studies in Literature and Language* 15 (1974): 833–850.

———. *The Scapegoat.* Translated by Yvonne Freccero. Baltimore: Johns Hopkins University Press, 1986.

———. *A Theater of Envy: William Shakespeare.* New York: Oxford University Press, 1991.

———. *Things Hidden since the Foundation of the World.* Translated by Stephen Bann and Michael Metteer. Stanford, CA: Stanford University Press, 1987.

———. *Violence and the Sacred.* Translated by Patrick Gregory. Baltimore: Johns Hopkins University Press, 1977.

Girard, René, with Pierpaolo Antonello and João Cezar de Castro Rocha. *Evolution and Conversion: Dialogues on the Origins of Culture.* New York and London: Continuum International Publishing, 2007.

Golsan, Richard J. *René Girard and Myth: An Introduction.* New York and London: Garland Publishing, 1993.

Gomme, A. W. *A Historical Commentary on Thucydides. The Ten Years' War.* Vol. 2, *Books II–III.* Oxford: Oxford University Press, 1956.

Gomme, A. W., A. Andrewes, and K. J. Dover. *A Historical Commentary on Thucydides*. Vol. 4, *Books V 25–VII*. Oxford: Oxford University Press, 1970.

Goodhart, Sandor. "Ληστὰς Ἔφασκε: Oedipus and Laius' Many Murderers." *Diacritics* 8 (1978): 55–71.

Gouldner, Alvin W. *Enter Plato: Classical Greece and the Origins of Social Theory*. New York: Basic Books, 1965.

Gribble, David. *Alcibiades and Athens: A Study in Literary Presentation*. Oxford: Oxford University Press, 1999.

Grote, George. *History of Greece*. Vol. 8. New York: Harper & Brothers, 1859.

Grube, G. M. A. *Plato's Thought*. Boston: Beacon Hill, 1958.

Gurd, Sean Alexander. *Iphigenias at Aulis: Textual Multiplicity, Radical Philology*. Ithaca: Cornell University Press, 2005.

Guthrie, W. K. C. *A History of Greek Philosophy*. Vol. 3, *The Fifth-Century Enlightenment*. Cambridge: Cambridge University Press, 1969.

———. *A History of Greek Philosophy*. Vol. 4, *Plato—The Man and His Dialogues: Earlier Period*. Cambridge: Cambridge University Press, 1975.

———. *Socrates*. Cambridge: Cambridge University Press, 1971.

Hall, Edith. *Inventing the Barbarian: Greek Self-Definition through Tragedy*. Oxford: Oxford University Press, 1989.

Halliwell, Stephen. *Greek Laughter: A Study of Cultural Psychology from Homer to Early Christianity*. Cambridge: Cambridge University Press, 2008.

Hammond, N. G. L. *A History of Greece to 322 B.C.* Oxford: Oxford University Press, 1959.

Harriott, Rosemary. *Poetry and Criticism before Plato*. London: Methuen, 1969.

Harrison, A. W. R. *The Law of Athens*. 2 Vols. Oxford: Clarendon Press, 1971.

Harrison, Jane Ellen. *Epilegomena to the Study of Greek Religion and Themis: A Study of the Social Origins of Greek Religion*. 1912. New Hyde Park, NY: University Books 1962.

———. *Prolegomena to the Study of Greek Religion*. Cambridge: Cambridge University Press, 1903.

Henderson, Jeffrey. *The Maculate Muse: Obscene Language in Attic Comedy*. 2nd ed. New York: Oxford University Press, 1991.

Hughes, Dennis D. *Human Sacrifice in Ancient Greece*. London: Routledge, 1991.

Inscriptionae Graecae, consilio et auctoritate Litterarum Borussicae. Berlin: Akademie der Wissenschaften, 1873– . Vol. 2: *Inscriptiones Atticae aetatis quae est inter Euclidis annum et Augusti tempora*.

Jacoby, F. *Die Fragmente der griechischen Historiker*. Vol. 3. Leiden, Netherlands: E. L. Brill, 1954.

Joyce, Michael, trans. "Symposium." In *The Collected Dialogues of Plato.* Bollingen Series, 71. Edited by Edith Hamilton and Huntington Cairns, 526–574. Pantheon Books: New York, 1961.

Kagan, D. "The Origin and Purposes of Ostracism." *Hesperia* 30 (1961): 393–401.

Kahn, Charles H. "Aeschines on Socratic Eros." In *The Socratic Movement,* edited by Paul A. Vander Waerdt, 87–106. Ithaca, NY: Cornell University Press, 1994.

Kennedy, George. *The Art of Persuasion in Greece.* Princeton, NJ: Princeton University Press, 1963.

Kerferd, G. B. *The Sophistic Movement.* Cambridge: Cambridge University Press, 1981.

Kirk, G. S. *The Songs of Homer.* Cambridge: Cambridge University Press, 1962.

———. "Methodological Reflections on the Myths of Heracles." In *Il mito greco: Atti del Convegno internazionale (Urbino 7–12 maggio 1973),* edited by B. Gentili and G. Paioni, 285–297. Rome: Edizioni dell' Ateneo & Bizzarri, 1977.

Kirwan, Michael, SJ. *Discovering Girard.* Cambridge, MA: Cowley Publications, 2005.

Klinkenborg, Verlyn. "If It Weren't for the Ox, We Wouldn't Be Where We Are." *Smithsonian* 24 (1993): 82–93.

Knox, Bernard M. W. "The Date of *the Oedipus Tyrannus* of Sophocles." *American Journal of Philology* 77 (1956): 144–147.

Kurke, Leslie. *The Traffic in Praise: Pindar and the Poetics of Social Economy.* Ithaca, NY: Cornell University Press, 1991.

Landfester, Manfred. *Die Ritter des Aristophanes.* Amsterdam: B. R. Grüner, 1967.

Lesky, Albin. *A History of Greek Literature.* Translated by James Willis and Cornelis de Heer. New York: Crowell, 1966.

Liddell, Henry George, and Robert Scott. *A Greek-English Lexicon. Revised Supplement.* Edited by Henry Stuart Jones with Roderick McKenzie. Oxford: Clarendon Press, 1996.

Loraux, Nicole. *The Children of Athena.* Translated by Caroline Levine. Princeton, N.J.: Princeton University Press, 1993.

Maas, Paul. *Textual Criticism.* Translated by Barbara Flower. Oxford: Oxford University Press, 1958.

Macleod, Colin. *Collected Essays.* Oxford: Oxford University Press, 1983.

Melville, Herman. *Moby Dick or the Whale.* 1920. London: Oxford University Press: 1958.

Miller, Stephen G. *The Prytaneion: Its Function and Architectural Form.* Berkeley: University of California Press, 1978.

Momigliano, A. *The Development of Greek Biography.* Cambridge, MA: Harvard University, 1971.

Montuori, Mario. *Socrates: Physiology of a Myth*. Translated by J. M. P. and M. Langdale. Amsterdam: J. C. Gieben, 1981.

Murray, Penelope. *Plato on Poetry: Ion; Republic 376e–398b9; Republic 595–608b10*. Cambridge: Cambridge University Press, 1966.

Nails, Debra. *The People of Plato: A Prosopography of Plato and Other Socratics*. Indianapolis: Hackett, 2002.

Nauk, Augustus. *Tragicorum Graecorum Fragmenta*. Hildesheim: G. Olms, 1964.

Nightingale, Andrea Wilson. *Genres in Dialogue: Plato and the Construct of Philosophy*. Cambridge: Cambridge University Press, 1995.

———. "Plato's *Gorgias* and Euripides' *Antiope:* A Study in Generic Transformation." *Classical Antiquity* 11 (1992): 121–141.

Nussbaum, Martha. "Aristophanes and Socrates on Learning Practical Wisdom." *Yale Classical Studies* 26 (1980): 43–97.

Ober, Josiah. *Mass and Elite in Democratic Athens*. Princeton, NJ: Princeton University Press, 1989.

Onians, Richard Broxton. *The Origins of European Thought About the Body, the Mind, the Soul, the World, Time and Fate: New Interpretations of Greek, Roman and Kindred Evidence also of some basic Jewish and Christian Beliefs*. 1951. Cambridge: Cambridge University Press, 1988.

Parke, H. W., and D. E. W. Wormell. *The Delphic Oracle*. Oxford: Blackwell, 1956.

———. *Festivals of the Athenians*. Ithaca, NY: Cornell University Press, 1977.

Perry, B. *Aesopica: A Series of Texts Relating to Aesop or Ascribed to Him or Closely Connected with the Literary Tradition*. Vol. 1. Urbana: University of Illinois Press, 1952.

Pickard-Cambridge, A. W. *Dithyramb, Tragedy and Comedy*. Oxford: Clarendon Press, 1927.

Plochmann, George Kimball, and Franklin E. Robinson. *A Friendly Companion to Plato's Gorgias*. Carbondale: Southern Illinois University Press, 1988.

Rabinowitz, Nancy Sorkin. *Anxiety Veiled: Euripides and the Traffic in Women*. Ithaca, NY: Cornell University Press, 1993.

Rinon, Yoav. "The Rhetoric of Jacques Derrida I: Plato's Pharmacy." *Review of Metaphysics* 46 (1992): 369–386.

Robinson, Richard. *Plato's Earlier Dialectic*. 2nd ed. Oxford: Oxford University Press, 1953.

Rudhardt, Jean. *Notions fondamentales de la pensée religieuse et actes constitutifs du culte dans la Grèce classique*. Geneva: Droz, 1958.

Saussure, Ferdinand de. *Course in General Linguistics*. Translated by W. Baskin. New York: Philosophical Library, 1959.

Seaford, Richard. *Reciprocity and Ritual: Homer and Tragedy in the Developing City-State*. Oxford: Oxford University Press, 1994.

Segal, Charles. "Aristophanes' Cloud-Chorus." *Arethusa* 2 (1969): 143–161.

———. *Tragedy and Civilization: An Interpretation of Sophocles.* Cambridge, MA: Harvard University Press, 1981.

Sidebottom, Harry. *Ancient Warfare: A Very Short Introduction.* Oxford: Oxford University Press, 2004.

Simon, Erika. *Festivals of Attica: An Archaeological Commentary.* Madison: University of Wisconsin Press, 1983.

Smyth, Herbert Weir. *Greek Grammar.* Cambridge, MA: Harvard University Press, 1956.

Snell, Bruno. *Pindari Carmina cum Fragmentis.* Lipzig: Teubner 1959 .

Sommerstein, Alan H. *Knights.* Warminster, Wilts, England: Aris & Phillips, 1981.

Stauffer, Devin. *The Unity of Plato's* Gorgias: *Rhetoric, Justice, and the Philosophic Life.* Cambridge, MA: Cambridge University Press, 2006.

Stewart, Patrick. *Patrick Stewart Performs Charles Dickens'* A Christmas Carol. Audio CD. 79382-9. New York: Simon & Schuster, 1991.

Strauss, Barry S. *Athens after the Peloponnesian War: Class Faction and Policy 403–386 B.C.* Ithaca, NY: Cornell University Press, 1986.

Taplin, O. *Greek Tragedy in Action.* Berkeley: University of California Press, 1978.

Taylor, A. E. *Plato: The Man and His Work.* New York: Meridian Books, 1956.

Tyrrell, Wm. Blake. *Amazons: A Study in Athenian Mythmaking.* Baltimore: Johns Hopkins University Press, 1984.

———. *The Smell of Sweat: Greek Athletics, Olympics, and Culture.* Wauconda, IL: Bolchazy-Carducci Publishers, 2004.

———. "The Unity of Sophocles' *Ajax.*" *Arethusa* 16 (1985): 155–185.

Tyrrell, Wm. Blake, and Larry Joe Bennett. "Sophocles' Enemy Sisters." *Contagion* 15/16 (2008/2009): 1–18.

Tyrrell, Wm. Blake, and Frieda S. Brown. *Athenian Myths and Institutions: Words in Action.* New York: Oxford University Press, 1991.

Vernant, Jean-Pierre. "Ambiguity and Reversal: On the Enigmatic Structure of Oedipus Rex." In *Myth and Tragedy in Ancient Greece,* 113–140. Translated by Janet Lloyd. Zone Books: New York, 1990.

———. *Mortals and Immortals: Collected Essays.* Edited by Froma I. Zeitlin. Princeton, NJ: Princeton University Press, 1991.

———. "Théorie générale du sacrifice et mise à mort dans la θυσία grecque." In *Le Sacrifice dans l'Antiquité: Huit Exposés Suivis de Discussions: Vandœuvres-Genève, 25–30 août 1980, Entretiens sur l'antiquité classique* 27 (1981): 1–21.

Versényi, Laszlo. *Holiness and Justice: An Interpretation of Plato's* Euthyphro. Washington, DC: University Press of America, 1982.

Webster, T. B. L. *Greek Theater Production.* London: Methuen, 1956.

West, Thomas G. *Plato's Apology of Socrates: An Interpretation, with a New Translation.* Ithaca, NY: Cornell University Press, 1979.

West, Thomas G., and Grace Starry West. *Four Texts on Socrates: Plato's* Euthyphro, Apology, *and* Crito, *and Aristophanes'* Clouds. Ithaca, NY: Cornell University Press, 1984.

Williams, James G. *The Bible, Violence, and the Sacred: Liberation from the Myth of Sanctioned Violence.* New York: HarperCollins, 1991.

Wilson, John. "'The Customary Meanings of Words Were Changed'—Or Were They? A Note on Thucydides 3.82.4." *Classical Quarterly* 32 (1982): 18–20.

Woodhead, W. D. "Gorgias." In *The Collected Dialogues of Plato,* 229–307. Edited by Edith Hamilton and Huntington Cairns. New York: Pantheon Books, 1961.

Young, David C. *The Olympic Myth of Greek Amateur Athletics.* Chicago: Ares, 1985.

Zanker, Paul. *The Mask of Socrates: The Image of the Intellectual in Antiquity.* Translated by Alan Shapiro. Berkeley: University of California Press, 1995.

Zeller, Eduard. *Plato and the Older Academy.* Translated by Sarah Frances Alleyne and Alfred Goodwin. New York: Russell & Russell, 1962.

Index

A

Achilles, 31, 137, 141, 147
Aelian, 102
Aeschines, 2, 16
Aeschylus: *Agamemnon,* xii, xiii, 50–52; *Eumenides,* 97; *Oresteia,* xii; *Seven Against Thebes,* 34
Aesop, 70, 96
Agamemnon, xii, xiii, 2, 31, 50, 51, 52, 96, 141; acquisitive desire, 91
Alcibiades, 75, 93, 95, 102, 110, 141–42
Ameipsias, 75, 77, 80, 106
Amphion, 24, 37–40
anêr agathos (brave man), 31, 141, 142
antitimêsis (counterpenalty), 125–34
Anytus, 92, 93, 94, 102, 103, 106
Apollonius of Tyana, 109–10
aretê (excellence), 31–32
Aristophanes, 2, 3, 106; *Birds,* 3, 80; *Clouds,* xviii, 74–90; *Frogs,* xii, 80; *Knights,* 62–70, 95
Aristotle, 2

B

Baile, Gil, 141
Bandera, Cesáreo, 143–44, 146, 152 (n. 14)
barrenness: in myths, 47
Bennett, Larry Joe, 160 (n. 46), 164 (n. 87)
Benveniste, Emile, 129
Bouphonia, 43–47
Brickhouse, Thomas C., 99–101, 111
bullshitting, 29–30
Burkert, Walter, 41
Burnet, John, 99, 105, 113

C

Callicles, 6, 8, 20, 24–40
Cervantes, Miguel de, xi, xii
Chaerephon, 25, 26, 77; Delphic oracle, 111–13
Clay, Diskin, 3, 127, 172 (n. 100)
Clytemnestra, xii, xiii, 52, 53, 55
Compton, Todd M., 57, 70
Connor, W. Robert, 79

X

Z